ZIPF MANEUVERS

ISBN (print): 978-1-916541-10-8
ISBN (ebook): 978-1-916541-11-5

First edition.

First published in 2025 by Erratum Press
Sheffield, UK
www.erratumpress.com

Design and typesetting by Ansgar Allen
Cover art by Miron Tee

ZIPF MANEUVERS

ON NON-REPRINTABLE MATERIALS

Andrew C. Wenaus
Germán Sierra

with an introduction by Steven Shaviro

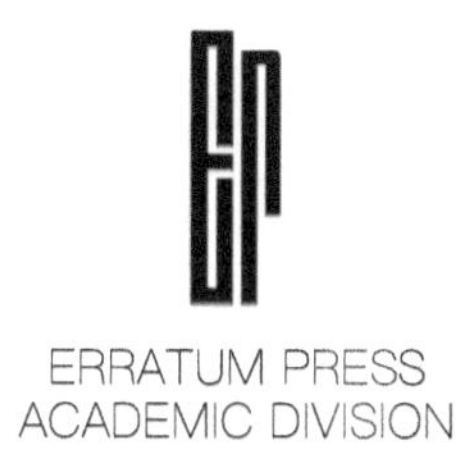

ERRATUM PRESS
ACADEMIC DIVISION

In Memory of Aaron Swartz

1986-2013

A live word does not denote an object but chooses freely, as if for an abode, this or that object notion, thingness, a dear body. And around the thing, a word wanders freely, as a soul around the abandoned but not forgotten body.

- Osip Mandelstam

INTRODUCTION TO: ZIPF MANEUVERS

What are words worth? This is a straightforward question, albeit one without any easy answer. Words have worth, or value, in many disparate senses and in many disparate situations. Words may serve to designate things and actions; they may convey information; they may express feelings, intentions, and moods; they may work as displays of virtuosity or as forms of propaganda; they may serve as parts of larger structures, such as sentences, paragraphs, philosophical arguments, poems, and books; and so on and so forth. The worth and value of words may be different in all these instances.

Also, worth and value can themselves be measured in many sorts of ways: in terms of money, in terms of efficiency, in terms of moral character, in terms of intrinsic beauty and aesthetic achievement, et cetera. The same word or words may have different meanings and effects in different circumstances: "Fire!" means one thing when issued as a command to a squad of men holding rifles, and another thing when shouted out in a crowded theater. Indeed, it means still another thing when sung in a hit single: "Fire", by The Crazy World of Arthur Brown, which reached #2 on the US Billboard Hot One Hundred chart in 1968, second only to the Beatles' "Hey Jude".

But there's even more to the question of what words are worth. We also need to consider the difference between spoken words and written words, not to mention sung words. And even beyond that, we need to reckon with the ambiguities intrinsic not only to particular words, but to the nature of language itself. The English language, or any other human language, consists of a store of words, together with complex rules for putting them together (syntax and grammar). Most linguists accept Noam Chomsky's assertion that these rules include the possibility of recursion: sentences can refer reflexively to other sentences, allowing for meta-levels of complexity.

In addition, there's the question of appreciating language in and for itself. What does it mean to appreciate a particular linguistic style, especially a complex one like that of William Faulkner or Marcel Proust? We know that words are all too often subordinated to their meanings, so that they function like windows, letting us better apprehend the world beyond them. But words can also be loved and appreciated in and of themselves, and for themselves. We can regard words as opaque pictures instead of as transparent windows. We can listen to spoken words themselves, or look at or look at written words themselves, instead of merely listening and looking *through* them. To give an example: Butterflies are beautiful animals; but the English word *butterfly* is also beautiful in its own right; and the equivalent German word *Schmetterling* even more so.

I ask the question with which this Introduction begins in all sincerity. But I also could have put those four words in quotation marks. If I had done so, I might have gotten into trouble. For in that case, I would be quoting a line from another hit song, "Wordy Rappinghood" by Tom Tom Club, which reached #1 on the US Billboard Top Eighty chart (officially known as "Dance Club Songs") in 1981. Song lyrics are legally subject to copyright; they may not be quoted without permission.

Sometimes permission to cite is freely granted. In 2003, when my book *Connected, or What It Means to Live in the Network Society* (University of Minnesota Press) was published, I received permission in writing (duly noted on the copyright page) to quote several lines of lyrics from songs on the hip hop album *Deltron 3030*, a collaboration between MC Del tha Funkee Homosapien, producer Dan the Automator, and DJ Kid Koala. In this particular instance, I was fortunate that the copyright holder, Happy Hemp Music (ASCAP), gave me permission to quote the lyrics without charging me a fee. But copyright holders are not obligated to give any such permission; they are free to deny permission to cite altogether, or to charge however much they want for the privilege. For instance, fifteen or so years ago, the Rolling Stones charged UK £500 for the right to quote one line from a song of theirs, and Beatles charged UK £735 for the same privilege.[1] The prices are likely much higher today.

So it is a good thing that I did not actually quote lyrics from "Wordy Rappinghood" at the beginning of this Introduction. I simply stated a question in my own words; and those words only accidentally, or contingently, resembled those of an actually-existing song lyric. I should note that, while the doctrine of "fair use" allows me to cite, without penalty, several lines from a novel that I am discussing as a literary critic, no such exemption exists in the case of song lyrics or poetry. Here, quoting a single line of three or four words, even with full attribution, is enough to constitute copyright violation.

Had I actually quoted song lyrics without permission, then, I could have been liable for both civil and criminal penalties. Civil penalties can include statutory damages of at least $750 and up to $30,000 per work infringed, as well as an additional fine of up to $150,000 per work infringed for willful infringement. Criminal penalties can include fines of up to $250,000 per

1 Morrison, Blake (2010). "Blake Morrison on the cost of quoting lyrics". *The Guardian*, April 30, 2010. https://www.theguardian.com/books/2010/may/01/blake-morrison-lyrics-copyright.

offense, as well as up to five years in prison for first-time offenders.[2] I should note that these penalties are for a first offense; the punishment for repeated acts of copyright violation can be considerably more severe.

Usually, so heavy a sentence as five years imprisonment is only imposed in the United States in cases that involve "using or carrying a firearm during a crime of violence or drug trafficking".[3] Evidently, modern society takes the issue of copyright violation quite seriously; quoting a line of somebody else's poem or song lyrics is a crime of similar gravity to bank robbery, arson, or assaulting an officer of the law.

Who is the victim in cases of copyright violation? When I referred in an earlier paragraph to "somebody else's poem or song lyrics", I was not being sufficiently specific. The question of *who owns* a certain text, or any other string of words, is not always a simple and obvious one. The person who actually conceived and wrote a given text is not necessarily the owner, and is not even always recognized as the author. For instance, the Beat poet Lew Welch wrote one of the most famous lines in advertising history: "Raid Kills Bugs Dead", a slogan widely used in insecticide commercials for fifty years, from 1956 to 2016. But these words do not "belong" to Welch, and never did. The legal creator of the slogan was the advertising agency for which Welch worked as an employee: Foote, Cone & Belding (FCB). And FCB, in its own turn, supplied the slogan to S. C. Johnson & Son, the company that manufactures the Raid brand of insecticide. Indeed, in 1986 this corporation registered the slogan as a trademark.[4]

In other words, just as the workers in an automobile factory do not own the cars that they have made, so the author of a text does not necessarily own the words that he or she has generated. Texts, like other commodities, can be alienated from their primary producers, in just the way Marx and Engels described. Often, the words of a text are owned, not by the writer, but instead by the publisher, broadcaster, or distributor. And even in cases where the author is granted copyright over the words themselves, ancillary rights are usually not included. Let me illustrate this with a personal example. I wrote a book about music videos, including a chapter on two music videos for songs written and performed by FKA twigs. I wanted to use a still image from one of these videos on the cover of the book. The director of the music video gave

2 Copyright Law of the United States, Title 17. "Chapter 5: Copyright Infringement and Remedies". https://www.copyright.gov/title17/92chap5.html.

3 Families for Justice Reform (2024). "Federal Mandatory Minimums". https://famm.org/wp-content/uploads/2018/04/Chart-All-Fed-MMs.pdf.

4 Wikipedia (2024). "Raid (insecticide)". https://en.wikipedia.org/wiki/Raid_(insecticide).

me permission; the producer of the music video gave me permission; and agents for FKA twigs also gave me permission. However, I was unable to obtain permission to reproduce the image from the record label that distributed the music video, and the album on which the song appeared. As a result, I was unable to use the image for the cover of my book.

All this brings me to *Zipf Maneuvers*, the book for which the current essay is the Introduction. This book is designed to accompany the re-release of Kenji Siratori's novel *Blood Electric*. Siratori is an experimental writer, and his words and paragraphs resist intelligibility. As Andrew Wenaus puts it, Siratori's often violent and affectively charged words "establish forceful interpretive reaction. However, this reaction is one that cannot be situated into a more structured semantic context". Instead, Siratori's language must be regarded "as a semantically void literary space". The words of Siratori's English prose are individually recognizable, but they do not congeal into meaningful representations. In this regard, Wenaus compares Siratori's work to the writing of such twentieth-century experimental authors as Antonin Artaud and William Burroughs.

At this point, given my adherence to the protocols of academic critical writing, the reader will expect me to provide a reference to Wenaus' text. However, there is a reason I will not do so. Andrew Wenaus and Germán Sierra have both published excellent scholarly articles about Siratori's writing, and their original intention was to append these essays to the new edition of *Blood Electric*. However, they were stymied by the copyright issues that I described earlier in this essay. In both cases, the copyrights to their previously published articles are held by large and powerful publishing companies. Due to the articles' prior publication in literary journals, Sierra's essay is owned by Springer/Nature, and Wenaus' essay is owned by Bloomsbury. When asked for permission to republish the essays alongside Siratori's original text, both publishers demanded large fees: indeed, they asked for payments that far exceed whatever monetary amount Wenaus and Sierra might reasonably expect to receive from this republication. (Ironically enough, it is fairly easy to find both essays online, and to download them for free to one's own machine).

The book in hand, *Zipf Maneuvers*, has been produced as a response to this situation. The title refers to a discovery by the linguist George Kingsley Zipf, who found that, in a given body of language, if you list all the words in the order of how frequently they are used, their frequency tends to be inversely proportional to their order in the list. That is to say, according to Zipf's Law the second-most-common word will be used roughly half as often as the firstmost-common word, the third-most-common-word will be used roughly one third as often as the first, and so on.

Wenaus and Sierra therefore wrote an algorithm that divided their essays into individual words, and recorded the frequency and the positions of each. In the original essays, the word "the" was used 308 times, the word "of" was used 271 times; and so on, all the way down to the more than five thousand words that were used only once each. The relative frequencies of all these words do not precisely fit into the distribution predicted by Zipf; but Zipf's Law is only an approximation, not an exact rule, and the numbers are close enough.

Zipf Maneuvers starts with a "Proem" that gives the Python script used to generate the data that constitute the main body of the text. In theory – though this would be quite difficult in practice – the contents of *Zipf Maneuvers* can be used to reconstitute the original texts. In this way, the book conforms to the "no-hiding theorem" of quantum mechanics, which states that information can be transformed, but can never be destroyed. The words are all there. Wenaus and Sierra have conformed to the often ridiculous strictures of copyright law, while at the same time reasserting their own acts of authorship, and their own claims, as literary critics, to respond to Siratori's texts.

Steven Shaviro

PROEM

```
import re
from collections import Counter
from docx import Document

def extract_words_and_positions(text):
    # Normalize and split the text into words
    words = re.findall(r'\b\w+\b', text.lower())
    return words

def word_frequency_and_positions(words):
    # Count word frequencies
    frequency = Counter(words)
    positions = {}

    # Track positions of each word
    for index, word in enumerate(words):
        if word not in positions:
            positions[word] = []
        positions[word].append(index + 1)

    return frequency, positions

def save  to  word(frequency, positions, filename):
    # Create a new Document
    doc = Document()
    doc.add_heading('Word Frequency and Positions', 0)

    # Sort words by frequency (Zipf's law)
    sorted_words = sorted(frequency.items(), key=lambda x: (-x[1], x[0]))

    for word, count in sorted_words:
        doc.add_paragraph(f'■ {word} ■')
        doc.add_paragraph(f'Occurrences: {count}')
        doc.add_paragraph('Positions:')
        doc.add_paragraph(', '.join(map(str, positions[word])))
        doc.add_paragraph()  # Add an empty paragraph for spacing
```

```
    # Save the Document
    doc.save(filename)

if __name__ == "__main__":
    # Replace the text below with your own text to emancipate prisoner article
or chapter
     = """ TEXT """

    # Extract words and their positions
    words = extract_words_and_positions(text)
    frequency, positions = word_frequency_and_positions(words)

    # Save the results to a Word document
    save_to_word(frequency, positions, 'word_positions.docx')
```

WORD FREQUENCY AND POSITIONS

■ the ■

Occurrences: 308

Positions:

5, 11, 19, 34, 45, 53, 177, 193, 223, 303, 314, 320, 343, 346, 366, 369, 407, 444, 453, 464, 470, 475, 514, 546, 553, 564, 573, 589, 594, 617, 642, 732, 747, 750, 773, 784, 787, 828, 830, 832, 834, 836, 841, 892, 899, 905, 919, 931, 973, 1106, 1116, 1126, 1164, 1167, 1228, 1241, 1267, 1338, 1342, 1352, 1401, 1435, 1438, 1474, 1478, 1484, 1500, 1526, 1540, 1566, 1572, 1579, 1588, 1599, 1616, 1656, 1659, 1661, 1700, 1752, 1755, 1761, 1778, 1811, 1815, 1872, 1897, 1929, 1964, 1997, 2004, 2007, 2013, 2016, 2021, 2036, 2047, 2061, 2064, 2075, 2080, 2102, 2108, 2117, 2120, 2133, 2159, 2170, 2179, 2190, 2235, 2264, 2267, 2273, 2295, 2298, 2301, 2315, 2318, 2321, 2327, 2330, 2348, 2357, 2373, 2385, 2419, 2422, 2431, 2446, 2464, 2470, 2483, 2502, 2532, 2543, 2607, 2624, 2655, 2671, 2680, 2692, 2718, 2747, 2754, 2758, 2766, 2775, 2785, 2788, 2801, 2805, 2823, 2826, 2832, 2837, 2853, 2860, 2873, 2919, 2940, 2967, 2971, 2980, 2995, 3006, 3037, 3045, 3108, 3130, 3142, 3146, 3156, 3160, 3179, 3193, 3212, 3231, 3242, 3247, 3250, 3264, 3267, 3280, 3290, 3304, 3307, 3333, 3351, 3376, 3393, 3405, 3423, 3519, 3523, 3532, 3546, 3554, 3562, 3566, 3656, 3665, 3669, 3683, 3713, 3747, 3779, 3789, 3796, 3804, 3809, 3812, 3818, 3821, 3841, 3846, 3852, 3865, 3874, 3924, 3960, 3965, 3968, 3971, 3978, 3984, 4014, 4027, 4059, 4067, 4074, 4122, 4138, 4214, 4253, 4261, 4270, 4281, 4295, 4314, 4338, 4356, 4371, 4407, 4414, 4418, 4461, 4510, 4524, 4532, 4543, 4548, 4576, 4583, 4594, 4601, 4614, 4631, 4644, 4690, 4716, 4723, 4752, 4762, 4791, 4812, 4841, 4850, 4853, 4870, 4882, 4915, 4951, 4957, 4968, 4974, 4982, 5025, 5047, 5083, 5089, 5108, 5194, 5208, 5227, 5246, 5263, 5357, 5360, 5376, 5388, 5406, 5422, 5438, 5470, 5505, 5523, 5532, 5550, 5558, 5562, 5578, 5585, 5595, 5625, 5679, 5806, 5820

■ of ■

Occurrences: 271

Positions:

7, 21, 49, 61, 68, 98, 106, 113, 188, 192, 243, 255, 265, 282, 306, 316, 322, 345, 368, 409, 420, 456, 472, 501, 516, 527, 544, 549, 568, 576, 593, 599, 614, 641, 646, 679, 735, 738, 749, 752, 759, 775, 797, 844, 883, 887, 894, 901, 907, 923, 934, 1007, 1044, 1051, 1057, 1084, 1119, 1128, 1134, 1150, 1166, 1199, 1227, 1275, 1303, 1308, 1323, 1334, 1337, 1341, 1351, 1380, 1410, 1437, 1477, 1487, 1502, 1545, 1560, 1578, 1609, 1615, 1658, 1699, 1702, 1754, 1760, 1763, 1785, 1788, 1806, 1836, 1874, 1903, 1910, 1920, 1928, 1932, 1966, 1990, 2009, 2038, 2050, 2063, 2086, 2119, 2135, 2154, 2178, 2192, 2211, 2263, 2269, 2275, 2297, 2310, 2317, 2326, 2333, 2387, 2421, 2428, 2473, 2526, 2534, 2560, 2566, 2657, 2661, 2673, 2679, 2688, 2717, 2749, 2777, 2790, 2807, 2825, 2828, 2839, 2842, 2856, 2863, 2881, 2884, 2888, 2897, 2912, 2923, 2951, 2976, 2998, 3008, 3040, 3048, 3058, 3093, 3141, 3162, 3197, 3239, 3245, 3249, 3253, 3270, 3283, 3292, 3306, 3310, 3335, 3355, 3378, 3383, 3398, 3407, 3426, 3513, 3522, 3542, 3561, 3609, 3650, 3658, 3668, 3691, 3756, 3799, 3820, 3833, 3864, 3878, 3905, 3931, 3934, 3974, 3980, 4102, 4107, 4118, 4242, 4255, 4260, 4283, 4298, 4309, 4337, 4358, 4374, 4391, 4409, 4427, 4456, 4464, 4468, 4473, 4495, 4506, 4512, 4526, 4534, 4570, 4578, 4586, 4596,

4605, 4626, 4633, 4659, 4708, 4754, 4761, 4765, 4827, 4840, 4844, 4852, 4872, 4884, 4925, 4986, 5007, 5027, 5049, 5055, 5196, 5210, 5265, 5269, 5356, 5392, 5410, 5424, 5437, 5460, 5507, 5534, 5542, 5552, 5566, 5572, 5598, 5615, 5635, 5645, 5658, 5664, 5681, 5693, 5764, 5783, 5822

■ and ■

Occurrences: 197

Positions:

3, 10, 25, 41, 43, 47, 70, 73, 78, 124, 130, 153, 196, 245, 261, 270, 298, 338, 391, 406, 440, 508, 521, 536, 584, 597, 667, 778, 804, 809, 821, 847, 857, 866, 875, 898, 911, 936, 939, 944, 962, 966, 975, 1003, 1024, 1028, 1086, 1108, 1171, 1188, 1194, 1201, 1220, 1255, 1282, 1369, 1433, 1470, 1536, 1547, 1621, 1674, 1709, 1736, 1800, 1826, 1843, 1914, 1922, 1985, 1992, 1996, 2011, 2034, 2066, 2096, 2157, 2215, 2225, 2272, 2287, 2320, 2343, 2353, 2382, 2445, 2453, 2460, 2479, 2506, 2518, 2528, 2554, 2564, 2593, 2602, 2636, 2670, 2697, 2707, 2721, 2781, 2811, 2819, 2859, 2917, 2973, 3010, 3084, 3153, 3175, 3178, 3195, 3214, 3259, 3262, 3275, 3287, 3396, 3416, 3553, 3583, 3591, 3600, 3678, 3710, 3722, 3835, 3902, 3939, 3950, 3962, 3996, 3999, 4016, 4053, 4121, 4134, 4153, 4168, 4182, 4198, 4224, 4232, 4252, 4266, 4303, 4330, 4341, 4343, 4379, 4439, 4490, 4515, 4529, 4555, 4558, 4566, 4590, 4665, 4742, 4758, 4773, 4782, 4829, 4928, 4939, 4984, 4996, 5004, 5014, 5023, 5065, 5088, 5101, 5123, 5129, 5145, 5158, 5184, 5226, 5245, 5293, 5310, 5342, 5349, 5371, 5379, 5456, 5536, 5612, 5620, 5641, 5671, 5778, 5797, 5831

■ a ■

Occurrences: 155

Positions:

95, 104, 145, 164, 215, 241, 286, 290, 385, 401, 417, 448, 473, 481, 499, 644, 694, 799, 881, 1035, 1049, 1054, 1058, 1082, 1131, 1141, 1151, 1156, 1218, 1234, 1244, 1270, 1391, 1426, 1454, 1466, 1511, 1607, 1610, 1627, 1685, 1728, 1757, 1783, 1804, 1834, 1869, 1875, 1886, 1954, 1978, 1983, 2042, 2069, 2142, 2186, 2197, 2208, 2308, 2392, 2399, 2404, 2436, 2511, 2523, 2580, 2591, 2619, 2634, 2658, 2713, 2768, 2793, 2798, 2843, 2864, 2898, 2908, 2924, 2927, 2933, 2935, 2943, 2946, 2949, 3027, 3056, 3113, 3138, 3236, 3273, 3300, 3314, 3399, 3439, 3481, 3489, 3507, 3558, 3581, 3589, 3743, 3754, 3831, 3889, 3990, 4007, 4035, 4042, 4100, 4105, 4114, 4132, 4144, 4159, 4164, 4180, 4183, 4289, 4299, 4318, 4396, 4442, 4449, 4453, 4465, 4474, 4503, 4608, 4650, 4796, 4801, 4820, 4867, 4868, 4888, 4920, 5000, 5011, 5096, 5103, 5162, 5348, 5353, 5373, 5380, 5451, 5540, 5610, 5622, 5633, 5652, 5656, 5685, 5762

■ in ■

Occurrences: 116

Positions:

16, 115, 163, 176, 186, 197, 325, 362, 397, 428, 431, 552, 588, 635, 663, 707, 726, 811, 918, 1034, 1074, 1140, 1181, 1196, 1393, 1406, 1457, 1468, 1581, 1596, 1612, 1676, 1733, 1741, 1776, 1818, 1881, 2116, 2234, 2251, 2290, 2363, 2408, 2499, 2531, 2630, 2727, 2753, 2771, 2784, 2831, 2989, 2992, 3112, 3186, 3289, 3296, 3327, 3331, 3347, 3437, 3464, 3483, 3531, 3644, 3680, 3773, 3808, 3845, 3873, 3923, 4005, 4013, 4029, 4041, 4104, 4131, 4141, 4154, 4222, 4273, 4278, 4287, 4304, 4325, 4349, 4376, 4395, 4413, 4441, 4502, 4509, 4573, 4642, 4656, 4670, 4677, 4711, 4722, 4756, 4917, 5021, 5178, 5255, 5262, 5276, 5344, 5359, 5367, 5390, 5408, 5463, 5469, 5588, 5594, 5802

■ to ■

Occurrences: 100

Positions:

33, 44, 274, 294, 302, 483, 489, 510, 623, 654, 661, 665, 681, 693, 783, 793, 825, 840, 869, 1038, 1191, 1238, 1312, 1508, 1525, 1584, 1587, 1623, 1644, 1667, 1689, 1726, 1766, 1832, 1858, 1867, 2001, 2026, 2167, 2188, 2203, 2228, 2279, 2283, 2293, 2366, 2390, 2398, 2403, 2509, 2556, 2584, 2589, 2605, 2616, 2622, 2643, 2690, 2736, 2814, 2822, 2900, 2903, 3005, 3015, 3089, 3126, 3219, 3321, 3339, 3570, 3688, 3726, 3760, 3803, 3859, 3920, 4055, 4150, 4157, 4175, 4187, 4195, 4202, 4293, 4714, 4816, 4848, 5181, 5474, 5479, 5521, 5529, 5538, 5546, 5668, 5674, 5702, 5800, 5812

■ is ■

Occurrences: 79

Positions:

203, 214, 350, 423, 434, 446, 479, 604, 675, 687, 705, 714, 754, 780, 791, 838, 1000, 1063, 1096, 1206, 1346, 1749, 1769, 1853, 1878, 1891, 1901, 1975, 2100, 2126, 2148, 2162, 2165, 2173, 2184, 2258, 2323, 2355, 2586, 2640, 3120, 3233, 3266, 3279, 3312, 3359, 3545, 3574, 3585, 3673, 3723, 3795, 3807, 3816, 3827, 3848, 3970, 3986, 4004, 4034, 4062, 4192, 4291, 4361, 4370, 4629, 4648, 4698, 4702, 4770, 4794, 4834, 5288, 5305, 5511, 5520, 5581, 5648, 5741

■ as ■

Occurrences: 74

Positions:

190, 201, 340, 374, 379, 459, 461, 498, 629, 699, 717, 880, 986, 1112, 1148, 1208, 1213, 1269, 1354, 1418, 1429, 1441, 1465, 1556, 1606, 1639, 1646, 1652, 1794, 1977, 2083, 2091, 2150, 2222, 2246, 2289, 2501, 2530, 2579, 2675, 2710, 2734, 2891, 3036, 3065, 3070, 3129, 3134, 3173, 3209, 3222, 3224, 3255, 3272, 3480, 3535, 3580, 3742, 3753, 3830, 3885, 4094, 4452, 4687, 4731, 4804, 4819, 5252, 5418, 5574, 5651, 5730, 5761, 5772

■ that ■

Occurrences: 68

Positions:

227, 253, 328, 450, 467, 577, 605, 817, 861, 1001, 1029, 1149, 1225, 1248, 1277, 1347, 1472, 1492, 1529, 1565, 1590, 1670, 1850, 1883, 1890, 1902, 1960, 2028, 2073, 2125, 2144, 2163, 2261, 2394, 2764, 2915, 2969, 2991, 3020, 3061, 3102, 3119, 3184, 3202, 3256, 3323, 3389, 3517, 3527, 3634, 3792, 3994, 4010, 4048, 4126, 4155, 4228, 4398, 4500, 4550, 4561, 4719, 4771, 5510, 5637, 5697, 5784, 5805

■ or ■

Occurrences: 57

Positions:

206, 353, 387, 426, 632, 786, 978, 993, 1015, 1317, 1331, 1443, 1497, 1796, 1798, 1865, 1938, 1969, 2231, 2254, 2441, 2685, 2739, 2804, 2902, 2926, 2959, 3117, 3353, 3432, 3506, 3601, 3615, 3619, 3625, 3630, 3638, 3646, 3654, 3675, 3705, 3823, 3896, 3910, 4072, 4087, 4116, 4161, 4484, 4545, 4592, 4777, 5421, 5655, 5767, 5789, 5814

■ are ■

Occurrences: 50

Positions:

64, 101, 259, 540, 560, 806, 818, 1018, 1077, 1087, 1294, 1349, 1362, 1530, 1591, 1618, 1654, 1738, 1823, 1827, 1844, 2175, 2724, 2877, 2964, 3337, 3456, 3469, 3635, 3784, 3918, 3936, 4084, 4111, 4130, 4217, 4257, 4268, 4346, 4381, 4431, 4479, 4501, 4521, 4551, 4720, 4785, 5719, 5746, 5781

■ by ■

Occurrences: 46

Positions:

76, 103, 135, 236, 342, 612, 701, 718, 728, 930,

942, 1081, 1115, 1400, 1462, 1480, 1515, 1539, 1743, 2340, 2665, 3026, 3495, 3550, 3893, 3899, 3907, 3912, 3941, 3945, 4058, 4076, 4113, 4460, 4471, 4517, 4523, 4531, 4618, 4694, 4806, 4859, 5513, 5688, 5705, 5759

■ be ■

Occurrences: 44

Positions:

484, 490, 523, 655, 671, 682, 1033, 1103, 1279, 1416, 1452, 1494, 1585, 1604, 1645, 1871, 2280, 2557, 2653, 2737, 3127, 3151, 3159, 3318, 3340, 3443, 3492, 3511, 3606, 3727, 3740, 3921, 4056, 4092, 4147, 4148, 4158, 4173, 4400, 4487, 4685, 4817, 5700, 5770

■ for ■

Occurrences: 38

Positions:

313, 319, 376, 384, 400, 851, 1090, 1315, 1425, 1434, 1571, 1648, 1655, 1679, 1751, 1861, 1893, 2300, 2329, 2568, 2803, 3226, 3302, 3344, 3473, 3746, 3766, 3839, 3977, 4179, 4227, 4276, 4568, 4661, 4666, 4705, 5525, 5609

■ an ■

Occurrences: 37

Positions:

232, 283, 309, 326, 487, 608, 794, 884, 1065, 1098, 1109, 1182, 1395, 1407, 1557, 1946, 1986, 2051, 2084, 2122, 2136, 2291, 2434, 2552, 3090, 3361, 3475, 3607, 3663, 3801, 3975, 3987, 4045, 4706, 4712, 5689, 5773

■ s ■

Occurrences: 37

Positions:

181, 199, 249, 525, 535, 538, 620, 639, 1137, 1518, 1772, 1936, 1941, 2182, 2306, 2369, 2455, 2570, 2628, 2648, 3294, 3372, 3386, 3486, 3501, 3538, 3613, 3730, 3814, 3955, 3959, 4307, 4321, 5217, 5386, 5433, 5828

■ it ■

Occurrences: 33

Positions:

204, 336, 380, 462, 524, 619, 658, 668, 790, 1205, 1386, 1548, 2206, 2257, 2521, 2547, 2895, 2983, 3124, 3316, 3371, 3385, 3390, 3584, 3604, 4003, 4020, 4033, 4178, 4191, 4837, 5206, 5580

■ media ■

Occurrences: 33

Positions:

1094, 1293, 1348, 1360, 2681, 3357, 3381, 3401, 3412, 3418, 3448, 3455, 3463, 3693, 3786, 3882, 4209, 4231, 4245, 5022, 5053, 5087, 5147, 5316, 5331, 5439, 5449, 5516, 5710, 5718, 5722, 5728, 5744

■ not ■

Occurrences: 33

Positions:

144, 171, 311, 480, 621, 651, 688, 781, 1207, 1252, 1635, 1739, 1854, 2356, 2396, 2878, 2942, 2945, 3200, 3234, 3387, 3457, 3577, 3849, 4085, 4193, 4362, 4434, 4630, 4795, 5713, 5720, 5809

■ which ■

Occurrences: 29

Positions:

359, 690, 1075, 1613, 1734, 1777, 1912, 2164, 2409, 2772, 3073, 3257, 3303, 3336, 3438, 3465, 3484, 4288, 4377, 4697, 4780, 4832, 5464, 5475, 5480, 5561, 5589, 5647, 5785

■ 2015 ■

Occurrences: 28

Positions:

189, 333, 533, 758, 1117, 1261, 1357, 1506, 1595, 2742, 2813, 3177, 3573, 3735, 3862, 4869, 4880, 4889, 4896, 4914, 5043, 5193, 5374, 5387, 5401, 5489, 5605, 5792

■ art ■

Occurrences: 28

Positions:

138, 208, 355, 364, 422, 551, 859, 990, 992, 996, 1353, 1375, 1382, 1458, 1724, 1968, 2286, 2702,

3373, 3454, 3869, 3982, 4357, 4497, 4701, 4919, 5086, 5261

■ but ■
Occurrences: 27
Positions:
318, 486, 657, 789, 957, 1287, 1576, 1745, 2402, 2883, 2948, 3241, 3460, 3576, 3770, 3855, 3915, 4190, 4365, 4388, 4436, 4560, 4637, 5478, 5726, 5737, 5817

■ human ■
Occurrences: 26
Positions:
50, 107, 902, 1367, 1481, 1490, 1503, 1567, 1693, 1707, 1971, 1984, 2076, 2087, 2106, 2115, 2130, 2212, 2342, 2352, 2871, 3757, 4564, 4675, 5465, 5544

■ from ■
Occurrences: 25
Positions:
57, 768, 1394, 1533, 2006, 2015, 2046, 2132, 2195, 2243, 2380, 2411, 2475, 2577, 2618, 2870, 2979, 3107, 3122, 3192, 3211, 3375, 3588, 4600, 5577

■ this ■
Occurrences: 25
Positions:
58, 120, 132, 357, 410, 600, 636, 1040, 1597, 1696, 1764, 1918, 2058, 2575, 2631, 3348, 3384, 3671, 3806, 3932, 3981, 4142, 4678, 5547, 5661

■ new ■
Occurrences: 24
Positions:
22, 54, 59, 86, 194, 826, 870, 908, 925, 1020, 1042, 1120, 1286, 2426, 2659, 3002, 3114, 3925, 4422, 4624, 4854, 5146, 5149, 5452

■ contemporary ■
Occurrences: 23
Positions:
421, 1070, 1231, 1264, 1359, 1374, 1600, 2284, 2360, 2700, 2905, 2962, 2993, 3414, 3868, 4238, 4274, 4428, 4627, 4700, 4918, 5526, 5590

■ on ■
Occurrences: 20
Positions:
126, 222, 684, 1499, 2101, 2107, 2966, 3079, 4026, 4039, 4582, 4593, 4891, 4900, 5046, 5114, 5120, 5164, 5224, 5243

■ postdigital ■
Occurrences: 20
Positions:
1, 92, 133, 555, 762, 776, 976, 1292, 1344, 2180, 2644, 2743, 3927, 4262, 4326, 4403, 4646, 4681, 4862, 5339

■ its ■
Occurrences: 19
Positions:
708, 719, 729, 765, 1175, 1862, 2516, 2598, 3276, 3718, 3856, 4030, 4050, 4080, 4671, 5393, 5411, 5517, 5601

■ computer ■
Occurrences: 17
Positions:
1013, 1686, 1694, 1703, 1870, 1972, 2054, 2071, 2143, 2155, 2237, 2344, 2354, 3514, 3639, 4954, 4971

■ has ■
Occurrences: 16
Positions:
30, 381, 413, 916, 1387, 1583, 1664, 1780, 1951, 3018, 3023, 3325, 3685, 3715, 4815, 5786

■ they ■
Occurrences: 16
Positions:
83, 958, 969, 1300, 1653, 2493, 2731, 3215, 3771, 4091, 4200, 4216, 4267, 5476, 5481, 5715

■ with ■
Occurrences: 16
Positions:
110, 211, 980, 1630, 1684, 1706, 2079, 2314, 2548, 3404, 3598, 4023, 4066, 4613, 5199, 5213

■ code ■
Occurrences: 15
Positions:

1014, 1062, 1179, 1431, 1857, 1991, 2010, 2024, 2082, 2111, 2147, 2271, 3525, 4952, 4969

■ press ■
Occurrences: 14
Positions:
4911, 4990, 5009, 5029, 5038, 5057, 5076, 5092, 5152, 5167, 5190, 5271, 5368, 5441

■ what ■
Occurrences: 14
Positions:
335, 1450, 2201, 2218, 2239, 3123, 3659, 3774, 3824, 3851, 4353, 4621, 5287, 5304

■ can ■
Occurrences: 13
Positions:
669, 1102, 1250, 1884, 3077, 3189, 4021, 4070, 4090, 4098, 4146, 5592, 5698

■ digital ■
Occurrences: 13
Positions:
147, 151, 437, 558, 785, 974, 981, 1030, 1157, 1633, 1993, 2683, 3692

■ might ■
Occurrences: 13
Positions:
371, 571, 1032, 1549, 2652, 3478, 3491, 3605, 3661, 3739, 4399, 4683, 5769

■ 2016 ■
Occurrences: 12
Positions:
1720, 2986, 3096, 3169, 3343, 4790, 5104, 5161, 5218, 5286, 5327, 5497

■ codes ■
Occurrences: 12
Positions:
9, 29, 55, 140, 853, 915, 926, 2600, 3358, 4591, 4692, 4725

■ language ■
Occurrences: 12
Positions:
2092, 2401, 2407, 2415, 2424, 2444, 2448, 2485, 2505, 2545, 2583, 2621

■ content ■
Occurrences: 11
Positions:
713, 742, 746, 753, 756, 1240, 3094, 3672, 3815, 3819, 3843

■ data ■
Occurrences: 11
Positions:
99, 457, 1052, 1173, 1411, 1413, 1447, 1994, 2098, 5514, 5565

■ e ■
Occurrences: 11
Positions:
167, 2141, 3612, 4977, 5013, 5081, 5229, 5234, 5295, 5300, 5351

■ internet ■
Occurrences: 11
Positions:
788, 995, 1268, 1948, 3543, 3563, 3567, 3728, 3737, 3748, 3880

■ into ■
Occurrences: 11
Positions:
1285, 1814, 2522, 2542, 2712, 3054, 3230, 3299, 4079, 4333, 5569

■ network ■
Occurrences: 11
Positions:
796, 1520, 3761, 3781, 3805, 4106, 4397, 4469, 4733, 4826, 4860

■ one ■
Occurrences: 11
Positions:
542, 592, 1336, 2103, 2410, 2800, 3539, 4197, 4760, 4839, 5827

■ own ■
Occurrences: 11
Positions:
496, 709, 1863, 2443, 3081, 3857, 4151, 4196, 4672, 5602, 5829

■ text ■
Occurrences: 11
Positions:
833, 1178, 1860, 2299, 2632, 2674, 2693, 3488, 3603, 3653, 4607

■ through ■
Occurrences: 11
Positions:
91, 616, 972, 1155, 1217, 1236, 1259, 2033, 5186, 5560, 5600

■ time ■
Occurrences: 11
Positions:
403, 777, 2161, 2729, 2760, 4226, 4351, 4360, 4420, 4458, 5436

■ been ■
Occurrences: 10
Positions:
383, 395, 724, 928, 1388, 1952, 3024, 3686, 4212, 5787

■ i ■
Occurrences: 10
Positions:
142, 169, 512, 518, 1160, 1223, 1721, 2140, 4447, 5582

■ just ■
Occurrences: 10
Positions:
541, 652, 1253, 1636, 2879, 3035, 3235, 3458, 3493, 5672

■ literature ■
Occurrences: 10
Positions:
770, 988, 2389, 2393, 2606, 2609, 4275, 4921, 5417, 5420

■ other ■
Occurrences: 10
Positions:
230, 1488, 1692, 2109, 2920, 3170, 3616, 3689, 4024, 5704

■ such ■
Occurrences: 10
Positions:
628, 985, 1793, 2090, 2221, 2245, 3172, 3534, 3884, 4730

■ visual ■
Occurrences: 10
Positions:
154, 182, 207, 354, 392, 1061, 1152, 2097, 3427, 4906

■ wark ■
Occurrences: 10
Positions:
703, 757, 3572, 3734, 3750, 3840, 3861, 5015, 5385, 5405

■ work ■
Occurrences: 10
Positions:
250, 393, 497, 1118, 1682, 1756, 1876, 3198, 3891, 5383

■ writing ■
Occurrences: 10
Positions:
139, 763, 955, 1768, 2497, 2703, 4498, 5035, 5073, 5425

■ artist ■
Occurrences: 9
Positions:
155, 1123, 1168, 1242, 1601, 1949, 2181, 3993, 4793

■ at ■
Occurrences: 9
Positions:
530, 582, 1829, 2003, 2012, 2158, 2757, 3655, 4417

■ both ■
Occurrences: 9
Positions:
23, 909, 1097, 1424, 2689, 2852, 4012, 4221, 4574

■ circulation ■
Occurrences: 9
Positions:
615, 686, 704, 727, 739, 751, 774, 849, 2669

■ have ■
Occurrences: 9
Positions:
372, 394, 927, 1550, 2774, 4210, 4556, 4749, 5482

■ meme ■
Occurrences: 9
Positions:
3564, 3568, 3714, 3813, 3822, 3847, 3853, 5389, 5407

■ more ■
Occurrences: 9
Positions:
441, 1200, 1202, 1296, 1541, 1943, 3674, 3866, 3963

■ novel ■
Occurrences: 9
Positions:
96, 815, 961, 1773, 2471, 3490, 3503, 4958, 4975

■ post ■
Occurrences: 9
Positions:
150, 945, 994, 2694, 3408, 3897, 4535, 4537, 5454

■ re ■
Occurrences: 9
Positions:
66, 562, 932, 970, 1132, 1283, 1301, 3369, 3696

■ some ■
Occurrences: 9
Positions:
85, 960, 1551, 1577, 1821, 1933, 3163, 3863, 3916

■ university ■
Occurrences: 9
Positions:
4910, 4989, 5006, 5026, 5037, 5054, 5151, 5189, 5268

■ 2 ■
Occurrences: 8
Positions:
1995, 2018, 2045, 2169, 2256, 5364, 5492, 5501

■ artistic ■
Occurrences: 8
Positions:
71, 937, 983, 1022, 1731, 2840, 3415, 4527

■ artworks ■
Occurrences: 8
Positions:
1232, 1324, 1735, 3917, 4239, 4429, 4628, 4682

■ com ■
Occurrences: 8
Positions:
4895, 4963, 5236, 5302, 5326, 5400, 5496, 5754

■ current ■
Occurrences: 8
Positions:
554, 1343, 3364, 3453, 4645, 4680, 4767, 4813

■ fiction ■
Occurrences: 8
Positions:
1026, 1767, 2716, 3366, 3870, 5317, 5332, 5340

■ http ■
Occurrences: 8
Positions:
4877, 4893, 4960, 5203, 5232, 5298, 5324, 5752

■ literary ■
Occurrences: 8
Positions:
28, 69, 127, 864, 914, 935, 3417, 4863

■ machine ■
Occurrences: 8
Positions:
51, 108, 287, 291, 903, 2599, 2836, 3148

■ non ■
Occurrences: 8
Positions:
26, 912, 1444, 1489, 2114, 3785, 4339, 5457

■ objects ■
Occurrences: 8
Positions:
1330, 1589, 4095, 4378, 4774, 4830, 5696, 5711

■ plantoid ■
Occurrences: 8
Positions:
3966, 3969, 3985, 4075, 4145, 4165, 4544, 5755

■ produced ■
Occurrences: 8
Positions:
235, 1740, 1747, 2725, 4347, 4459, 4522, 4858

■ self ■
Occurrences: 8
Positions:
209, 213, 258, 445, 476, 643, 831, 3991

■ symbols ■
Occurrences: 8

Positions:
100, 805, 1053, 1107, 1412, 1414, 1448, 4589

■ their ■
Occurrences: 8
Positions:
1239, 2495, 3080, 4128, 4392, 4482, 4634, 4638

■ we ■
Occurrences: 8
Positions:
570, 1185, 1249, 2651, 2773, 2930, 3660, 3825

■ 2010 ■
Occurrences: 7
Positions:
772, 2378, 4741, 4748, 5060, 5274, 5415

■ agency ■
Occurrences: 7
Positions:
1368, 1580, 2872, 4559, 4565, 4781, 4833

■ all ■
Occurrences: 7
Positions:
398, 526, 1378, 2536, 2750, 2816, 3284

■ automation ■
Occurrences: 7
Positions:
2699, 2789, 2809, 2838, 2978, 3221, 3762

■ avedissian ■
Occurrences: 7

Positions:
162, 251, 332, 432, 477, 532, 638

■ becomes ■
Occurrences: 7
Positions:
607, 740, 1390, 2112, 2207, 2433, 3105

■ between ■
Occurrences: 7
Positions:
38, 890, 1982, 2032, 2351, 2439, 3937

■ deep ■
Occurrences: 7
Positions:
4133, 5315, 5330, 5435, 5709, 5717, 5743

■ different ■
Occurrences: 7
Positions:
111, 1321, 1830, 2477, 2582, 3446, 5662

■ form ■
Occurrences: 7
Positions:
2911, 3252, 3309, 4032, 4775, 5254, 5541

■ goring ■
Occurrences: 7
Positions:
157, 180, 237, 248, 278, 493, 537

■ her ■
Occurrences: 7

Positions:
159, 256, 299, 495, 1146, 1624, 2442

■ like ■
Occurrences: 7
Positions:
810, 2646, 3075, 3498, 3703, 4542, 4547

■ linguistic ■
Occurrences: 7
Positions:
24, 27, 910, 913, 2429, 2489, 2513

■ many ■
Occurrences: 7
Positions:
1226, 1263, 1649, 2262, 2961, 4237, 4410

■ negarestani ■
Occurrences: 7
Positions:
2377, 2468, 2613, 3228, 3342, 5272, 5284

■ no ■
Occurrences: 7
Positions:
212, 676, 1383, 2127, 3319, 5322, 5483

■ p ■
Occurrences: 7
Positions:
2449, 2491, 2610, 2956, 5093, 5442, 5835

■ poetry ■
Occurrences: 7

Positions:
200, 205, 352, 3428, 3516, 3544, 4907

■ real ■
Occurrences: 7
Positions:
2728, 2795, 3131, 3636, 3782, 3842, 4350

■ same ■
Occurrences: 7
Positions:
590, 2160, 2755, 2759, 4139, 4415, 4419

■ sierra ■
Occurrences: 7
Positions:
4264, 4367, 4445, 5312, 5335, 5336, 5749

■ social ■
Occurrences: 7
Positions:
1093, 3109, 3213, 3411, 3881, 4929, 5721

■ technological ■
Occurrences: 7
Positions:
36, 730, 888, 2676, 2786, 2861, 3447

■ technologies ■
Occurrences: 7
Positions:
559, 1361, 1634, 1638, 2876, 2880, 3188

■ thought ■
Occurrences: 7

Positions:
2088, 2156, 2168, 2194, 2200, 2204, 3332

■ universal ■
Occurrences: 7
Positions:
8, 852, 1008, 1059, 1271, 3356, 4724

■ 2013 ■
Occurrences: 6
Positions:
1048, 1775, 1896, 4947, 4979, 5170

■ although ■
Occurrences: 6
Positions:
761, 1262, 2612, 2730, 3736, 4385

■ any ■
Occurrences: 6
Positions:
624, 1332, 1373, 2487, 2686, 3087

■ artists ■
Occurrences: 6
Positions:
42, 891, 2963, 3345, 5282, 5760

■ could ■
Occurrences: 6
Positions:
1278, 1415, 1451, 1603, 3442, 3510

■ defined ■
Occurrences: 6

Positions:
1461, 1976, 2664, 4448, 4516, 5748

■ forms ■
Occurrences: 6
Positions:
872, 1204, 1379, 2253, 3050, 3690

■ fully ■
Occurrences: 6
Positions:
12, 2594, 2637, 2698, 2844, 4553

■ instance ■
Occurrences: 6
Positions:
1680, 3474, 3541, 4277, 5394, 5412

■ itself ■
Occurrences: 6
Positions:
349, 2145, 3111, 3998, 4002, 4152

■ japanese ■
Occurrences: 6
Positions:
386, 2538, 2549, 2578, 2595, 2638

■ kind ■
Occurrences: 6
Positions:
645, 3755, 3933, 4426, 5634, 5663

■ lütticken ■
Occurrences: 6

Positions:
2985, 3016, 3095, 3100, 3168, 5216

■ networked ■
Occurrences: 6
Positions:
2762, 2875, 4423, 4450, 4477, 4519

■ only ■
Occurrences: 6
Positions:
312, 1498, 2358, 3487, 5699, 5810

■ our ■
Occurrences: 6
Positions:
736, 1197, 1257, 1534, 2817, 4359

■ performance ■
Occurrences: 6
Positions:
116, 1392, 1981, 2288, 2677, 4476

■ philosophy ■
Occurrences: 6
Positions:
1980, 3271, 3293, 3324, 5289, 5306

■ possibility ■
Occurrences: 6
Positions:
2796, 2824, 3315, 4577, 4595, 4632

■ set ■
Occurrences: 6

Positions:
60, 273, 3326, 3832, 4101, 4117

■ synchronic ■
Occurrences: 6
Positions:
601, 846, 1002, 2714, 4334, 4462

■ system ■
Occurrences: 6
Positions:
1073, 1427, 1439, 2934, 4125, 5686

■ techno ■
Occurrences: 6
Positions:
565, 695, 2833, 3204, 4123, 4695

■ texts ■
Occurrences: 6
Positions:
856, 1101, 1325, 1737, 2311, 2645

■ understood ■
Occurrences: 6
Positions:
716, 1417, 4588, 4686, 4818, 5650

■ using ■
Occurrences: 6
Positions:
136, 1105, 1637, 1855, 2629, 3445

■ way ■
Occurrences: 6

Positions:
500, 1184, 1258, 4137, 4143, 4156

■ while ■
Occurrences: 6
Positions:
492, 1839, 2451, 4181, 4208, 5660

■ works ■
Occurrences: 6
Positions:
128, 539, 1289, 2265, 2337, 3871

■ 1 ■
Occurrences: 5
Positions:
1371, 5135, 5323, 5431, 5445

■ 1987 ■
Occurrences: 5
Positions:
1523, 2384, 4736, 4999, 5176

■ 2011 ■
Occurrences: 5
Positions:
405, 1291, 3430, 4904, 5033

■ 2014 ■
Occurrences: 5
Positions:
2339, 5017, 5030, 5082, 5623

■ also ■
Occurrences: 5

Positions:
1161, 2312, 4530, 4684, 5818

■ archive ■
Occurrences: 5
Positions:
488, 640, 649, 829, 4916

■ author ■
Occurrences: 5
Positions:
1779, 1873, 4799, 4803, 4814

■ become ■
Occurrences: 5
Positions:
308, 373, 2232, 5467, 5714

■ being ■
Occurrences: 5
Positions:
1079, 1592, 3055, 3360, 4383

■ bernico ■
Occurrences: 5
Positions:
1464, 1505, 1509, 1594, 4886

■ capitalism ■
Occurrences: 5
Positions:
2994, 3034, 4696, 4710, 5003

■ century ■
Occurrences: 5
Positions:
179, 4244, 4809, 5052, 5448

■ combination ■
Occurrences: 5
Positions:
950, 1333, 1701, 1919, 2687

■ constructed ■
Occurrences: 5
Positions:
929, 1790, 1989, 3374, 4312

■ cultural ■
Occurrences: 5
Positions:
566, 2722, 3115, 3349, 4344

■ english ■
Occurrences: 5
Positions:
2484, 2500, 2544, 2585, 2608

■ evolving ■
Occurrences: 5
Positions:
820, 1067, 1305, 4825, 4856

■ experimental ■
Occurrences: 5
Positions:
2701, 2886, 2977, 3365, 4496

■ features ■
Occurrences: 5
Positions:
88, 575, 965, 1340, 4259

■ flux ■
Occurrences: 5
Positions:
4507, 5230, 5235, 5296, 5301

■ g ■
Occurrences: 5
Positions:
4978, 4995, 5059, 5313, 5337

■ humans ■
Occurrences: 5
Positions:
1673, 1681, 4097, 4772, 4828

■ images ■
Occurrences: 5
Positions:
254, 264, 1176, 1327, 3497

■ includes ■
Occurrences: 5
Positions:
228, 279, 1169, 3518, 5819

■ interactions ■
Occurrences: 5
Positions:
52, 63, 904, 1404, 4065

■ interesting ■
Occurrences: 5
Positions:
87, 963, 2260, 3867, 4492

■ irritant ■
Occurrences: 5
Positions:
1774, 1799, 1899, 2649, 5171

■ jameson ■
Occurrences: 5
Positions:
2988, 3012, 3017, 3098, 5125

■ larson ■
Occurrences: 5
Positions:
1771, 1808, 1848, 3901, 5168

■ means ■
Occurrences: 5
Positions:
613, 3367, 4472, 5677, 5811

■ most ■
Occurrences: 5
Positions:
922, 1229, 1614, 2456, 2503

■ neither ■
Occurrences: 5
Positions:
3063, 4432, 4800, 5219, 5238

■ networks ■
Occurrences: 5
Positions:
618, 798, 1528, 4776, 5670

■ notes ■
Occurrences: 5
Positions:
4890, 4899, 5223, 5242, 5444

■ number ■
Occurrences: 5
Positions:
886, 1784, 1805, 4467, 5692

■ often ■
Occurrences: 5
Positions:
65, 2704, 3575, 3698, 4703

■ outside ■
Occurrences: 5
Positions:
2005, 2017, 2153, 2191, 5579

■ perception ■
Occurrences: 5
Positions:
1370, 1504, 1546, 1561, 1582

■ performative ■
Occurrences: 5
Positions:
1955, 2048, 2349, 4225, 4691

■ public ■
Occurrences: 5
Positions:
896, 4043, 4060, 4068, 5803

■ r ■
Occurrences: 5
Positions:
3776, 4934, 5273, 5285, 5619

■ sense ■
Occurrences: 5
Positions:
637, 1598, 4679, 5597, 5821

■ something ■
Occurrences: 5
Positions:
296, 1889, 3329, 5816, 5824

■ space ■
Occurrences: 5
Positions:
134, 578, 4044, 4457, 4483

■ symbolic ■
Occurrences: 5
Positions:
871, 1009, 1422, 4663, 5253

■ syntopic ■
Occurrences: 5
Positions:
602, 848, 1004, 2715, 4335

■ them ■
Occurrences: 5
Positions:
1894, 3752, 3794, 4189, 4207

■ theory ■
Occurrences: 5
Positions:
1521, 4734, 4757, 4811, 4847

■ where ■
Occurrences: 5
Positions:
94, 557, 802, 4019, 5143

■ within ■
Occurrences: 5
Positions:
1905, 1916, 2196, 2463, 2482

■ you ■
Occurrences: 5
Positions:
4170, 4171, 4204, 4949, 4966

■ 2007 ■
Occurrences: 4
Positions:
874, 4746, 4935, 5250

■ 2016b ■
Occurrences: 4
Positions:
4368, 4446, 5338, 5750

■ about ■
Occurrences: 4
Positions:
337, 436, 442, 1210

■ aesthetic ■
Occurrences: 4
Positions:
964, 4046, 5228, 5247

■ archives ■
Occurrences: 4
Positions:
2735, 4494, 5757, 5777

■ around ■
Occurrences: 4
Positions:
1791, 2035, 4313, 4317

■ automatism ■
Occurrences: 4
Positions:
949, 2997, 5222, 5241

■ autonomous ■
Occurrences: 4
Positions:
2866, 3106, 3210, 4162

■ autonomy ■
Occurrences: 4
Positions:
2996, 3047, 5225, 5244

■ because ■
Occurrences: 4
Positions:
673, 698, 3382, 3788

■ beyond ■
Occurrences: 4
Positions:
2851, 3044, 3422, 5639

■ books ■
Occurrences: 4
Positions:
1937, 4250, 5068, 5173

■ capital ■
Occurrences: 4
Positions:
3022, 3052, 3066, 5131

■ centaur ■
Occurrences: 4
Positions:
1663, 1677, 1723, 1967

■ computosophy ■
Occurrences: 4
Positions:
1959, 1974, 2029, 5500

■ concept ■
Occurrences: 4
Positions:
748, 1512, 2386, 4604

■ counter ■
Occurrences: 4
Positions:
648, 4493, 5776, 5779

■ culture ■
Occurrences: 4
Positions:
3621, 3729, 5128, 5142

■ deleuze ■
Occurrences: 4
Positions:
2381, 2452, 4994, 5642

■ developed ■
Occurrences: 4
Positions:
75, 941, 3922, 4693

■ distributed ■
Occurrences: 4
Positions:
1475, 4481, 4786, 4836

■ does ■
Occurrences: 4
Positions:
650, 2395, 3067, 3072

■ electronic ■
Occurrences: 4
Positions:
429, 769, 987, 5416

■ environment ■
Occurrences: 4
Positions:
556, 603, 1043, 3350

■ even ■
Occurrences: 4
Positions:
2797, 3706, 4783, 5826

■ ever ■
Occurrences: 4
Positions:
1066, 1396, 4824, 4855

■ everything ■
Occurrences: 4
Positions:
517, 580, 586, 2791

■ example ■
Occurrences: 4
Positions:
543, 1056, 1759, 2325

■ f ■
Occurrences: 4
Positions:
4998, 5100, 5126, 5192

■ feed ■
Occurrences: 4
Positions:
4073, 5044, 5553, 5555

■ finance ■
Occurrences: 4
Positions:
3011, 3021, 3051, 5130

■ future ■
Occurrences: 4
Positions:
2708, 3379, 5048, 5377

■ galloway ■
Occurrences: 4
Positions:
2893, 2953, 3777, 5010

■ gannis ■
Occurrences: 4
Positions:
1125, 1144, 5201, 5215

■ global ■
Occurrences: 4
Positions:
35, 62, 766, 858

■ hansen ■
Occurrences: 4
Positions:
1356, 5039, 5488, 5604

■ he ■
Occurrences: 4
Positions:
1877, 2627, 3135, 3768

■ here ■
Occurrences: 4
Positions:
999, 1725, 2615, 5678

■ hybrid ■
Occurrences: 4
Positions:
1203, 2070, 3461, 4008

■ image ■
Occurrences: 4
Positions:
3547, 3596, 3608, 3664

■ insanecomputer ■
Occurrences: 4
Positions:
1945, 2019, 2057, 2172

■ intelligence ■
Occurrences: 4
Positions:
2138, 3254, 3311, 5116

■ languages ■
Occurrences: 4
Positions:
2345, 2467, 2480, 4857

■ latour ■
Occurrences: 4
Positions:
1517, 1522, 4735, 5174

■ main ■
Occurrences: 4
Positions:
574, 1339, 4763, 4842

■ major ■
Occurrences: 4
Positions:
595, 2405, 2423, 2447

■ making ■
Occurrences: 4
Positions:
288, 506, 550, 3800

■ may ■
Occurrences: 4
Positions:
1493, 4166, 4172, 4185

■ mechanical ■
Occurrences: 4
Positions:
4037, 4051, 4541, 4635

■ methods ■
Occurrences: 4
Positions:
72, 938, 1314, 3468

■ minor ■
Occurrences: 4
Positions:
2346, 2388, 2400, 2662

■ mit ■
Occurrences: 4
Positions:
5075, 5091, 5166, 5440

■ modern ■
Occurrences: 4
Positions:
77, 943, 946, 2302

■ much ■
Occurrences: 4
Positions:
460, 1209, 1295, 1364

■ must ■
Occurrences: 4
Positions:
2030, 2931, 2938, 3206

■ nor ■
Occurrences: 4
Positions:
3068, 4089, 5221, 5240

■ nostalgia ■
Occurrences: 4
Positions:
4235, 4364, 4873, 4885

■ now ■
Occurrences: 4
Positions:
1643, 2783, 3724, 4218

■ performing ■
Occurrences: 4
Positions:
1363, 1420, 1711, 4653

■ place ■
Occurrences: 4
Positions:
591, 779, 2756, 4416

■ practice ■
Occurrences: 4
Positions:
202, 1147, 1376, 1732

■ present ■
Occurrences: 4
Positions:
84, 2719, 4340, 4845

■ process ■
Occurrences: 4
Positions:
412, 1222, 1575, 2124

■ processes ■
Occurrences: 4
Positions:
1617, 2089, 4569, 5473

■ project ■
Occurrences: 4
Positions:
1957, 1999, 2025, 2059

■ reality ■
Occurrences: 4
Positions:
569, 3906, 5197, 5211

■ seen ■
Occurrences: 4
Positions:
1846, 2149, 3341, 3741

■ siratori ■
Occurrences: 4
Positions:
2368, 2535, 2569, 5277

■ so ■
Occurrences: 4
Positions:
334, 1372, 1626, 2650

■ symbiopoiesis ■
Occurrences: 4
Positions:
1459, 1510, 4892, 4901

■ those ■
Occurrences: 4
Positions:
1335, 1419, 4425, 4766

■ timespaces ■
Occurrences: 4
Positions:
2763, 4424, 4478, 4520

■ traditional ■
Occurrences: 4
Positions:
863, 2620, 3424, 3466

■ ultimate ■
Occurrences: 4
Positions:
3243, 3251, 3268, 3308

■ use ■
Occurrences: 4
Positions:
20, 906, 1313, 1722

■ used ■
Occurrences: 4
Positions:
1089, 2682, 3125, 5799

■ very ■
Occurrences: 4
Positions:
720, 1729, 2176, 2794

■ without ■
Occurrences: 4
Positions:
755, 2486, 3086, 5382

■ working ■
Occurrences: 4
Positions:
1428, 1440, 2965, 3346

■ world ■
Occurrences: 4
Positions:
3132, 4018, 5381, 5419

■ www ■
Occurrences: 4
Positions:
4961, 5204, 5233, 5299

■ 3 ■
Occurrences: 3
Positions:
2890, 4931, 5502

■ 8 ■
Occurrences: 3
Positions:
4514, 4932, 5793

■ according ■
Occurrences: 3
Positions:
1507, 3014, 3569

■ across ■
Occurrences: 3
Positions:
2425, 4779, 5107

■ action ■
Occurrences: 3
Positions:
1025, 4533, 5179

■ activity ■
Occurrences: 3
Positions:
4528, 5683, 5740

■ aesthetics ■
Occurrences: 3
Positions:
1046, 4985, 5260

■ against ■
Occurrences: 3
Positions:
1691, 2982, 3145

■ al ■
Occurrences: 3
Positions:
1719, 2955, 4789

■ algorithm ■
Occurrences: 3
Positions:
1688, 1746, 4655

■ already ■
Occurrences: 3
Positions:
715, 723, 2151

■ always ■
Occurrences: 3
Positions:
382, 2152, 3578

■ am ■
Occurrences: 3
Positions:
143, 513, 520

■ among ■
Occurrences: 3
Positions:
229, 4269, 4831

■ analysis ■
Occurrences: 3
Positions:
835, 1538, 1657

■ another ■
Occurrences: 3
Positions:
2324, 2412, 2623

■ artificial ■
Occurrences: 3
Positions:
2137, 2867, 5115

■ arts ■
Occurrences: 3
Positions:
4215, 4759, 4927

■ artwork ■
Occurrences: 3
Positions:
837, 4606, 4647

■ assemblages ■
Occurrences: 3
Positions:
109, 1307, 4778

■ authors ■
Occurrences: 3
Positions:
1265, 2361, 3171

■ automated ■
Occurrences: 3
Positions:
13, 2845, 4554

■ automatic ■
Occurrences: 3
Positions:
2835, 2847, 3203

■ automatically ■
Occurrences: 3
Positions:
1316, 1319, 2417

■ available ■
Occurrences: 3
Positions:
1310, 2751, 4411

■ avantgarde ■
Occurrences: 3
Positions:
14, 2846, 2848

■ avedisian ■
Occurrences: 3
Positions:
534, 2741, 4866

■ b ■
Occurrences: 3
Positions:
4946, 5041, 5175

■ bohn ■
Occurrences: 3
Positions:
404, 3429, 4902

■ born ■
Occurrences: 3
Positions:
146, 854, 982

■ cannot ■
Occurrences: 3
Positions:
3158, 4205, 4486

■ carla ■
Occurrences: 3
Positions:
1124, 5200, 5214

■ cherished ■
Occurrences: 3
Positions:
491, 656, 2738

■ chess ■
Occurrences: 3
Positions:
1678, 1687, 1714

■ circulate ■
Occurrences: 3
Positions:
662, 3085, 3860

■ clearly ■
Occurrences: 3
Positions:
1513, 3150, 3155

■ collaborative ■
Occurrences: 3
Positions:
118, 1979, 3890

■ completely ■
Occurrences: 3
Positions:
427, 1619, 2865

■ consciousness ■
Occurrences: 3
Positions:
5487, 5573, 5591

■ continuously ■
Occurrences: 3
Positions:
561, 819, 4822

■ creation ■
Occurrences: 3
Positions:
1212, 1476, 1753

■ critical ■
Occurrences: 3
Positions:
4810, 4846, 5132

■ develop ■
Occurrences: 3
Positions:
2031, 3208, 3872

■ dominant ■
Occurrences: 3
Positions:
2406, 2465, 2504

■ emoji ■
Occurrences: 3
Positions:
1064, 1095, 1129

■ entity ■
Occurrences: 3
Positions:
1988, 2055, 4009

■ et ■
Occurrences: 3
Positions:
1718, 2954, 4788

■ etc ■
Occurrences: 3
Positions:
1180, 3452, 4251

■ explains ■
Occurrences: 3
Positions:
252, 1358, 1849

■ fictions ■
Occurrences: 3
Positions:
1446, 4327, 5745

■ former ■
Occurrences: 3
Positions:
257, 4328, 4393

■ forward ■
Occurrences: 3
Positions:
5045, 5554, 5556

■ generated ■
Occurrences: 3
Positions:
3515, 3640, 5512

■ gif ■
Occurrences: 3
Positions:
3477, 3502, 3670

■ goes ■
Occurrences: 3
Positions:
2849, 3043, 5638

■ guattari ■
Occurrences: 3
Positions:
2383, 2454, 4997

■ harman ■
Occurrences: 3
Positions:
4740, 4747, 5058

■ his ■
Occurrences: 3
Positions:
1851, 2364, 2440

■ how ■
Occurrences: 3
Positions:
1385, 5180, 5742

■ however ■
Occurrences: 3
Positions:
82, 3133, 4352

■ identities ■
Occurrences: 3
Positions:
2696, 2720, 4342

■ if ■
Occurrences: 3
Positions:
712, 4948, 4965

■ including ■
Occurrences: 3
Positions:
1377, 2597, 3694

■ instead ■
Occurrences: 3
Positions:
2067, 2896, 2922

■ interview ■
Occurrences: 3
Positions:
1143, 5198, 5212

■ journal ■
Occurrences: 3
Positions:
4924, 5237, 5303

■ k ■
Occurrences: 3
Positions:
5032, 5071, 5278

■ less ■
Occurrences: 3
Positions:
435, 2413, 3676

■ literatures ■
Occurrences: 3
Positions:
2347, 2663, 5358

■ lost ■
Occurrences: 3
Positions:
175, 4296, 4384

■ m ■
Occurrences: 3
Positions:
4887, 5016, 5040

■ machines ■
Occurrences: 3
Positions:
2498, 4539, 5074

■ madness ■
Occurrences: 3
Positions:
5636, 5665, 5676

■ material ■
Occurrences: 3
Positions:
876, 1276, 1748

■ mediascape ■
Occurrences: 3
Positions:
1345, 1398, 1611

■ mediation ■
Occurrences: 3
Positions:
2914, 3370, 5024

■ memes ■
Occurrences: 3
Positions:
3738, 3763, 3783

■ models ■
Occurrences: 3
Positions:
267, 1544, 1563

■ movements ■
Occurrences: 3
Positions:
81, 948, 2540

■ music ■
Occurrences: 3
Positions:
277, 1326, 4248

■ n ■
Occurrences: 3
Positions:
5042, 5070, 5370

■ named ■
Occurrences: 3
Positions:
238, 1958, 2056

■ nature ■
Occurrences: 3
Positions:
711, 721, 734

■ objective ■
Occurrences: 3
Positions:
697, 1852, 3277

■ once ■
Occurrences: 3
Positions:
531, 583, 1842

■ open ■
Occurrences: 3
Positions:
1071, 1099, 5450

■ part ■
Occurrences: 3
Positions:
191, 5290, 5307

■ particular ■
Occurrences: 3
Positions:
625, 3540, 4475

■ philosopher ■
Occurrences: 3
Positions:
2139, 2375, 5796

■ philosophical ■
Occurrences: 3
Positions:
2219, 4728, 4768

■ plantoids ■
Occurrences: 3
Positions:
4083, 4108, 4120

■ pop ■
Occurrences: 3
Positions:
2854, 3620, 3744

■ printed ■
Occurrences: 3
Positions:
1329, 3508, 4249

■ producing ■
Occurrences: 3
Positions:
814, 1019, 1320

■ production ■
Occurrences: 3
Positions:
1198, 3000, 3064

■ program ■
Occurrences: 3
Positions:
2121, 3274, 3301

■ quite ■
Occurrences: 3
Positions:
1962, 2259, 4135

■ realism ■
Occurrences: 3
Positions:
2226, 4744, 5063

■ recent ■
Occurrences: 3
Positions:
17, 1142, 4727

■ recently ■
Occurrences: 3
Positions:
1665, 1944, 3964

■ recognizes ■
Occurrences: 3
Positions:
1473, 3136, 3261

■ reproduction ■
Occurrences: 3
Positions:
2882, 4571, 4636

■ scott ■
Occurrences: 3
Positions:
702, 3571, 5404

■ sex ■
Occurrences: 3
Positions:
2371, 4323, 5280

■ signs ■
Occurrences: 3
Positions:
680, 803, 1076

■ sound ■
Occurrences: 3
Positions:
2285, 2336, 3711

■ speculative ■
Occurrences: 3
Positions:
3400, 4743, 5062

■ srnicek ■
Occurrences: 3
Positions:
2810, 3174, 5369

■ symbiopoietic ■
Occurrences: 3
Positions:
1408, 1455, 1562

■ synchronicity ■
Occurrences: 3
Positions:
2, 443, 579

■ synchronization ■
Occurrences: 3
Positions:
2744, 4405, 5707

■ syntactic ■
Occurrences: 3
Positions:
2562, 3409, 5630

■ syntopy ■
Occurrences: 3
Positions:
4, 585, 2745

■ systems ■
Occurrences: 3
Positions:
865, 1010, 1669

■ t ■
Occurrences: 3
Positions:
670, 1569, 3765

■ techniques ■
Occurrences: 3
Positions:
1482, 3419, 3837

■ technology ■
Occurrences: 3
Positions:
744, 3009, 3240

■ terms ■
Occurrences: 3
Positions:
511, 3682, 4676

■ textual ■
Occurrences: 3
Positions:
390, 1060, 1381

■ than ■
Occurrences: 3
Positions:
1297, 1366, 1713

■ there ■
Occurrences: 3
Positions:
674, 2185, 3485

■ today ■
Occurrences: 3
Positions:
1163, 2929, 5429

■ together ■
Occurrences: 3
Positions:
1683, 1803, 2078

■ trying ■
Occurrences: 3
Positions:
1190, 1866, 4292

■ two ■
Occurrences: 3
Positions:
2921, 5291, 5308

■ universe ■
Occurrences: 3
Positions:
97, 1050, 1409

■ us ■
Occurrences: 3
Positions:
3218, 3767, 4879

■ via ■
Occurrences: 3
Positions:
4064, 5486, 5549

■ well ■
Occurrences: 3
Positions:
1963, 2850, 4219

■ when ■
Occurrences: 3
Positions:
89, 968, 2205

■ whole ■
Occurrences: 3
Positions:
471, 1041, 1573

■ will ■
Occurrences: 3
Positions:
522, 4955, 4972

■ williams ■
Occurrences: 3
Positions:
2812, 3176, 5372

■ words ■
Occurrences: 3
Positions:
433, 1792, 2567

■ would ■
Occurrences: 3
Positions:
691, 3149, 3317

■ writer ■
Occurrences: 3
Positions:
1602, 1887, 2432

■ writers ■
Occurrences: 3
Positions:
39, 378, 2474

■ york ■
Occurrences: 3
Positions:
1121, 4942, 5150

■ 10 ■
Occurrences: 2
Positions:
5443, 5836

■ 12 ■
Occurrences: 2
Positions:
3888, 4881

■ 16 ■
Occurrences: 2
Positions:
4876, 5118

■ 182 ■
Occurrences: 2
Positions:
2450, 2611

■ 1997 ■
Occurrences: 2
Positions:
3013, 5127

■ 2002 ■
Occurrences: 2
Positions:
879, 5072

■ 2006 ■
Occurrences: 2
Positions:
3436, 5140

■ 2008 ■
Occurrences: 2
Positions:
5434, 5834

■ 2016a ■
Occurrences: 2
Positions:
4265, 5314

■ 24 ■
Occurrences: 2
Positions:
5079, 5134

■ 4 ■
Occurrences: 2
Positions:
3182, 5608

■ 5 ■
Occurrences: 2
Positions:
3413, 5629

■ 6 ■
Occurrences: 2
Positions:
3967, 5751

■ 69 ■
Occurrences: 2
Positions:
5231, 5297

■ 7 ■
Occurrences: 2
Positions:
4499, 5756

■ aaai ■
Occurrences: 2
Positions:
5112, 5117

■ abstract ■
Occurrences: 2
Positions:
15, 2334

■ accelerated ■
Occurrences: 2
Positions:
31, 415

■ access ■
Occurrences: 2
Positions:
5485, 5545

■ actor ■
Occurrences: 2
Positions:
1519, 4732

■ adopting ■
Occurrences: 2
Positions:
2266, 4689

■ after ■
Occurrences: 2
Positions:
2782, 4177

■ again ■
Occurrences: 2
Positions:
1847, 3099

■ age ■
Occurrences: 2
Positions:
3749, 5264

■ ahead ■
Occurrences: 2
Positions:
1350, 4220

■ alexander ■
Occurrences: 2
Positions:
2892, 3775

■ algorithms ■
Occurrences: 2
Positions:
1306, 1744

■ allows ■
Occurrences: 2
Positions:
2746, 4406

■ alphabet ■
Occurrences: 2
Positions:
370, 1100

■ amaranth ■
Occurrences: 2
Positions:
3942, 3946

■ animals ■
Occurrences: 2
Positions:
2952, 3617

■ animated ■
Occurrences: 2
Positions:
3476, 3496

■ anomalies ■
Occurrences: 2
Positions:
2430, 2529

■ apocalypse ■
Occurrences: 2
Positions:
3410, 5631

■ appropriated ■
Occurrences: 2
Positions:
2558, 2740

■ attempt ■
Occurrences: 2
Positions:
2292, 4713

■ autocracy ■
Occurrences: 2
Positions:
5220, 5239

■ based ■
Occurrences: 2
Positions:
149, 1122

■ becoming ■
Occurrences: 2
Positions:
2510, 5659

■ belong ■
Occurrences: 2
Positions:
2397, 5477

■ biological ■
Occurrences: 2
Positions:
633, 4546

■ blocks ■
Occurrences: 2
Positions:
1787, 1813

■ book ■
Occurrences: 2
Positions:
3509, 3533

■ borsuk ■
Occurrences: 2
Positions:
3943, 3947

■ boscacci ■
Occurrences: 2
Positions:
4912, 5791

■ brassier ■
Occurrences: 2
Positions:
4745, 4933

■ build ■
Occurrences: 2
Positions:
4950, 4967

■ building ■
Occurrences: 2
Positions:
1786, 1812

■ butler ■
Occurrences: 2
Positions:
1895, 4945

■ c ■
Occurrences: 2
Positions:
5157, 5346

■ call ■
Occurrences: 2
Positions:
572, 850

■ capitalist ■
Occurrences: 2
Positions:
2834, 3103

■ central ■
Occurrences: 2
Positions:
2414, 5518

■ centrality ■
Occurrences: 2
Positions:
2517, 4753

■ challenges ■
Occurrences: 2
Positions:
598, 4843

■ chicago ■
Occurrences: 2
Positions:
5028, 5056

■ circular ■
Occurrences: 2
Positions:
710, 733

■ circulates ■
Occurrences: 2
Positions:
743, 745

■ coded ■
Occurrences: 2
Positions:
2039, 2081

■ coleman ■
Occurrences: 2
Positions:
1047, 4976

■ collaboration ■
Occurrences: 2
Positions:
1629, 1973

■ collections ■
Occurrences: 2
Positions:
1302, 5782

■ come ■
Occurrences: 2
Positions:
1666, 4167

■ communication ■
Occurrences: 2
Positions:
1091, 2277

■ complex ■
Occurrences: 2
Positions:
1235, 1856

■ composed ■
Occurrences: 2
Positions:
3494, 5687

■ computational ■
Occurrences: 2
Positions:
2193, 2199

■ computers ■
Occurrences: 2
Positions:
1675, 1715

■ conceived ■
Occurrences: 2
Positions:
1389, 1605

■ consequently ■
Occurrences: 2
Positions:
2507, 3838

■ consider ■
Occurrences: 2
Positions:
1266, 3662

■ creates ■
Occurrences: 2
Positions:
1243, 2068

■ cultures ■
Occurrences: 2
Positions:
399, 2478

■ curated ■
Occurrences: 2
Positions:
1280, 3892

■ cyborg ■
Occurrences: 2
Positions:
2065, 2695

■ cycles ■
Occurrences: 2
Positions:
1904, 1906

■ d ■
Occurrences: 2
Positions:
5154, 5169

■ darby ■
Occurrences: 2
Positions:
1770, 3900

■ database ■
Occurrences: 2
Positions:
5251, 5259

■ decay ■
Occurrences: 2
Positions:
4366, 4369

■ defines ■
Occurrences: 2
Positions:
1145, 4355

■ describe ■
Occurrences: 2
Positions:
1668, 2391

■ described ■
Occurrences: 2
Positions:
4617, 5771

■ desirable ■
Occurrences: 2
Positions:
2799, 3237

■ determined ■
Occurrences: 2
Positions:
4112, 4489

■ devices ■
Occurrences: 2
Positions:
74, 940

■ digicult ■
Occurrences: 2
Positions:
5202, 5205

■ discarded ■
Occurrences: 2
Positions:
2726, 4348

■ discourses ■
Occurrences: 2
Positions:
4718, 4769

■ diversification ■
Occurrences: 2
Positions:
48, 2527

■ do ■
Occurrences: 2
Positions:
3199, 5712

■ domain ■
Occurrences: 2
Positions:
5533, 5548

■ due ■
Occurrences: 2
Positions:
32, 3004

■ each ■
Occurrences: 2
Positions:
3529, 5703

■ economy ■
Occurrences: 2
Positions:
4871, 4883

■ edge ■
Occurrences: 2
Positions:
2359, 2968

■ emerging ■
Occurrences: 2
Positions:
56, 2656

■ emojification ■
Occurrences: 2
Positions:
5195, 5209

■ enlightenment ■
Occurrences: 2
Positions:
3166, 4938

■ entities ■
Occurrences: 2
Positions:
3060, 4025

■ environments ■
Occurrences: 2
Positions:
93, 977

■ essential ■
Occurrences: 2
Positions:
1750, 3362

■ ethics ■
Occurrences: 2
Positions:
4983, 5122

■ examples ■
Occurrences: 2
Positions:
2458, 3930

■ excess ■
Occurrences: 2
Positions:
5391, 5409

■ existing ■
Occurrences: 2
Positions:
529, 581

■ experience ■
Occurrences: 2
Positions:
2217, 5593

■ extended ■
Occurrences: 2
Positions:
1730, 3687

■ far ■
Occurrences: 2
Positions:
3223, 3421

■ fast ■
Occurrences: 2
Positions:
1304, 1631

■ film ■
Occurrences: 2
Positions:
4301, 4324

■ final ■
Occurrences: 2
Positions:
2625, 4609

■ find ■
Occurrences: 2
Positions:
1192, 1224

■ first ■
Occurrences: 2
Positions:
5051, 5447

■ font ■
Occurrences: 2
Positions:
234, 3643

■ format ■
Occurrences: 2
Positions:
430, 3565

■ formats ■
Occurrences: 2
Positions:
3394, 3883

■ free ■
Occurrences: 2
Positions:
3190, 4160

■ full ■
Occurrences: 2
Positions:
1742, 2808

■ furious ■
Occurrences: 2
Positions:
2885, 3780

■ futures ■
Occurrences: 2
Positions:
4234, 4331

■ generation ■
Occurrences: 2
Positions:
2372, 5281

■ gifs ■
Occurrences: 2
Positions:
281, 1177

■ goldsmith ■
Occurrences: 2
Positions:
1290, 5031

■ good ■
Occurrences: 2
Positions:
1055, 3265

■ guerrilla ■
Occurrences: 2
Positions:
2370, 5279

■ h ■
Occurrences: 2
Positions:
5139, 5160

■ hand ■
Occurrences: 2
Positions:
2104, 2110

■ happening ■
Occurrences: 2
Positions:
587, 1405

■ hatcher ■
Occurrences: 2
Positions:
2305, 3952

■ hayles ■
Occurrences: 2
Positions:
878, 5069

■ https ■
Occurrences: 2
Positions:
5397, 5493

■ hyperpresent ■
Occurrences: 2
Positions:
2767, 2787

■ ian ■
Occurrences: 2
Positions:
2304, 3951

■ idea ■
Occurrences: 2
Positions:
1765, 1965

■ ikoniadou ■
Occurrences: 2
Positions:
2338, 5080

■ immanent ■
Occurrences: 2
Positions:
2123, 2166

■ indeed ■
Occurrences: 2
Positions:
685, 3313

■ industrial ■
Occurrences: 2
Positions:
284, 3033

■ inside ■
Occurrences: 2
Positions:
2008, 2014

■ intermediations ■
Occurrences: 2
Positions:
37, 889

■ interpretation ■
Occurrences: 2
Positions:
933, 1133

■ introduction ■
Occurrences: 2
Positions:
141, 2365

■ isaksen ■
Occurrences: 2
Positions:
1717, 5095

■ j ■
Occurrences: 2
Positions:
5098, 5414

■ jenkins ■
Occurrences: 2
Positions:
3435, 5138

■ joselit ■
Occurrences: 2
Positions:
4787, 5153

■ kindle ■
Occurrences: 2
Positions:
5490, 5606

■ kinds ■
Occurrences: 2
Positions:
1322, 4625

■ l ■
Occurrences: 2
Positions:
4913, 5249

■ late ■
Occurrences: 2
Positions:
4709, 4807

■ live ■
Occurrences: 2
Positions:
3078, 5599

■ lobster ■
Occurrences: 2
Positions:
240, 246

■ look ■
Occurrences: 2
Positions:
2002, 4176

■ lorenzin ■
Occurrences: 2
Positions:
1260, 5191

■ made ■
Occurrences: 2
Positions:
3512, 5758

■ mainly ■
Occurrences: 2
Positions:
4649, 5649

■ make ■
Occurrences: 2
Positions:
468, 1868

■ man ■
Occurrences: 2
Positions:
1795, 2944

■ manovich ■
Occurrences: 2
Positions:
873, 5248

■ meaning ■
Occurrences: 2
Positions:
1195, 1789

■ meaningful ■
Occurrences: 2
Positions:
1892, 4389

■ meanings ■
Occurrences: 2
Positions:
827, 967

■ mechanics ■
Occurrences: 2
Positions:
305, 4643

■ memories ■
Occurrences: 2
Positions:
2723, 4345

■ memory ■
Occurrences: 2
Positions:
4256, 5343

■ mind ■
Occurrences: 2
Positions:
2072, 2238

■ mixed ■
Occurrences: 2
Positions:
979, 3459

■ mode ■
Occurrences: 2
Positions:
3798, 5587

■ modernist ■
Occurrences: 2
Positions:
3049, 4603

■ movement ■
Occurrences: 2
Positions:
3557, 3667

■ multi ■
Occurrences: 2
Positions:
1214, 3380

■ musicality ■
Occurrences: 2
Positions:
2296, 2332

■ mutation ■
Occurrences: 2
Positions:
845, 4572

■ my ■
Occurrences: 2
Positions:
173, 997

■ myself ■
Occurrences: 2
Positions:
503, 505

■ narrative ■
Occurrences: 2
Positions:
1442, 1445

■ narratives ■
Occurrences: 2
Positions:
2752, 4336

■ necessarily ■
Occurrences: 2
Positions:
3207, 4480

■ needs ■
Occurrences: 2
Positions:
660, 2818

■ object ■
Occurrences: 2
Positions:
4611, 4737

■ off ■
Occurrences: 2
Positions:
452, 3717

■ offering ■
Occurrences: 2
Positions:
3759, 3802

■ old ■
Occurrences: 2
Positions:
4230, 5144

■ opening ■
Occurrences: 2
Positions:
2761, 4421

■ operation ■
Occurrences: 2
Positions:
5551, 5559

■ operations ■
Occurrences: 2
Positions:
1423, 4110

■ order ■
Occurrences: 2
Positions:
664, 4375

■ original ■
Occurrences: 2
Positions:
233, 677

■ originally ■
Occurrences: 2
Positions:
220, 3850

■ over ■
Occurrences: 2
Positions:
166, 1554

■ owned ■
Occurrences: 2
Positions:
3992, 4093

■ page ■
Occurrences: 2
Positions:
218, 3938

■ para ■
Occurrences: 2
Positions:
2023, 4674

■ paradigms ■
Occurrences: 2
Positions:
2220, 2242

■ past ■
Occurrences: 2
Positions:
2706, 4233

■ perceived ■
Occurrences: 2
Positions:
1593, 3128

■ perspective ■
Occurrences: 2
Positions:
2049, 2134

■ phenomenological ■
Occurrences: 2
Positions:
5455, 5596

■ physical ■
Occurrences: 2
Positions:
4015, 4031

■ play ■
Occurrences: 2
Positions:
3039, 3057

■ poem ■
Occurrences: 2
Positions:
2928, 3530

■ poet ■
Occurrences: 2
Positions:
152, 389

■ poetic ■
Occurrences: 2
Positions:
3559, 4404

■ political ■
Occurrences: 2
Positions:
2241, 2972

■ popular ■
Occurrences: 2
Positions:
1069, 3679

■ possible ■
Occurrences: 2
Positions:
3225, 4194

■ postmodern ■
Occurrences: 2
Positions:
79, 3038

■ potential ■
Occurrences: 2
Positions:
5524, 5657

■ potentiality ■
Occurrences: 2
Positions:
2889, 5503

■ pp ■
Occurrences: 2
Positions:
4991, 5077

■ practices ■
Occurrences: 2
Positions:
3288, 4864

■ pre ■
Occurrences: 2
Positions:
626, 4488

■ primarily ■
Occurrences: 2
Positions:
659, 5667

■ processing ■
Occurrences: 2
Positions:
1632, 2099

■ programs ■
Occurrences: 2
Positions:
5292, 5309

■ projects ■
Occurrences: 2
Positions:
1651, 2574

■ properly ■
Occurrences: 2
Positions:
4363, 5453

■ provide ■
Occurrences: 2
Positions:
1233, 1833

■ prsentation ■
Occurrences: 2
Positions:
2748, 4408

■ radical ■
Occurrences: 2
Positions:
2666, 5575

■ radically ■
Occurrences: 2
Positions:
2476, 2581

■ realizabilities ■
Occurrences: 2
Positions:
5294, 5311

■ realm ■
Occurrences: 2
Positions:
3118, 4511

■ recurrent ■
Occurrences: 2
Positions:
4271, 5731

■ references ■
Occurrences: 2
Positions:
301, 4865

■ refers ■
Occurrences: 2
Positions:
1524, 2614

■ related ■
Occurrences: 2
Positions:
2282, 5701

■ remains ■
Occurrences: 2
Positions:
360, 4838

■ repetition ■
Occurrences: 2
Positions:
951, 1921

■ representational ■
Occurrences: 2
Positions:
2093, 2213

■ review ■
Occurrences: 2
Positions:
4922, 5614

■ reza ■
Occurrences: 2
Positions:
2376, 3227

■ rhizome ■
Occurrences: 2
Positions:
198, 347

■ role ■
Occurrences: 2
Positions:
1165, 3295

■ schizophrenia ■
Occurrences: 2
Positions:
5005, 5646

■ science ■
Occurrences: 2
Positions:
4930, 5177

■ sculpture ■
Occurrences: 2
Positions:
3989, 4038

■ seamless ■
Occurrences: 2
Positions:
1970, 3926

■ search ■
Occurrences: 2
Positions:
2328, 4658

■ see ■
Occurrences: 2
Positions:
3201, 5617

■ seems ■
Occurrences: 2
Positions:
1642, 2792

■ sensibility ■
Occurrences: 2
Positions:
5535, 5567

■ sentences ■
Occurrences: 2
Positions:
1807, 1822

■ shared ■
Occurrences: 2
Positions:
3697, 5724

■ shift ■
Occurrences: 2
Positions:
1456, 1467

■ simply ■
Occurrences: 2
Positions:
1879, 3216

■ simultaneously ■
Occurrences: 2
Positions:
185, 2779

■ since ■
Occurrences: 2
Positions:
365, 416

■ society ■
Occurrences: 2
Positions:
5124, 5187

■ sometimes ■
Occurrences: 2
Positions:
3592, 4552

■ source ■
Occurrences: 2
Positions:
1274, 2270

■ steve ■
Occurrences: 2
Positions:
1939, 3551

■ storytelling ■
Occurrences: 2
Positions:
3434, 3467

■ structures ■
Occurrences: 2
Positions:
1817, 2563

■ subjectivity ■
Occurrences: 2
Positions:
4755, 5725

■ subtle ■
Occurrences: 2
Positions:
300, 4387

■ tabbi ■
Occurrences: 2
Positions:
771, 5413

■ task ■
Occurrences: 2
Positions:
3244, 3269

■ teleological ■
Occurrences: 2
Positions:
696, 4717

■ term ■
Occurrences: 2
Positions:
1662, 2022

■ themselves ■
Occurrences: 2
Positions:
824, 1917

■ then ■
Occurrences: 2
Positions:
1801, 1809

■ these ■
Occurrences: 2
Positions:
924, 4623

■ think ■
Occurrences: 2
Positions:
1162, 2189

■ third ■
Occurrences: 2
Positions:
2909, 2936

■ thoroughly ■
Occurrences: 2
Positions:
2105, 2129

■ tools ■
Occurrences: 2
Positions:
1641, 1882

■ transition ■
Occurrences: 2
Positions:
2576, 2617

■ translating ■
Occurrences: 2
Positions:
2590, 2633

■ twenty ■
Occurrences: 2
Positions:
5050, 5446

■ type ■
Occurrences: 2
Positions:
2660, 3092

■ uncreative ■
Occurrences: 2
Positions:
1288, 5034

■ understanding ■
Occurrences: 2
Positions:
1469, 2672

■ unknown ■
Occurrences: 2
Positions:
297, 1620

■ upgraded ■
Occurrences: 2
Positions:
485, 672

■ value ■
Occurrences: 2
Positions:
2999, 4664

■ vice ■
Occurrences: 2
Positions:
4959, 4962

■ videogame ■
Occurrences: 2
Positions:
2596, 2639

■ violent ■
Occurrences: 2
Positions:
2592, 2635

■ vis ■
Occurrences: 2
Positions:
3030, 3032

■ vol ■
Occurrences: 2
Positions:
5320, 5363

■ was ■
Occurrences: 2
Positions:
519, 1460

■ western ■
Occurrences: 2
Positions:
363, 377

■ why ■
Occurrences: 2
Positions:
3811, 4699

■ widely ■
Occurrences: 2
Positions:
1088, 1309

■ wonderful ■
Occurrences: 2
Positions:
1758, 3929

■ wordpress ■
Occurrences: 2
Positions:
5399, 5495

■ write ■
Occurrences: 2
Positions:
4956, 4973

■ writes ■
Occurrences: 2
Positions:
2416, 3769

■ written ■
Occurrences: 2
Positions:
1104, 3449

■ xenotext ■
Occurrences: 2
Positions:
3961, 4549

■ your ■
Occurrences: 2
Positions:
4953, 4970

■ youth ■
Occurrences: 2
Positions:
174, 317

■ zielinski ■
Occurrences: 2
Positions:
5432, 5833

■ 01 ■
Occurrences: 1
Positions:
5328

■ 02 ■
Occurrences: 1
Positions:
4898

■ 03 ■
Occurrences: 1
Positions:
5498

■ 04 ■
Occurrences: 1
Positions:
5329

■ 05 ■
Occurrences: 1
Positions:
5499

■ 06 ■
Occurrences: 1
Positions:
4897

■ 09 ■
Occurrences: 1
Positions:
5402

■ 11 ■
Occurrences: 1
Positions:
4992

■ 15 ■
Occurrences: 1
Positions:
4993

■ 1529 ■
Occurrences: 1
Positions:
5491

■ 183 ■
Occurrences: 1
Positions:
2492

■ 19 ■
Occurrences: 1
Positions:
5094

■ 20th ■
Occurrences: 1
Positions:
178

■ 21 ■
Occurrences: 1
Positions:
5078

■ 264 ■
Occurrences: 1
Positions:
5136

■ 265 ■
Occurrences: 1
Positions:
5137

■ 30 ■
Occurrences: 1
Positions:
5403

■ 31 ■
Occurrences: 1
Positions:
5430

■ 3d ■
Occurrences: 1
Positions:
1328

■ 63 ■
Occurrences: 1
Positions:
2957

■ 736 ■
Occurrences: 1
Positions:
5607

■ ability ■
Occurrences: 1
Positions:
3858

■ abra ■
Occurrences: 1
Positions:
3944

■ absolute ■
Occurrences: 1
Positions:
2857

■ absolution ■
Occurrences: 1
Positions:
4282

■ abuín ■
Occurrences: 1
Positions:
5347

■ accelerate ■
Occurrences: 1
Positions:
5624

■ accelerationism ■
Occurrences: 1
Positions:
5616

■ accelerationist ■
Occurrences: 1
Positions:
5626

■ accelerationists ■
Occurrences: 1
Positions:
3181

■ accessed ■
Occurrences: 1
Positions:
5564

■ accountable ■
Occurrences: 1
Positions:
1570

■ accounts ■
Occurrences: 1
Positions:
4241

■ acestes ■
Occurrences: 1
Positions:
4285

■ achieve ■
Occurrences: 1
Positions:
1888

■ achievement ■
Occurrences: 1
Positions:
3282

■ acknowledging ■
Occurrences: 1
Positions:
545

■ acquire ■
Occurrences: 1
Positions:
959

■ activation ■
Occurrences: 1
Positions:
4463

■ actors ■
Occurrences: 1
Positions:
1491

■ actually ■
Occurrences: 1
Positions:
4354

■ added ■
Occurrences: 1
Positions:
1080

■ address ■
Occurrences: 1
Positions:
4849

■ adequately ■
Occurrences: 1
Positions:
3260

■ adopts ■
Occurrences: 1
Positions:
3392

■ advantage ■
Occurrences: 1
Positions:
1698

■ advantageous ■
Occurrences: 1
Positions:
1036

■ advantages ■
Occurrences: 1
Positions:
1553

■ aesthetical ■
Occurrences: 1
Positions:
2974

■ affects ■
Occurrences: 1
Positions:
5666

■ agent ■
Occurrences: 1
Positions:
4163

■ agents ■
Occurrences: 1
Positions:
1085

■ ai ■
Occurrences: 1
Positions:
5121

■ aim ■
Occurrences: 1
Positions:
5519

■ aims ■
Occurrences: 1
Positions:
2000

■ albeit ■
Occurrences: 1
Positions:
1246

■ alexis ■
Occurrences: 1
Positions:
161

■ allcaps ■
Occurrences: 1
Positions:
3645

■ allowed ■
Occurrences: 1
Positions:
4174

■ almost ■
Occurrences: 1
Positions:
1272

■ alone ■
Occurrences: 1
Positions:
1716

■ along ■
Occurrences: 1
Positions:
1092

■ alongside ■
Occurrences: 1
Positions:
1483

■ alt ■
Occurrences: 1
Positions:
3555

■ alter ■
Occurrences: 1
Positions:
1913

■ alternative ■
Occurrences: 1
Positions:
5765

■ amorphous ■
Occurrences: 1
Positions:
1987

■ amplified ■
Occurrences: 1
Positions:
2233

■ analog ■
Occurrences: 1
Positions:
4246

■ analogy ■
Occurrences: 1
Positions:
310

■ anarchival ■
Occurrences: 1
Positions:
5774

■ ancestral ■
Occurrences: 1
Positions:
2240

■ android ■
Occurrences: 1
Positions:
3976

■ annihilates ■
Occurrences: 1
Positions:
2918

■ anonymous ■
Occurrences: 1
Positions:
1947

■ anthology ■
Occurrences: 1
Positions:
183

■ apparatus ■
Occurrences: 1
Positions:
2319

■ appear ■
Occurrences: 1
Positions:
1841

■ appearing ■
Occurrences: 1
Positions:
2481

■ applicable ■
Occurrences: 1
Positions:
2642

■ application ■
Occurrences: 1
Positions:
1762

■ appreciated ■
Occurrences: 1
Positions:
4057

■ appreciation ■
Occurrences: 1
Positions:
4061

■ appropriation ■
Occurrences: 1
Positions:
3560

■ apropriation ■
Occurrences: 1
Positions:
3352

■ aq ■
Occurrences: 1
Positions:
4874

■ aramcheck ■
Occurrences: 1
Positions:
3909

■ arborescent ■
Occurrences: 1
Positions:
1543

■ archeology ■
Occurrences: 1
Positions:
3402

■ architectures ■
Occurrences: 1
Positions:
2604

■ aren ■
Occurrences: 1
Positions:
3764

■ argued ■
Occurrences: 1
Positions:
3019

■ arrangements ■
Occurrences: 1
Positions:
119

■ article ■
Occurrences: 1
Positions:
121

■ artictic ■
Occurrences: 1
Positions:
2829

■ artifacts ■
Occurrences: 1
Positions:
2214

■ artwoks ■
Occurrences: 1
Positions:
3935

■ asemic ■
Occurrences: 1
Positions:
954

■ asked ■
Occurrences: 1
Positions:
341

■ asking ■
Occurrences: 1
Positions:
2174

■ assertion ■
Occurrences: 1
Positions:
4764

■ assimetrical ■
Occurrences: 1
Positions:
5695

■ associated ■
Occurrences: 1
Positions:
3834

■ associations ■
Occurrences: 1
Positions:
3721

■ assured ■
Occurrences: 1
Positions:
158

■ atopic ■
Occurrences: 1
Positions:
895

■ attached ■
Occurrences: 1
Positions:
622

■ attaching ■
Occurrences: 1
Positions:
823

■ audio ■
Occurrences: 1
Positions:
3708

■ auratic ■
Occurrences: 1
Positions:
4615

■ authored ■
Occurrences: 1
Positions:
4861

■ auto ■
Occurrences: 1
Positions:
4652

■ autocratic ■
Occurrences: 1
Positions:
3165

■ automating ■
Occurrences: 1
Positions:
3187

■ autonomization ■
Occurrences: 1
Positions:
3029

■ autonomized ■
Occurrences: 1
Positions:
3041

■ autopoiesis ■
Occurrences: 1
Positions:
1555

■ autopoietic ■
Occurrences: 1
Positions:
3988

■ availability ■
Occurrences: 1
Positions:
4585

■ avanesian ■
Occurrences: 1
Positions:
5621

■ avangardist ■
Occurrences: 1
Positions:
80

■ avantgardist ■
Occurrences: 1
Positions:
947

■ avenues ■
Occurrences: 1
Positions:
4310

■ balloon ■
Occurrences: 1
Positions:
1797

■ basic ■
Occurrences: 1
Positions:
3790

■ beatty ■
Occurrences: 1
Positions:
5156

■ beauty ■
Occurrences: 1
Positions:
4052

■ beckett ■
Occurrences: 1
Positions:
2461

■ before ■
Occurrences: 1
Positions:
2780

■ begin ■
Occurrences: 1
Positions:
2227

■ beginning ■
Occurrences: 1
Positions:
367

■ begs ■
Occurrences: 1
Positions:
4054

■ behind ■
Occurrences: 1
Positions:
4213

■ believe ■
Occurrences: 1
Positions:
3183

■ benjamin ■
Occurrences: 1
Positions:
4620

■ benjamins ■
Occurrences: 1
Positions:
5366

■ best ■
Occurrences: 1
Positions:
5747

■ better ■
Occurrences: 1
Positions:
1712

■ biology ■
Occurrences: 1
Positions:
1017

■ birth ■
Occurrences: 1
Positions:
868

■ bitcoin ■
Occurrences: 1
Positions:
4081

■ bleed ■
Occurrences: 1
Positions:
2541

■ blending ■
Occurrences: 1
Positions:
411

■ blockchain ■
Occurrences: 1
Positions:
4028

■ blogs ■
Occurrences: 1
Positions:
3903

■ boards ■
Occurrences: 1
Positions:
3712

■ body ■
Occurrences: 1
Positions:
2322

■ bok ■
Occurrences: 1
Positions:
3958

■ boomed ■
Occurrences: 1
Positions:
917

■ borrows ■
Occurrences: 1
Positions:
2379

■ bosch ■
Occurrences: 1
Positions:
1136

■ bought ■
Occurrences: 1
Positions:
4086

■ brandon ■
Occurrences: 1
Positions:
4305

■ brings ■
Occurrences: 1
Positions:
3053

■ broader ■
Occurrences: 1
Positions:
3681

■ brow ■
Occurrences: 1
Positions:
3627

■ bruno ■
Occurrences: 1
Positions:
1516

■ bugs ■
Occurrences: 1
Positions:
2601

■ built ■
Occurrences: 1
Positions:
4641

■ buried ■
Occurrences: 1
Positions:
5790

■ burst ■
Occurrences: 1
Positions:
5716

■ cadences ■
Occurrences: 1
Positions:
2274

■ called ■
Occurrences: 1
Positions:
1453

■ calls ■
Occurrences: 1
Positions:
3778

■ case ■
Occurrences: 1
Positions:
2533

■ cases ■
Occurrences: 1
Positions:
4575

■ catalog ■
Occurrences: 1
Positions:
1186

■ cats ■
Occurrences: 1
Positions:
3610

■ causal ■
Occurrences: 1
Positions:
5508

■ celebrities ■
Occurrences: 1
Positions:
3618

■ challenged ■
Occurrences: 1
Positions:
4751

■ change ■
Occurrences: 1
Positions:
1925

■ changing ■
Occurrences: 1
Positions:
1397

■ chaotic ■
Occurrences: 1
Positions:
1402

■ chaplin ■
Occurrences: 1
Positions:
4320

■ characteristics ■
Occurrences: 1
Positions:
2420

■ characterizes ■
Occurrences: 1
Positions:
4622

■ charged ■
Occurrences: 1
Positions:
4612

■ charles ■
Occurrences: 1
Positions:
4319

■ chemical ■
Occurrences: 1
Positions:
812

■ chinese ■
Occurrences: 1
Positions:
388

■ christian ■
Occurrences: 1
Positions:
3957

■ cinq ■
Occurrences: 1
Positions:
5319

■ circuitous ■
Occurrences: 1
Positions:
1247

■ circulating ■
Occurrences: 1
Positions:
3732

■ circumstances ■
Occurrences: 1
Positions:
548

■ class ■
Occurrences: 1
Positions:
2249

■ classic ■
Occurrences: 1
Positions:
5640

■ clear ■
Occurrences: 1
Positions:
741

■ click ■
Occurrences: 1
Positions:
1256

■ clips ■
Occurrences: 1
Positions:
3709

■ close ■
Occurrences: 1
Positions:
1628

■ closely ■
Occurrences: 1
Positions:
2281

■ clouds ■
Occurrences: 1
Positions:
3649

■ co ■
Occurrences: 1
Positions:
4562

■ coalescence ■
Occurrences: 1
Positions:
2316

■ coder ■
Occurrences: 1
Positions:
2077

■ coding ■
Occurrences: 1
Positions:
4980

■ cognition ■
Occurrences: 1
Positions:
5675

■ cognitive ■
Occurrences: 1
Positions:
5653

■ coherently ■
Occurrences: 1
Positions:
3258

■ collage ■
Occurrences: 1
Positions:
953

■ colleague ■
Occurrences: 1
Positions:
160

■ collection ■
Occurrences: 1
Positions:
2309

■ collective ■
Occurrences: 1
Positions:
5723

■ collide ■
Occurrences: 1
Positions:
5148

■ colliding ■
Occurrences: 1
Positions:
808

■ colour ■
Occurrences: 1
Positions:
3648

■ columbia ■
Occurrences: 1
Positions:
5036

■ combinations ■
Occurrences: 1
Positions:
1820

■ combines ■
Occurrences: 1
Positions:
2916

■ combining ■
Occurrences: 1
Positions:
2341

■ comic ■
Occurrences: 1
Positions:
3651

■ coming ■
Occurrences: 1
Positions:
509

■ communities ■
Occurrences: 1
Positions:
897

■ comparative ■
Occurrences: 1
Positions:
5354

■ comparison ■
Occurrences: 1
Positions:
2626

■ compelling ■
Occurrences: 1
Positions:
1230

■ compete ■
Occurrences: 1
Positions:
1690

■ comprise ■
Occurrences: 1
Positions:
2765

■ comprised ■
Occurrences: 1
Positions:
1399

■ computation ■
Occurrences: 1
Positions:
2095

■ conception ■
Occurrences: 1
Positions:
737

■ conceptual ■
Occurrences: 1
Positions:
1552

■ conceptualism ■
Occurrences: 1
Positions:
956

■ conceptualizations ■
Occurrences: 1
Positions:
567

■ concerned ■
Occurrences: 1
Positions:
2313

■ conclusion ■
Occurrences: 1
Positions:
4726

■ condensed ■
Occurrences: 1
Positions:
3829

■ condition ■
Occurrences: 1
Positions:
4263

■ conditions ■
Occurrences: 1
Positions:
627

■ conference ■
Occurrences: 1
Positions:
5113

■ confluence ■
Occurrences: 1
Positions:
2350

■ conform ■
Occurrences: 1
Positions:
4491

■ confront ■
Occurrences: 1
Positions:
2932

■ confronts ■
Occurrences: 1
Positions:
2907

■ confused ■
Occurrences: 1
Positions:
4704

■ conscious ■
Occurrences: 1
Positions:
1537

■ consciously ■
Occurrences: 1
Positions:
2958

■ consciusness ■
Occurrences: 1
Positions:
4784

■ consequences ■
Occurrences: 1
Positions:
3334

■ considerations ■
Occurrences: 1
Positions:
634

■ consistently ■
Occurrences: 1
Positions:
4382

■ constantly ■
Occurrences: 1
Positions:
1078

■ constraint ■
Occurrences: 1
Positions:
5427

■ consume ■
Occurrences: 1
Positions:
3826

■ consumed ■
Occurrences: 1
Positions:
3844

■ consumerism ■
Occurrences: 1
Positions:
307

■ consumption ■
Occurrences: 1
Positions:
3069

■ contains ■
Occurrences: 1
Positions:
3854

■ context ■
Occurrences: 1
Positions:
3291

■ contingent ■
Occurrences: 1
Positions:
3836

■ continuum ■
Occurrences: 1
Positions:
801

■ contract ■
Occurrences: 1
Positions:
4115

■ contracts ■
Occurrences: 1
Positions:
4119

■ contructed ■
Occurrences: 1
Positions:
3587

■ conventional ■
Occurrences: 1
Positions:
1542

■ convergence ■
Occurrences: 1
Positions:
5141

■ conversation ■
Occurrences: 1
Positions:
165

■ conveys ■
Occurrences: 1
Positions:
1900

■ convinctions ■
Occurrences: 1
Positions:
5832

■ cooper ■
Occurrences: 1
Positions:
3500

■ coordinated ■
Occurrences: 1
Positions:
4579

■ coordination ■
Occurrences: 1
Positions:
4525

■ countermemory ■
Occurrences: 1
Positions:
5768

■ couroux ■
Occurrences: 1
Positions:
3914

■ course ■
Occurrences: 1
Positions:
760

■ craft ■
Occurrences: 1
Positions:
3248

■ create ■
Occurrences: 1
Positions:
295

■ created ■
Occurrences: 1
Positions:
221

■ creating ■
Occurrences: 1
Positions:
2041

■ creations ■
Occurrences: 1
Positions:
1660

■ creative ■
Occurrences: 1
Positions:
1650

■ creativity ■
Occurrences: 1
Positions:
1708

■ critically ■
Occurrences: 1
Positions:
122

■ criticism ■
Occurrences: 1
Positions:
2906

■ cult ■
Occurrences: 1
Positions:
4300

■ cultivated ■
Occurrences: 1
Positions:
3285

■ cut ■
Occurrences: 1
Positions:
260

■ cyber ■
Occurrences: 1
Positions:
2572

■ cyberspace ■
Occurrences: 1
Positions:
3076

■ cyclical ■
Occurrences: 1
Positions:
330

■ dark ■
Occurrences: 1
Positions:
2524

■ darwinist ■
Occurrences: 1
Positions:
3720

■ databased ■
Occurrences: 1
Positions:
1430

■ databases ■
Occurrences: 1
Positions:
1299

■ dead ■
Occurrences: 1
Positions:
4802

■ death ■
Occurrences: 1
Positions:
315

■ debates ■
Occurrences: 1
Positions:
5804

■ decades ■
Occurrences: 1
Positions:
921

■ december ■
Occurrences: 1
Positions:
4875

■ decide ■
Occurrences: 1
Positions:
4201

■ def ■
Occurrences: 1
Positions:
3624

■ defense ■
Occurrences: 1
Positions:
3140

■ define ■
Occurrences: 1
Positions:
1727

■ defining ■
Occurrences: 1
Positions:
4667

■ deleuzian ■
Occurrences: 1
Positions:
4536

■ deligts ■
Occurrences: 1
Positions:
1130

■ deliriously ■
Occurrences: 1
Positions:
3164

■ demand ■
Occurrences: 1
Positions:
2802

■ dennis ■
Occurrences: 1
Positions:
3499

■ describes ■
Occurrences: 1
Positions:
494

■ description ■
Occurrences: 1
Positions:
1471

■ desires ■
Occurrences: 1
Positions:
2820

■ desolation ■
Occurrences: 1
Positions:
4308

■ destiny ■
Occurrences: 1
Positions:
4373

■ detailed ■
Occurrences: 1
Positions:
5611

■ developing ■
Occurrences: 1
Positions:
1953

■ development ■
Occurrences: 1
Positions:
3354

■ dickinson ■
Occurrences: 1
Positions:
4909

■ did ■
Occurrences: 1
Positions:
170

■ dietmar ■
Occurrences: 1
Positions:
5794

■ differently ■
Occurrences: 1
Positions:
4599

■ dimension ■
Occurrences: 1
Positions:
3116

■ direct ■
Occurrences: 1
Positions:
5484

■ directly ■
Occurrences: 1
Positions:
5530

■ director ■
Occurrences: 1
Positions:
4302

■ discrete ■
Occurrences: 1
Positions:
4466

■ disctintive ■
Occurrences: 1
Positions:
4258

■ disease ■
Occurrences: 1
Positions:
5654

■ disintegrate ■
Occurrences: 1
Positions:
2255

■ display ■
Occurrences: 1
Positions:
4040

■ easily ■
Occurrences: 1
Positions:
3695

■ easy ■
Occurrences: 1
Positions:
1311

■ ebooks ■
Occurrences: 1
Positions:
5283

■ echovirus ■
Occurrences: 1
Positions:
3887

■ economics ■
Occurrences: 1
Positions:
3205

■ ecosystems ■
Occurrences: 1
Positions:
3928

■ ed ■
Occurrences: 1
Positions:
5258

■ eds ■
Occurrences: 1
Positions:
5352

■ eduardo ■
Occurrences: 1
Positions:
3953

■ efficacy ■
Occurrences: 1
Positions:
5509

■ efficient ■
Occurrences: 1
Positions:
5738

■ electro ■
Occurrences: 1
Positions:
4540

■ elements ■
Occurrences: 1
Positions:
4470

■ elicits ■
Occurrences: 1
Positions:
5632

■ embeddable ■
Occurrences: 1
Positions:
3707

■ embedded ■
Occurrences: 1
Positions:
4721

■ embracement ■
Occurrences: 1
Positions:
2975

■ emergence ■
Occurrences: 1
Positions:
2472

■ emergent ■
Occurrences: 1
Positions:
609

■ emotional ■
Occurrences: 1
Positions:
647

■ empire ■
Occurrences: 1
Positions:
2514

■ encourage ■
Occurrences: 1
Positions:
3217

■ end ■
Occurrences: 1
Positions:
3810

■ endless ■
Occurrences: 1
Positions:
1273

■ engineers ■
Occurrences: 1
Positions:
5185

■ enjoy ■
Occurrences: 1
Positions:
4099

■ enlarged ■
Occurrences: 1
Positions:
792

■ entering ■
Occurrences: 1
Positions:
129

■ enters ■
Occurrences: 1
Positions:
5568

■ environmental ■
Occurrences: 1
Positions:
5472

■ epic ■
Occurrences: 1
Positions:
219

■ epiphenomenal ■
Occurrences: 1
Positions:
3817

■ epiphenomenon ■
Occurrences: 1
Positions:
4707

■ equivalent ■
Occurrences: 1
Positions:
3973

■ era ■
Occurrences: 1
Positions:
327

■ essay ■
Occurrences: 1
Positions:
5333

■ essays ■
Occurrences: 1
Positions:
5064

■ essence ■
Occurrences: 1
Positions:
4006

■ essentially ■
Occurrences: 1
Positions:
2587

■ esteems ■
Occurrences: 1
Positions:
329

■ european ■
Occurrences: 1
Positions:
2466

■ evanescent ■
Occurrences: 1
Positions:
3876

■ event ■
Occurrences: 1
Positions:
5085

■ eventuallity ■
Occurrences: 1
Positions:
843

■ eventually ■
Occurrences: 1
Positions:
4000

■ everchanging ■
Occurrences: 1
Positions:
4654

■ evil ■
Occurrences: 1
Positions:
3147

■ evocative ■
Occurrences: 1
Positions:
4240

■ explain ■
Occurrences: 1
Positions:
2027

■ explained ■
Occurrences: 1
Positions:
700

■ explanatory ■
Occurrences: 1
Positions:
1558

■ explicit ■
Occurrences: 1
Positions:
4136

■ exploration ■
Occurrences: 1
Positions:
2183

■ explores ■
Occurrences: 1
Positions:
5504

■ exploring ■
Occurrences: 1
Positions:
131

■ expressions ■
Occurrences: 1
Positions:
984

■ extense ■
Occurrences: 1
Positions:
5613

■ extension ■
Occurrences: 1
Positions:
2085

■ extinction ■
Occurrences: 1
Positions:
4940

■ extraordinary ■
Occurrences: 1
Positions:
5690

■ extreme ■
Occurrences: 1
Positions:
3368

■ facilitate ■
Occurrences: 1
Positions:
5539

■ factory ■
Occurrences: 1
Positions:
285

■ fairleigh ■
Occurrences: 1
Positions:
4908

■ famous ■
Occurrences: 1
Positions:
1138

■ faster ■
Occurrences: 1
Positions:
1365

■ fear ■
Occurrences: 1
Positions:
2806

■ feel ■
Occurrences: 1
Positions:
1251

■ feeling ■
Occurrences: 1
Positions:
1898

■ feels ■
Occurrences: 1
Positions:
1926

■ feign ■
Occurrences: 1
Positions:
5813

■ fields ■
Occurrences: 1
Positions:
1027

■ filmed ■
Occurrences: 1
Positions:
3451

■ films ■
Occurrences: 1
Positions:
4297

■ finances ■
Occurrences: 1
Positions:
3997

■ flowers ■
Occurrences: 1
Positions:
269

■ flows ■
Occurrences: 1
Positions:
2565

■ follow ■
Occurrences: 1
Positions:
5182

■ follows ■
Occurrences: 1
Positions:
2987

■ footer ■
Occurrences: 1
Positions:
3602

■ foreign ■
Occurrences: 1
Positions:
1622

■ forgiving ■
Occurrences: 1
Positions:
504

■ formula ■
Occurrences: 1
Positions:
3745

■ forthcoming ■
Occurrences: 1
Positions:
2874

■ foster ■
Occurrences: 1
Positions:
5159

■ found ■
Occurrences: 1
Positions:
3590

■ fragment ■
Occurrences: 1
Positions:
3042

■ fragments ■
Occurrences: 1
Positions:
463

■ frameworks ■
Occurrences: 1
Positions:
3425

■ francae ■
Occurrences: 1
Positions:
1012

■ freedom ■
Occurrences: 1
Positions:
4981

■ frequent ■
Occurrences: 1
Positions:
2362

■ frequently ■
Occurrences: 1
Positions:
3391

■ frogs ■
Occurrences: 1
Positions:
3614

■ frozen ■
Occurrences: 1
Positions:
3520

■ fulfill ■
Occurrences: 1
Positions:
2815

■ funcion ■
Occurrences: 1
Positions:
3479

■ funeral ■
Occurrences: 1
Positions:
276

■ further ■
Occurrences: 1
Positions:
3028

■ futural ■
Occurrences: 1
Positions:
5570

■ gallery ■
Occurrences: 1
Positions:
4184

■ games ■
Occurrences: 1
Positions:
5106

■ garden ■
Occurrences: 1
Positions:
1127

■ gathered ■
Occurrences: 1
Positions:
1802

■ gender ■
Occurrences: 1
Positions:
2247

■ general ■
Occurrences: 1
Positions:
1930

■ generalized ■
Occurrences: 1
Positions:
4584

■ genesis ■
Occurrences: 1
Positions:
3956

■ geographical ■
Occurrences: 1
Positions:
631

■ german ■
Occurrences: 1
Positions:
5334

■ gertrud ■
Occurrences: 1
Positions:
1934

■ gesture ■
Occurrences: 1
Positions:
5763

■ ghostly ■
Occurrences: 1
Positions:
454

■ give ■
Occurrences: 1
Positions:
867

■ glacial ■
Occurrences: 1
Positions:
1923

■ glass ■
Occurrences: 1
Positions:
1159

■ glitch ■
Occurrences: 1
Positions:
991

■ glyph ■
Occurrences: 1
Positions:
1072

■ go ■
Occurrences: 1
Positions:
3420

■ governs ■
Occurrences: 1
Positions:
4127

■ graphics ■
Occurrences: 1
Positions:
3633

■ greatest ■
Occurrences: 1
Positions:
3281

■ group ■
Occurrences: 1
Positions:
2941

■ growth ■
Occurrences: 1
Positions:
324

■ guattarian ■
Occurrences: 1
Positions:
5643

■ hacked ■
Occurrences: 1
Positions:
4402

■ hacker ■
Occurrences: 1
Positions:
1045

■ hacking ■
Occurrences: 1
Positions:
4987

■ happens ■
Occurrences: 1
Positions:
2202

■ harvard ■
Occurrences: 1
Positions:
5188

■ haunted ■
Occurrences: 1
Positions:
3504

■ having ■
Occurrences: 1
Positions:
722

■ header ■
Occurrences: 1
Positions:
3599

■ hegemonic ■
Occurrences: 1
Positions:
2512

■ heights ■
Occurrences: 1
Positions:
3003

■ hell ■
Occurrences: 1
Positions:
239

■ help ■
Occurrences: 1
Positions:
1885

■ helvetica ■
Occurrences: 1
Positions:
244

■ heresy ■
Occurrences: 1
Positions:
2044

■ hermeneutics ■
Occurrences: 1
Positions:
2901

■ heterogenous ■
Occurrences: 1
Positions:
2209

■ hi ■
Occurrences: 1
Positions:
3623

■ hidden ■
Occurrences: 1
Positions:
304

■ hieronymus ■
Occurrences: 1
Positions:
1135

■ highlights ■
Occurrences: 1
Positions:
2469

■ highly ■
Occurrences: 1
Positions:
1068

■ highways ■
Occurrences: 1
Positions:
860

■ him ■
Occurrences: 1
Positions:
1625

■ historical ■
Occurrences: 1
Positions:
4223

■ history ■
Occurrences: 1
Positions:
5355

■ hobson ■
Occurrences: 1
Positions:
4306

■ house ■
Occurrences: 1
Positions:
3505

■ humanist ■
Occurrences: 1
Positions:
3139

■ humanities ■
Occurrences: 1
Positions:
1031

■ humanity ■
Occurrences: 1
Positions:
2244

■ hyperstitional ■
Occurrences: 1
Positions:
2769

■ hypothesis ■
Occurrences: 1
Positions:
998

■ iberian ■
Occurrences: 1
Positions:
5361

■ icon ■
Occurrences: 1
Positions:
1110

■ idealism ■
Occurrences: 1
Positions:
2223

■ ideas ■
Occurrences: 1
Positions:
5644

■ identity ■
Occurrences: 1
Positions:
606

■ illudere ■
Occurrences: 1
Positions:
5808

■ illusions ■
Occurrences: 1
Positions:
4513

■ immediately ■
Occurrences: 1
Positions:
2113

■ immortality ■
Occurrences: 1
Positions:
458

■ impact ■
Occurrences: 1
Positions:
3642

■ implementation ■
Occurrences: 1
Positions:
2827

■ implicated ■
Occurrences: 1
Positions:
5468

■ implication ■
Occurrences: 1
Positions:
114

■ implode ■
Occurrences: 1
Positions:
4332

■ imploding ■
Occurrences: 1
Positions:
2711

■ important ■
Occurrences: 1
Positions:
1647

■ impossibility ■
Occurrences: 1
Positions:
321

■ impossible ■
Occurrences: 1
Positions:
2555

■ improvements ■
Occurrences: 1
Positions:
3185

■ impulse ■
Occurrences: 1
Positions:
5775

■ increase ■
Occurrences: 1
Positions:
46

■ increasing ■
Occurrences: 1
Positions:
885

■ independence ■
Occurrences: 1
Positions:
4557

■ independent ■
Occurrences: 1
Positions:
3121

■ independently ■
Occurrences: 1
Positions:
2678

■ indignity ■
Occurrences: 1
Positions:
3196

■ indirect ■
Occurrences: 1
Positions:
5543

■ infection ■
Occurrences: 1
Positions:
1006

■ infernal ■
Occurrences: 1
Positions:
2496

■ infesting ■
Occurrences: 1
Positions:
2546

■ influenced ■
Occurrences: 1
Positions:
1514

■ information ■
Occurrences: 1
Positions:
5266

■ inherits ■
Occurrences: 1
Positions:
764

■ initially ■
Occurrences: 1
Positions:
1781

■ innovative ■
Occurrences: 1
Positions:
137

■ inquiries ■
Occurrences: 1
Positions:
5020

■ inquiry ■
Occurrences: 1
Positions:
5133

■ insist ■
Occurrences: 1
Positions:
5801

■ insists ■
Occurrences: 1
Positions:
478

■ inspirational ■
Occurrences: 1
Positions:
3699

■ installation ■
Occurrences: 1
Positions:
3983

■ instantaneous ■
Occurrences: 1
Positions:
4597

■ instructions ■
Occurrences: 1
Positions:
1432

■ insurgent ■
Occurrences: 1
Positions:
2435

■ intangible ■
Occurrences: 1
Positions:
1496

■ integrate ■
Occurrences: 1
Positions:
1672

■ inteligence ■
Occurrences: 1
Positions:
2868

■ intended ■
Occurrences: 1
Positions:
3579

■ intense ■
Occurrences: 1
Positions:
5734

■ intensive ■
Occurrences: 1
Positions:
5515

■ interact ■
Occurrences: 1
Positions:
4022

■ interaction ■
Occurrences: 1
Positions:
4103

■ interested ■
Occurrences: 1
Positions:
1880

■ interfere ■
Occurrences: 1
Positions:
4715

■ internal ■
Occurrences: 1
Positions:
3082

■ international ■
Occurrences: 1
Positions:
4923

■ interpretations ■
Occurrences: 1
Positions:
67

■ intervals ■
Occurrences: 1
Positions:
1831

■ intervention ■
Occurrences: 1
Positions:
4567

■ kept ■
Occurrences: 1
Positions:
1824

■ knowledge ■
Occurrences: 1
Positions:
5766

■ laing ■
Occurrences: 1
Positions:
4286

■ lambert ■
Occurrences: 1
Positions:
5155

■ landscapes ■
Occurrences: 1
Positions:
1023

■ lantz ■
Occurrences: 1
Positions:
5099

■ large ■
Occurrences: 1
Positions:
5691

■ largely ■
Occurrences: 1
Positions:
1531

■ larger ■
Occurrences: 1
Positions:
5471

■ last ■
Occurrences: 1
Positions:
920

■ later ■
Occurrences: 1
Positions:
3137

■ latourian ■
Occurrences: 1
Positions:
4538

■ launched ■
Occurrences: 1
Positions:
184

■ layered ■
Occurrences: 1
Positions:
1215

■ leave ■
Occurrences: 1
Positions:
4203

■ leaving ■
Occurrences: 1
Positions:
4386

■ lectures ■
Occurrences: 1
Positions:
5066

■ left ■
Occurrences: 1
Positions:
3180

■ legal ■
Occurrences: 1
Positions:
4124

■ legend ■
Occurrences: 1
Positions:
4316

■ liberal ■
Occurrences: 1
Positions:
4926

■ library ■
Occurrences: 1
Positions:
1111

■ limit ■
Occurrences: 1
Positions:
3657

■ limited ■
Occurrences: 1
Positions:
782

■ limits ■
Occurrences: 1
Positions:
2037

■ line ■
Occurrences: 1
Positions:
1237

■ lines ■
Occurrences: 1
Positions:
3526

■ linguae ■
Occurrences: 1
Positions:
1011

■ liquid ■
Occurrences: 1
Positions:
293

■ lit ■
Occurrences: 1
Positions:
3556

■ lived ■
Occurrences: 1
Positions:
465

■ living ■
Occurrences: 1
Positions:
2778

■ lo ■
Occurrences: 1
Positions:
3626

■ lone ■
Occurrences: 1
Positions:
3143

■ long ■
Occurrences: 1
Positions:
402

■ longer ■
Occurrences: 1
Positions:
2128

■ looking ■
Occurrences: 1
Positions:
1158

■ loop ■
Occurrences: 1
Positions:
2770

■ looped ■
Occurrences: 1
Positions:
3666

■ looping ■
Occurrences: 1
Positions:
280

■ low ■
Occurrences: 1
Positions:
3594

■ lsrson ■
Occurrences: 1
Positions:
2647

■ machinic ■
Occurrences: 1
Positions:
2276

■ mackay ■
Occurrences: 1
Positions:
5618

■ macmillan ■
Occurrences: 1
Positions:
4944

■ macro ■
Occurrences: 1
Positions:
3548

■ mail ■
Occurrences: 1
Positions:
168

■ majority ■
Occurrences: 1
Positions:
419

■ manifesting ■
Occurrences: 1
Positions:
3110

■ manipulate ■
Occurrences: 1
Positions:
1859

■ manipulation ■
Occurrences: 1
Positions:
6

■ manipulator ■
Occurrences: 1
Positions:
1608

■ manufacture ■
Occurrences: 1
Positions:
4129

■ manupulated ■
Occurrences: 1
Positions:
102

■ marc ■
Occurrences: 1
Positions:
3913

■ march ■
Occurrences: 1
Positions:
187

■ mark ■
Occurrences: 1
Positions:
1355

■ marked ■
Occurrences: 1
Positions:
3025

■ market ■
Occurrences: 1
Positions:
438

■ mashup ■
Occurrences: 1
Positions:
952

■ materialism ■
Occurrences: 1
Positions:
2224

■ materialisms ■
Occurrences: 1
Positions:
5165

■ materialist ■
Occurrences: 1
Positions:
2335

■ matt ■
Occurrences: 1
Positions:
1463

■ mattbernico ■
Occurrences: 1
Positions:
4894

■ matter ■
Occurrences: 1
Positions:
1384

■ maybe ■
Occurrences: 1
Positions:
356

■ me ■
Occurrences: 1
Positions:
528

■ meaningless ■
Occurrences: 1
Positions:
5736

■ mediate ■
Occurrences: 1
Positions:
5531

■ mediatic ■
Occurrences: 1
Positions:
3797

■ mere ■
Occurrences: 1
Positions:
1640

■ merging ■
Occurrences: 1
Positions:
396

■ metabolisms ■
Occurrences: 1
Positions:
3083

■ metaphor ■
Occurrences: 1
Positions:
1193

■ metaphors ■
Occurrences: 1
Positions:
877

■ metastable ■
Occurrences: 1
Positions:
4440

■ method ■
Occurrences: 1
Positions:
2187

■ microcomputational ■
Occurrences: 1
Positions:
5527

■ minimal ■
Occurrences: 1
Positions:
3731

■ minnesota ■
Occurrences: 1
Positions:
5270

■ minnessota ■
Occurrences: 1
Positions:
5008

■ mix ■
Occurrences: 1
Positions:
242

■ mixes ■
Occurrences: 1
Positions:
2074

■ mixture ■
Occurrences: 1
Positions:
2210

■ model ■
Occurrences: 1
Positions:
1559

■ modes ■
Occurrences: 1
Positions:
112

■ modified ■
Occurrences: 1
Positions:
3593

■ molecular ■
Occurrences: 1
Positions:
1016

■ moments ■
Occurrences: 1
Positions:
5571

■ monetary ■
Occurrences: 1
Positions:
3059

■ money ■
Occurrences: 1
Positions:
3071

■ monfort ■
Occurrences: 1
Positions:
3537

■ monuments ■
Occurrences: 1
Positions:
5780

■ moreover ■
Occurrences: 1
Positions:
339

■ morph ■
Occurrences: 1
Positions:
2229

■ mostly ■
Occurrences: 1
Positions:
4211

■ motion ■
Occurrences: 1
Positions:
3328

■ movie ■
Occurrences: 1
Positions:
3482

■ movies ■
Occurrences: 1
Positions:
4247

■ moving ■
Occurrences: 1
Positions:
4508

■ ms ■
Occurrences: 1
Positions:
3631

■ multimedia ■
Occurrences: 1
Positions:
3431

■ museum ■
Occurrences: 1
Positions:
195

■ mutate ■
Occurrences: 1
Positions:
2230

■ mutated ■
Occurrences: 1
Positions:
2053

■ mythology ■
Occurrences: 1
Positions:
2862

■ names ■
Occurrences: 1
Positions:
5557

■ narrated ■
Occurrences: 1
Positions:
3444

■ narrating ■
Occurrences: 1
Positions:
1154

■ nealon ■
Occurrences: 1
Positions:
5102

■ need ■
Occurrences: 1
Positions:
3062

■ neo ■
Occurrences: 1
Positions:
3719

■ net ■
Occurrences: 1
Positions:
989

■ networking ■
Occurrences: 1
Positions:
4580

■ neuro ■
Occurrences: 1
Positions:
2571

■ never ■
Occurrences: 1
Positions:
1845

■ newhive ■
Occurrences: 1
Positions:
226

■ news ■
Occurrences: 1
Positions:
5207

■ nicholas ■
Occurrences: 1
Positions:
4279

■ nick ■
Occurrences: 1
Positions:
3536

■ nihil ■
Occurrences: 1
Positions:
4936

■ nonhuman ■
Occurrences: 1
Positions:
2216

■ noon ■
Occurrences: 1
Positions:
3895

■ north ■
Occurrences: 1
Positions:
3904

■ notion ■
Occurrences: 1
Positions:
2062

■ nowadays ■
Occurrences: 1
Positions:
4792

■ nude ■
Occurrences: 1
Positions:
266

■ nueva ■
Occurrences: 1
Positions:
4941

■ numerical ■
Occurrences: 1
Positions:
2094

■ numerocinqmagazine ■
Occurrences: 1
Positions:
5325

■ numéro ■
Occurrences: 1
Positions:
5318

■ occurring ■
Occurrences: 1
Positions:
611

■ okhaos ■
Occurrences: 1
Positions:
5753

■ older ■
Occurrences: 1
Positions:
3091

■ omnipresent ■
Occurrences: 1
Positions:
842

■ ongoing ■
Occurrences: 1
Positions:
3875

■ online ■
Occurrences: 1
Positions:
1956

■ ontology ■
Occurrences: 1
Positions:
4739

■ operationality ■
Occurrences: 1
Positions:
5603

■ opt ■
Occurrences: 1
Positions:
4563

■ orbits ■
Occurrences: 1
Positions:
1909

■ oriented ■
Occurrences: 1
Positions:
4738

■ ornaments ■
Occurrences: 1
Positions:
4047

■ others ■
Occurrences: 1
Positions:
1840

■ outcoming ■
Occurrences: 1
Positions:
3238

■ overflow ■
Occurrences: 1
Positions:
5267

■ overlaid ■
Occurrences: 1
Positions:
3597

■ owns ■
Occurrences: 1
Positions:
3995

■ pace ■
Occurrences: 1
Positions:
408

■ pack ■
Occurrences: 1
Positions:
2950

■ paint ■
Occurrences: 1
Positions:
3632

■ painted ■
Occurrences: 1
Positions:
3450

■ painting ■
Occurrences: 1
Positions:
1139

■ palgrave ■
Occurrences: 1
Positions:
4943

■ pandemonium ■
Occurrences: 1
Positions:
2559

■ paper ■
Occurrences: 1
Positions:
4444

■ paracode ■
Occurrences: 1
Positions:
5494

■ paradoxes ■
Occurrences: 1
Positions:
596

■ paroxysmal ■
Occurrences: 1
Positions:
5735

■ parsing ■
Occurrences: 1
Positions:
1172

■ partially ■
Occurrences: 1
Positions:
425

■ participate ■
Occurrences: 1
Positions:
3772

■ pasts ■
Occurrences: 1
Positions:
4329

■ path ■
Occurrences: 1
Positions:
1245

■ patterns ■
Occurrences: 1
Positions:
5708

■ peace ■
Occurrences: 1
Positions:
507

■ peculiarities ■
Occurrences: 1
Positions:
4851

■ peninsula ■
Occurrences: 1
Positions:
5362

■ penny ■
Occurrences: 1
Positions:
156

■ people ■
Occurrences: 1
Positions:
3191

■ perfectly ■
Occurrences: 1
Positions:
2641

■ perhaps ■
Occurrences: 1
Positions:
5825

■ periphery ■
Occurrences: 1
Positions:
1501

■ permanent ■
Occurrences: 1
Positions:
4504

■ permanently ■
Occurrences: 1
Positions:
807

■ permeates ■
Occurrences: 1
Positions:
4236

■ perpetual ■
Occurrences: 1
Positions:
4657

■ persist ■
Occurrences: 1
Positions:
2250

■ person ■
Occurrences: 1
Positions:
474

■ personal ■
Occurrences: 1
Positions:
323

■ phase ■
Occurrences: 1
Positions:
5459

■ phenomenology ■
Occurrences: 1
Positions:
2904

■ philosophizes ■
Occurrences: 1
Positions:
2146

■ philosopy ■
Occurrences: 1
Positions:
3246

■ photo ■
Occurrences: 1
Positions:
3628

■ phrases ■
Occurrences: 1
Positions:
3700

■ piece ■
Occurrences: 1
Positions:
4455

■ pieces ■
Occurrences: 1
Positions:
1942

■ places ■
Occurrences: 1
Positions:
1810

■ planning ■
Occurrences: 1
Positions:
1705

■ plant ■
Occurrences: 1
Positions:
3972

■ plastic ■
Occurrences: 1
Positions:
4821

■ plateaus ■
Occurrences: 1
Positions:
5002

■ platform ■
Occurrences: 1
Positions:
225

■ playing ■
Occurrences: 1
Positions:
5105

■ plus ■
Occurrences: 1
Positions:
217

■ poetically ■
Occurrences: 1
Positions:
4401

■ poetics ■
Occurrences: 1
Positions:
5428

■ point ■
Occurrences: 1
Positions:
3157

■ pool ■
Occurrences: 1
Positions:
2525

■ popularized ■
Occurrences: 1
Positions:
3549

■ portrait ■
Occurrences: 1
Positions:
210

■ position ■
Occurrences: 1
Positions:
1037

■ positions ■
Occurrences: 1
Positions:
5830

■ possibly ■
Occurrences: 1
Positions:
4673

■ postcapitalism ■
Occurrences: 1
Positions:
5378

■ presence ■
Occurrences: 1
Positions:
4394

■ presented ■
Occurrences: 1
Positions:
424

■ presents ■
Occurrences: 1
Positions:
2705

■ presupposes ■
Occurrences: 1
Positions:
3793

■ prevous ■
Occurrences: 1
Positions:
4443

■ primary ■
Occurrences: 1
Positions:
3647

■ princeton ■
Occurrences: 1
Positions:
4988

■ principal ■
Occurrences: 1
Positions:
5586

■ print ■
Occurrences: 1
Positions:
2684

■ prior ■
Occurrences: 1
Positions:
2488

■ prism ■
Occurrences: 1
Positions:
449

■ private ■
Occurrences: 1
Positions:
4322

■ problem ■
Occurrences: 1
Positions:
2925

■ product ■
Occurrences: 1
Positions:
482

■ profoundly ■
Occurrences: 1
Positions:
4750

■ programmatic ■
Occurrences: 1
Positions:
2043

■ prominent ■
Occurrences: 1
Positions:
2457

■ promises ■
Occurrences: 1
Positions:
455

■ prone ■
Occurrences: 1
Positions:
2508

■ property ■
Occurrences: 1
Positions:
610

■ proposed ■
Occurrences: 1
Positions:
1998

■ propossed ■
Occurrences: 1
Positions:
4805

■ prosthesis ■
Occurrences: 1
Positions:
2307

■ prosthetic ■
Occurrences: 1
Positions:
5458

■ protecting ■
Occurrences: 1
Positions:
502

■ punk ■
Occurrences: 1
Positions:
2573

■ pure ■
Occurrences: 1
Positions:
2913

■ purpose ■
Occurrences: 1
Positions:
3979

■ purposed ■
Occurrences: 1
Positions:
1284

■ push ■
Occurrences: 1
Positions:
3220

■ pushing ■
Occurrences: 1
Positions:
3229

■ put ■
Occurrences: 1
Positions:
725

■ puts ■
Occurrences: 1
Positions:
2894

■ python ■
Occurrences: 1
Positions:
3524

■ qualities ■
Occurrences: 1
Positions:
4616

■ question ■
Occurrences: 1
Positions:
358

■ questionnaire ■
Occurrences: 1
Positions:
5163

■ questions ■
Occurrences: 1
Positions:
2171

■ quoting ■
Occurrences: 1
Positions:
3097

■ race ■
Occurrences: 1
Positions:
2248

■ rag ■
Occurrences: 1
Positions:
271

■ range ■
Occurrences: 1
Positions:
1486

■ rather ■
Occurrences: 1
Positions:
4096

■ reaches ■
Occurrences: 1
Positions:
3001

■ reactions ■
Occurrences: 1
Positions:
813

■ read ■
Occurrences: 1
Positions:
4964

■ reader ■
Occurrences: 1
Positions:
5627

■ reading ■
Occurrences: 1
Positions:
4905

■ realizability ■
Occurrences: 1
Positions:
3305

■ realization ■
Occurrences: 1
Positions:
3278

■ realizes ■
Occurrences: 1
Positions:
3263

■ rearranged ■
Occurrences: 1
Positions:
262

■ reason ■
Occurrences: 1
Positions:
4229

■ rebellion ■
Occurrences: 1
Positions:
2830

■ recognizable ■
Occurrences: 1
Positions:
1021

■ recognize ■
Occurrences: 1
Positions:
1564

■ recombinant ■
Occurrences: 1
Positions:
3462

■ recombination ■
Occurrences: 1
Positions:
2887

■ recover ■
Occurrences: 1
Positions:
4294

■ recreation ■
Occurrences: 1
Positions:
1216

■ recurrence ■
Occurrences: 1
Positions:
5680

■ redundant ■
Occurrences: 1
Positions:
4437

■ reference ■
Occurrences: 1
Positions:
3088

■ reflects ■
Occurrences: 1
Positions:
125

■ regime ■
Occurrences: 1
Positions:
678

■ regressive ■
Occurrences: 1
Positions:
3152

■ reich ■
Occurrences: 1
Positions:
1940

■ reinvent ■
Occurrences: 1
Positions:
2494

■ reiteration ■
Occurrences: 1
Positions:
1911

■ reivindication ■
Occurrences: 1
Positions:
4254

■ relationships ■
Occurrences: 1
Positions:
4380

■ relative ■
Occurrences: 1
Positions:
3046

■ relegated ■
Occurrences: 1
Positions:
1586

■ relies ■
Occurrences: 1
Positions:
4581

■ remail ■
Occurrences: 1
Positions:
2732

■ remain ■
Occurrences: 1
Positions:
2462

■ reminiscent ■
Occurrences: 1
Positions:
1927

■ remix ■
Occurrences: 1
Positions:
1189

■ remixed ■
Occurrences: 1
Positions:
1281

■ remnants ■
Occurrences: 1
Positions:
3406

■ rendered ■
Occurrences: 1
Positions:
447

■ repeat ■
Occurrences: 1
Positions:
1915

■ repeated ■
Occurrences: 1
Positions:
1828

■ repetitive ■
Occurrences: 1
Positions:
2603

■ replenishment ■
Occurrences: 1
Positions:
331

■ replicative ■
Occurrences: 1
Positions:
4651

■ represent ■
Occurrences: 1
Positions:
1449

■ representative ■
Occurrences: 1
Positions:
2177

■ represents ■
Occurrences: 1
Positions:
1961

■ reproduce ■
Occurrences: 1
Positions:
2691

■ reproduces ■
Occurrences: 1
Positions:
4001

■ reproducibility ■
Occurrences: 1
Positions:
2858

■ reproducting ■
Occurrences: 1
Positions:
4640

■ require ■
Occurrences: 1
Positions:
653

■ research ■
Occurrences: 1
Positions:
5396

■ researcher ■
Occurrences: 1
Positions:
3144

■ reshaping ■
Occurrences: 1
Positions:
4823

■ resistance ■
Occurrences: 1
Positions:
2981

■ resolution ■
Occurrences: 1
Positions:
3595

■ resonating ■
Occurrences: 1
Positions:
361

■ resource ■
Occurrences: 1
Positions:
3363

■ restless ■
Occurrences: 1
Positions:
2437

■ restricted ■
Occurrences: 1
Positions:
2668

■ result ■
Occurrences: 1
Positions:
882

■ resuscitation ■
Occurrences: 1
Positions:
3161

■ retroactively ■
Occurrences: 1
Positions:
3828

■ return ■
Occurrences: 1
Positions:
2899

■ reverses ■
Occurrences: 1
Positions:
2060

■ reviewing ■
Occurrences: 1
Positions:
247

■ reviews ■
Occurrences: 1
Positions:
123

■ rhizomatic ■
Occurrences: 1
Positions:
1527

■ rhythm ■
Occurrences: 1
Positions:
1838

■ rhythmic ■
Occurrences: 1
Positions:
5739

■ rise ■
Occurrences: 1
Positions:
893

■ risk ■
Occurrences: 1
Positions:
4518

■ risking ■
Occurrences: 1
Positions:
5823

■ roberto ■
Occurrences: 1
Positions:
4284

■ roggenbruck ■
Occurrences: 1
Positions:
3552

■ rogue ■
Occurrences: 1
Positions:
2198

■ romantic ■
Occurrences: 1
Positions:
4602

■ romantically ■
Occurrences: 1
Positions:
4797

■ rombes ■
Occurrences: 1
Positions:
4280

■ ruins ■
Occurrences: 1
Positions:
3377

■ run ■
Occurrences: 1
Positions:
971

■ rythmic ■
Occurrences: 1
Positions:
5084

■ said ■
Occurrences: 1
Positions:
4149

■ sake ■
Occurrences: 1
Positions:
1864

■ sans ■
Occurrences: 1
Positions:
3652

■ sapega ■
Occurrences: 1
Positions:
5350

■ say ■
Occurrences: 1
Positions:
3322

■ scaled ■
Occurrences: 1
Positions:
1908

■ scenes ■
Occurrences: 1
Positions:
3622

■ schlocky ■
Occurrences: 1
Positions:
3677

■ scientists ■
Occurrences: 1
Positions:
5183

■ scinetists ■
Occurrences: 1
Positions:
40

■ scope ■
Occurrences: 1
Positions:
767

■ screen ■
Occurrences: 1
Positions:
3940

■ scroll ■
Occurrences: 1
Positions:
1254

■ secondariliy ■
Occurrences: 1
Positions:
5673

■ seem ■
Occurrences: 1
Positions:
2278

■ sef ■
Occurrences: 1
Positions:
4639

■ seizing ■
Occurrences: 1
Positions:
5682

■ seizures ■
Occurrences: 1
Positions:
5733

■ select ■
Occurrences: 1
Positions:
1187

■ selective ■
Occurrences: 1
Positions:
1219

■ semi ■
Occurrences: 1
Positions:
1318

■ sending ■
Occurrences: 1
Positions:
4077

■ sensation ■
Occurrences: 1
Positions:
2776

■ sensoriomotor ■
Occurrences: 1
Positions:
5669

■ sensors ■
Occurrences: 1
Positions:
5528

■ sensotial ■
Occurrences: 1
Positions:
1574

■ sentence ■
Occurrences: 1
Positions:
1816

■ separated ■
Occurrences: 1
Positions:
2869

■ separates ■
Occurrences: 1
Positions:
2970

■ serve ■
Occurrences: 1
Positions:
692

■ seventy ■
Occurrences: 1
Positions:
216

■ sfaq ■
Occurrences: 1
Positions:
4878

■ shall ■
Occurrences: 1
Positions:
5583

■ shaping ■
Occurrences: 1
Positions:
563

■ shopped ■
Occurrences: 1
Positions:
3629

■ short ■
Occurrences: 1
Positions:
3701

■ should ■
Occurrences: 1
Positions:
4199

■ silenced ■
Occurrences: 1
Positions:
5788

■ similar ■
Occurrences: 1
Positions:
2588

■ simple ■
Occurrences: 1
Positions:
1298

■ simulate ■
Occurrences: 1
Positions:
5815

■ single ■
Occurrences: 1
Positions:
4433

■ singular ■
Occurrences: 1
Positions:
1211

■ singularity ■
Occurrences: 1
Positions:
3232

■ size ■
Occurrences: 1
Positions:
4485

■ slang ■
Occurrences: 1
Positions:
2550

■ sloughed ■
Occurrences: 1
Positions:
3716

■ slow ■
Occurrences: 1
Positions:
1837

■ small ■
Occurrences: 1
Positions:
4454

■ sociologist ■
Occurrences: 1
Positions:
5798

■ sold ■
Occurrences: 1
Positions:
4088

■ somewhere ■
Occurrences: 1
Positions:
2733

■ sonic ■
Occurrences: 1
Positions:
5090

■ sort ■
Occurrences: 1
Positions:
1835

■ sounds ■
Occurrences: 1
Positions:
2561

■ spacetime ■
Occurrences: 1
Positions:
800

■ spatiotemporal ■
Occurrences: 1
Positions:
547

■ specific ■
Occurrences: 1
Positions:
3787

■ specimens ■
Occurrences: 1
Positions:
816

■ spurting ■
Occurrences: 1
Positions:
292

■ stable ■
Occurrences: 1
Positions:
4435

■ stablished ■
Occurrences: 1
Positions:
1782

■ standard ■
Occurrences: 1
Positions:
3879

■ starting ■
Occurrences: 1
Positions:
3919

■ state ■
Occurrences: 1
Positions:
4505

■ states ■
Occurrences: 1
Positions:
3101

■ static ■
Occurrences: 1
Positions:
1825

■ stein ■
Occurrences: 1
Positions:
1935

■ stop ■
Occurrences: 1
Positions:
4206

■ story ■
Occurrences: 1
Positions:
3441

■ storyteller ■
Occurrences: 1
Positions:
1153

■ strablishing ■
Occurrences: 1
Positions:
4662

■ strange ■
Occurrences: 1
Positions:
2252

■ strategies ■
Occurrences: 1
Positions:
3397

■ strategy ■
Occurrences: 1
Positions:
1710

■ structure ■
Occurrences: 1
Positions:
1931

■ style ■
Occurrences: 1
Positions:
2551

■ stylistic ■
Occurrences: 1
Positions:
2539

■ subject ■
Occurrences: 1
Positions:
3167

■ subjected ■
Occurrences: 1
Positions:
839

■ substrate ■
Occurrences: 1
Positions:
731

■ success ■
Occurrences: 1
Positions:
4669

■ suggest ■
Occurrences: 1
Positions:
5584

■ sum ■
Occurrences: 1
Positions:
515

■ superintelligence ■
Occurrences: 1
Positions:
5109

■ supremely ■
Occurrences: 1
Positions:
3074

■ surprising ■
Occurrences: 1
Positions:
3388

■ sven ■
Occurrences: 1
Positions:
2984

■ swarm ■
Occurrences: 1
Positions:
5727

■ sweeping ■
Occurrences: 1
Positions:
2418

■ syntax ■
Occurrences: 1
Positions:
2268

■ synthesis ■
Occurrences: 1
Positions:
3007

■ tactical ■
Occurrences: 1
Positions:
1704

■ tactics ■
Occurrences: 1
Positions:
3395

■ taken ■
Occurrences: 1
Positions:
3725

■ takes ■
Occurrences: 1
Positions:
1697

■ teams ■
Occurrences: 1
Positions:
1695

■ technical ■
Occurrences: 1
Positions:
5461

■ technically ■
Occurrences: 1
Positions:
5563

■ technique ■
Occurrences: 1
Positions:
3791

■ technodrome ■
Occurrences: 1
Positions:
5275

■ technoscience ■
Occurrences: 1
Positions:
3104

■ temporal ■
Occurrences: 1
Positions:
630

■ temporalily ■
Occurrences: 1
Positions:
822

■ tendencies ■
Occurrences: 1
Positions:
4729

■ territories ■
Occurrences: 1
Positions:
2427

■ textoids ■
Occurrences: 1
Positions:
4412

■ textworks ■
Occurrences: 1
Positions:
4430

■ thacker ■
Occurrences: 1
Positions:
5012

■ thematize ■
Occurrences: 1
Positions:
5522

■ themes ■
Occurrences: 1
Positions:
4272

■ theorist ■
Occurrences: 1
Positions:
1950

■ thereby ■
Occurrences: 1
Positions:
5537

■ thing ■
Occurrences: 1
Positions:
4140

■ things ■
Occurrences: 1
Positions:
231

■ thinking ■
Occurrences: 1
Positions:
3298

■ thirtieth ■
Occurrences: 1
Positions:
5111

■ thoughts ■
Occurrences: 1
Positions:
3286

■ thousand ■
Occurrences: 1
Positions:
5001

■ three ■
Occurrences: 1
Positions:
5019

■ throughout ■
Occurrences: 1
Positions:
5684

■ thus ■
Occurrences: 1
Positions:
2131

■ tightly ■
Occurrences: 1
Positions:
1671

■ times ■
Occurrences: 1
Positions:
2709

■ timespace ■
Occurrences: 1
Positions:
4451

■ tinkering ■
Occurrences: 1
Positions:
3403

■ tip ■
Occurrences: 1
Positions:
4071

■ title ■
Occurrences: 1
Positions:
344

■ togelius ■
Occurrences: 1
Positions:
5097

■ tokens ■
Occurrences: 1
Positions:
4078

■ towards ■
Occurrences: 1
Positions:
5061

■ traces ■
Occurrences: 1
Positions:
4390

■ transcriptions ■
Occurrences: 1
Positions:
3521

■ transcriptive ■
Occurrences: 1
Positions:
1221

■ transfect ■
Occurrences: 1
Positions:
862

■ transforming ■
Occurrences: 1
Positions:
3297

■ translated ■
Occurrences: 1
Positions:
855

■ translation ■
Occurrences: 1
Positions:
4598

■ transmedia ■
Occurrences: 1
Positions:
3433

■ transmedialeblog ■
Occurrences: 1
Positions:
5398

■ trapped ■
Occurrences: 1
Positions:
706

■ turned ■
Occurrences: 1
Positions:
3470

■ turning ■
Occurrences: 1
Positions:
2520

■ twentieth ■
Occurrences: 1
Positions:
4243

■ twitter ■
Occurrences: 1
Positions:
3886

■ twntieth ■
Occurrences: 1
Positions:
4808

■ typical ■
Occurrences: 1
Positions:
3440

■ uel ■
Occurrences: 1
Positions:
3908

■ uk ■
Occurrences: 1
Positions:
148

■ unavoidable ■
Occurrences: 1
Positions:
4372

■ unbound ■
Occurrences: 1
Positions:
4937

■ unbounded ■
Occurrences: 1
Positions:
2236

■ uncanny ■
Occurrences: 1
Positions:
2331

■ unconsciuosly ■
Occurrences: 1
Positions:
2960

■ under ■
Occurrences: 1
Positions:
5426

■ undermining ■
Occurrences: 1
Positions:
2515

■ understated ■
Occurrences: 1
Positions:
1924

■ undoubtedly ■
Occurrences: 1
Positions:
414

■ undrestands ■
Occurrences: 1
Positions:
3751

■ unequal ■
Occurrences: 1
Positions:
5694

■ unevenly ■
Occurrences: 1
Positions:
4835

■ unexpected ■
Occurrences: 1
Positions:
5732

■ unhelpful ■
Occurrences: 1
Positions:
3154

■ unique ■
Occurrences: 1
Positions:
4610

■ unit ■
Occurrences: 1
Positions:
3733

■ universality ■
Occurrences: 1
Positions:
5423

■ universalization ■
Occurrences: 1
Positions:
900

■ universally ■
Occurrences: 1
Positions:
4587

■ unnatural ■
Occurrences: 1
Positions:
5706

■ unprecedented ■
Occurrences: 1
Positions:
1183

■ unpredictable ■
Occurrences: 1
Positions:
1403

■ unremitting ■
Occurrences: 1
Positions:
2553

■ unseen ■
Occurrences: 1
Positions:
1495

■ unsubjective ■
Occurrences: 1
Positions:
5729

■ untold ■
Occurrences: 1
Positions:
4311

■ up ■
Occurrences: 1
Positions:
469

■ update ■
Occurrences: 1
Positions:
2294

■ upgrading ■
Occurrences: 1
Positions:
689

■ upon ■
Occurrences: 1
Positions:
263

■ upside ■
Occurrences: 1
Positions:
3471

■ urban ■
Occurrences: 1
Positions:
4315

■ urbanomic ■
Occurrences: 1
Positions:
5628

■ users ■
Occurrences: 1
Positions:
1436

■ uses ■
Occurrences: 1
Positions:
2020

■ usually ■
Occurrences: 1
Positions:
3586

■ variety ■
Occurrences: 1
Positions:
105

■ variously ■
Occurrences: 1
Positions:
1907

■ varying ■
Occurrences: 1
Positions:
1819

■ vast ■
Occurrences: 1
Positions:
418

■ verb ■
Occurrences: 1
Positions:
5807

■ verso ■
Occurrences: 1
Positions:
5384

■ vesna ■
Occurrences: 1
Positions:
5256

■ vibratory ■
Occurrences: 1
Positions:
4438

■ victoria ■
Occurrences: 1
Positions:
5257

■ videos ■
Occurrences: 1
Positions:
3702

■ vii ■
Occurrences: 1
Positions:
5321

■ vines ■
Occurrences: 1
Positions:
3704

■ violently ■
Occurrences: 1
Positions:
2519

■ virtual ■
Occurrences: 1
Positions:
4017

■ viruses ■
Occurrences: 1
Positions:
4688

■ visible ■
Occurrences: 1
Positions:
1479

■ vision ■
Occurrences: 1
Positions:
1535

■ visit ■
Occurrences: 1
Positions:
4169

■ votive ■
Occurrences: 1
Positions:
3758

■ w ■
Occurrences: 1
Positions:
4903

■ wallet ■
Occurrences: 1
Positions:
4082

■ walter ■
Occurrences: 1
Positions:
4619

■ want ■
Occurrences: 1
Positions:
172

■ wards ■
Occurrences: 1
Positions:
451

■ ways ■
Occurrences: 1
Positions:
4660

■ web ■
Occurrences: 1
Positions:
224

■ welded ■
Occurrences: 1
Positions:
4036

■ whether ■
Occurrences: 1
Positions:
1174

■ white ■
Occurrences: 1
Positions:
3641

■ who ■
Occurrences: 1
Positions:
4069

■ whose ■
Occurrences: 1
Positions:
4109

■ wide ■
Occurrences: 1
Positions:
1485

■ wish ■
Occurrences: 1
Positions:
4186

■ witnessing ■
Occurrences: 1
Positions:
2654

■ woman ■
Occurrences: 1
Positions:
2947

■ wonderfully ■
Occurrences: 1
Positions:
1113

■ word ■
Occurrences: 1
Positions:
3684

■ worked ■
Occurrences: 1
Positions:
683

■ workshop ■
Occurrences: 1
Positions:
5119

■ wrote ■
Occurrences: 1
Positions:
3528

■ xenaudial ■
Occurrences: 1
Positions:
3911

■ years ■
Occurrences: 1
Positions:
18

■ yet ■
Occurrences: 1
Positions:
3338

■ zero ■
Occurrences: 1
Positions:
5067

■ à ■
Occurrences: 1
Positions:
3031

WORD FREQUENCY AND POSITIONS

■ the ■

Occurrences: 1076

Positions:

10, 20, 23, 30, 33, 38, 44, 49, 53, 80, 85, 100, 104, 112, 115, 167, 179, 190, 193, 215, 221, 237, 253, 256, 271, 282, 298, 317, 347, 355, 380, 386, 397, 401, 421, 431, 443, 448, 454, 495, 497, 505, 509, 551, 559, 570, 577, 599, 610, 613, 656, 677, 690, 700, 713, 719, 723, 727, 734, 775, 781, 797, 815, 820, 827, 832, 836, 859, 869, 920, 938, 950, 961, 967, 973, 988, 1039, 1052, 1061, 1066, 1087, 1095, 1134, 1163, 1167, 1209, 1217, 1263, 1276, 1295, 1307, 1317, 1325, 1332, 1350, 1356, 1370, 1404, 1442, 1453, 1456, 1465, 1472, 1476, 1488, 1499, 1513, 1518, 1530, 1540, 1543, 1547, 1552, 1561, 1571, 1597, 1624, 1628, 1638, 1656, 1660, 1665, 1682, 1697, 1701, 1711, 1731, 1740, 1745, 1756, 1760, 1767, 1770, 1777, 1781, 1804, 1822, 1869, 1888, 1925, 1949, 1952, 1961, 1978, 1998, 2030, 2041, 2053, 2066, 2069, 2098, 2107, 2142, 2160, 2166, 2173, 2184, 2187, 2197, 2255, 2267, 2270, 2297, 2318, 2357, 2407, 2444, 2454, 2470, 2485, 2494, 2504, 2581, 2591, 2603, 2609, 2619, 2625, 2655, 2668, 2681, 2691, 2696, 2707, 2712, 2715, 2744, 2749, 2760, 2767, 2786, 2793, 2813, 2853, 2885, 2906, 2941, 2991, 3000, 3022, 3048, 3085, 3119, 3141, 3158, 3217, 3225, 3235, 3293, 3318, 3323, 3333, 3345, 3368, 3375, 3380, 3389, 3399, 3409, 3417, 3449, 3454, 3457, 3461, 3469, 3490, 3493, 3507, 3514, 3540, 3554, 3584, 3599, 3629, 3633, 3639, 3659, 3682, 3731, 3734, 3740, 3744, 3754, 3764, 3767, 3781, 3796, 3802, 3814, 3833, 3862, 3866, 3873, 3884, 3892, 3911, 3947, 3955, 3959, 3969, 3973, 3978, 3982, 3993, 4020, 4026, 4065, 4069, 4078, 4086, 4102, 4105, 4126, 4137, 4145, 4150, 4154, 4158, 4162, 4166, 4188, 4191, 4212, 4228, 4247, 4255, 4317, 4322, 4326, 4342, 4345, 4363, 4374, 4387, 4409, 4412, 4414, 4448, 4458, 4462, 4489, 4492, 4503, 4527, 4530, 4533, 4560, 4569, 4587, 4604, 4611, 4620, 4650, 4653, 4662, 4677, 4701, 4719, 4725, 4741, 4746, 4749, 4777, 4781, 4788, 4800, 4818, 4834, 4841, 4845, 4852, 4884, 4890, 4902, 4961, 5011, 5026, 5036, 5043, 5055, 5062, 5066, 5085, 5088, 5101, 5109, 5116, 5127, 5145, 5153, 5167, 5174, 5181, 5194, 5219, 5223, 5227, 5247, 5258, 5273, 5280, 5284, 5288, 5302, 5323, 5334, 5347, 5411, 5441, 5455, 5466, 5469, 5502, 5521, 5525, 5529, 5567, 5572, 5575, 5594, 5597, 5604, 5608, 5615, 5651, 5657, 5660, 5711, 5737, 5747, 5758, 5777, 5787, 5792, 5804, 5809, 5822, 5859, 5882, 5900, 5909, 5916, 5919, 5927, 5931, 5949, 5964, 5969, 5980, 5987, 5991, 5993, 6008, 6011, 6017, 6065, 6069, 6073, 6098, 6104, 6108, 6145, 6162, 6188, 6202, 6256, 6267, 6271, 6293, 6305, 6316, 6343, 6364, 6369, 6407, 6415, 6446, 6454, 6462, 6467, 6476, 6502, 6515, 6588, 6603, 6620, 6628, 6636, 6649, 6654, 6727, 6730, 6741, 6747, 6754, 6758, 6765, 6768, 6780, 6783, 6798, 6804, 6820, 6826, 6854, 6873, 6897, 6916, 6934, 6940, 6948, 6963, 6968, 6993, 7006, 7010, 7014, 7053, 7075, 7096, 7104, 7116, 7120, 7128, 7161, 7173, 7187, 7192, 7243, 7252, 7258, 7268, 7302, 7307, 7313, 7319, 7335, 7341, 7366, 7370, 7375, 7380, 7414, 7417, 7425, 7430, 7451, 7466, 7497, 7501, 7505, 7540, 7554, 7578, 7587, 7624, 7632, 7636, 7645, 7653, 7673, 7677, 7688, 7756, 7787, 7820, 7824, 7831, 7835, 7840, 7845, 7850, 7856, 7863, 7874, 7891, 7906, 7928, 7982, 8019, 8026, 8032, 8037, 8040, 8047, 8076, 8080, 8108, 8112,

8116, 8124, 8139, 8147, 8150, 8162, 8174, 8191, 8201, 8209, 8222, 8227, 8236, 8240, 8267, 8300, 8317, 8322, 8337, 8343, 8346, 8367, 8386, 8393, 8397, 8409, 8421, 8434, 8443, 8452, 8455, 8463, 8498, 8613, 8623, 8626, 8643, 8655, 8661, 8679, 8719, 8723, 8726, 8731, 8746, 8749, 8753, 8761, 8785, 8801, 8814, 8839, 8861, 8928, 8981, 8989, 9034, 9064, 9086, 9110, 9116, 9137, 9163, 9182, 9202, 9207, 9259, 9280, 9308, 9332, 9345, 9375, 9440, 9478, 9529, 9539, 9545, 9548, 9582, 9596, 9601, 9632, 9644, 9653, 9660, 9674, 9684, 9701, 9738, 9768, 9781, 9792, 9802, 9806, 9813, 9837, 9841, 9850, 9856, 9860, 9862, 9868, 9872, 9885, 9888, 9902, 9906, 9914, 9923, 9926, 9956, 9963, 9974, 9977, 9992, 9998, 10042, 10057, 10095, 10104, 10111, 10149, 10185, 10197, 10200, 10215, 10225, 10254, 10281, 10310, 10313, 10317, 10326, 10338, 10348, 10379, 10382, 10389, 10431, 10468, 10476, 10487, 10495, 10514, 10520, 10525, 10530, 10537, 10542, 10549, 10555, 10558, 10573, 10577, 10603, 10614, 10626, 10643, 10667, 10676, 10694, 10708, 10728, 10749, 10754, 10756, 10770, 10779, 10786, 10791, 10795, 10798, 10811, 10824, 10828, 10838, 10841, 10848, 10851, 10866, 10874, 10878, 10881, 10886, 10900, 10905, 10908, 10917, 10920, 10938, 10952, 10958, 10961, 10968, 10972, 10980, 10984, 11017, 11036, 11046, 11162, 11166, 11181, 11217, 11228, 11240, 11244, 11248, 11251, 11257, 11287, 11291, 11319, 11325, 11329, 11338, 11390, 11402, 11438, 11467, 11476, 11480, 11500, 11535, 11539, 11543, 11556, 11563, 11565, 11576, 11581, 11608, 11631, 11666, 11673, 11678, 11688, 11691, 11698, 11713, 11717, 11720, 11731, 11738, 11748, 11758, 11766, 11782, 11790, 11818, 11822, 11826, 11830, 11854, 11857, 11867, 11892, 11905, 11944, 11947, 11978, 12005, 12020, 12047, 12059, 12097, 12100, 12112, 12131, 12159, 12176, 12221, 12224, 12287, 12295, 12311, 12356, 12361, 12369, 12413, 12424, 12432, 12447, 12464, 12514, 12530, 12549, 12565, 12572, 12581, 12630, 12638, 12643, 12646, 12651, 12657, 12661, 12663, 12708, 12717, 12734, 12743, 12760, 12766, 12777, 12790, 12793, 12799, 12804, 12808, 12821, 12824, 12830, 12844, 12853, 12857, 12862, 12867, 12875, 12878, 12884, 12888, 12899, 12902, 12929, 12934, 12937, 12950, 12985, 13040, 13046, 13051, 13061, 13069, 13100, 13103, 13159, 13170, 13175, 13203, 13222, 13226, 13252, 13255, 13261, 13266, 13282, 13307, 13311, 13323, 13328, 13352, 13358, 13360, 13366, 13380, 13406, 13443, 13462, 13469, 13477, 13484, 13490, 13502, 13510, 13513, 13525, 13532, 13555, 13560, 13579, 13585, 13602, 13617, 13685, 13690, 13702, 13713, 13720, 13724, 13746, 13752, 13787, 13804, 13806, 13832, 13837, 13844, 13847, 13853, 13856, 13866, 13871, 13882, 13929, 13938, 13964, 13970, 14005, 14014, 14025, 14028, 14049, 14055, 14069, 14103, 14106, 14160, 14164, 14168, 14171, 14202, 14206, 14212, 14215, 14235, 14250, 14259, 14272, 14278, 14299, 14308, 14312, 14323, 14329, 14336, 14339, 14348, 14354, 14364, 14372, 14379, 14383, 14394, 14443, 14485, 14506, 14515, 14545, 14550, 14571, 14574, 14582, 14586, 14593, 14626, 14648, 14668, 14675, 14681, 14742, 14746,

14751, 14772, 14780, 14782, 14795, 14806, 14822, 14826, 14832, 14835, 14838, 14842, 14849, 14866, 14886, 14889, 14903, 14909, 14913, 14921, 14926, 14932, 14945, 14978, 14981, 14988, 14992, 15011, 15024, 15026, 15032, 15042, 15056, 15065, 15095, 15102, 15113, 15142, 15175, 15180, 15183, 15198, 15203, 15220, 15241, 15268, 15274, 15290, 15312, 15317, 15322, 15329, 15334, 15341, 15347, 15350, 15359, 15376, 15390, 15394, 15438, 15471, 15480, 15486, 15498, 15504, 15511, 15515, 15538, 15548, 15551, 15592, 15595, 15599, 15603

■ of ■

Occurrences: 774

Positions:

13, 22, 35, 41, 52, 84, 99, 114, 149, 162, 169, 182, 195, 204, 214, 255, 259, 274, 279, 284, 336, 342, 354, 400, 412, 424, 445, 481, 555, 561, 573, 580, 593, 621, 658, 692, 712, 722, 761, 779, 801, 817, 840, 871, 890, 895, 923, 941, 963, 975, 990, 996, 1012, 1016, 1054, 1069, 1089, 1097, 1105, 1140, 1166, 1246, 1257, 1266, 1279, 1286, 1298, 1306, 1327, 1334, 1341, 1345, 1354, 1358, 1369, 1372, 1390, 1406, 1413, 1455, 1468, 1475, 1483, 1490, 1502, 1520, 1528, 1536, 1542, 1550, 1557, 1573, 1584, 1610, 1623, 1627, 1641, 1652, 1688, 1700, 1710, 1755, 1759, 1769, 1780, 1797, 1818, 1871, 1890, 1923, 1928, 1945, 1954, 1971, 1997, 2000, 2009, 2033, 2040, 2055, 2075, 2081, 2089, 2101, 2144, 2147, 2165, 2168, 2200, 2269, 2276, 2287, 2296, 2359, 2453, 2456, 2496, 2528, 2542, 2550, 2557, 2562, 2580, 2645, 2660, 2674, 2693, 2701, 2709, 2714, 2725, 2728, 2735, 2747, 2781, 2856, 2880, 2884, 2890, 2892, 2908, 2956, 2971, 2993, 3052, 3058, 3064, 3070, 3080, 3087, 3108, 3122, 3128, 3131, 3143, 3161, 3180, 3183, 3193, 3228, 3240, 3251, 3255, 3265, 3277, 3322, 3335, 3367, 3371, 3414, 3451, 3460, 3471, 3509, 3516, 3545, 3557, 3607, 3623, 3635, 3643, 3686, 3718, 3733, 3743, 3749, 3760, 3766, 3780, 3799, 3813, 3816, 3835, 3865, 3936, 3950, 3958, 3975, 3981, 4022, 4028, 4080, 4088, 4104, 4140, 4153, 4164, 4190, 4203, 4257, 4295, 4300, 4321, 4328, 4348, 4355, 4366, 4389, 4397, 4411, 4424, 4446, 4450, 4461, 4468, 4496, 4529, 4538, 4562, 4571, 4590, 4615, 4652, 4665, 4676, 4689, 4721, 4743, 4748, 4787, 4807, 4836, 4883, 4894, 4905, 4931, 4963, 4968, 4984, 5028, 5045, 5057, 5065, 5111, 5119, 5129, 5143, 5148, 5160, 5163, 5196, 5200, 5206, 5226, 5234, 5241, 5252, 5283, 5292, 5295, 5316, 5340, 5390, 5398, 5401, 5404, 5418, 5423, 5468, 5524, 5541, 5555, 5569, 5607, 5619, 5653, 5659, 5707, 5713, 5726, 5749, 5757, 5776, 5789, 5808, 5842, 5861, 5926, 5933, 5953, 5956, 5968, 5985, 5997, 6010, 6033, 6058, 6064, 6071, 6110, 6137, 6139, 6147, 6164, 6190, 6249, 6262, 6269, 6339, 6345, 6368, 6409, 6456, 6504, 6514, 6529, 6575, 6596, 6606, 6608, 6622, 6630, 6638, 6656, 6666, 6668, 6695, 6732, 6738, 6760, 6801, 6806, 6822, 6828, 6856, 6862, 6875, 6892, 6900, 6915, 6918, 6970, 7022, 7029, 7042, 7077, 7106, 7126, 7130, 7151, 7230, 7247, 7256, 7260, 7264, 7272, 7277, 7292, 7306, 7312, 7337, 7359, 7372, 7408, 7416, 7442, 7447, 7460, 7476, 7503, 7556, 7591, 7631, 7639, 7647, 7652, 7655, 7675, 7744, 7748, 7826, 7839, 7893, 7905, 7985, 8025, 8036, 8079, 8114, 8149, 8154, 8173, 8239, 8275, 8302, 8314, 8319, 8324, 8332, 8340, 8348, 8366, 8389, 8400, 8411, 8423, 8492, 8495, 8501, 8628, 8657, 8666, 8681, 8685, 8714, 8718, 8721, 8725, 8730, 8748, 8751, 8755, 8763, 8779, 8781,

8805, 8816, 8863, 8889, 8895, 8976, 8994, 8997, 9016, 9024, 9030, 9077, 9088, 9098, 9113, 9126, 9184, 9228, 9312, 9334, 9355, 9392, 9413, 9425, 9498, 9506, 9531, 9541, 9547, 9584, 9592, 9598, 9619, 9641, 9646, 9655, 9676, 9689, 9715, 9729, 9784, 9839, 9871, 9887, 9928, 9936, 9946, 9976, 9981, 9988, 9994, 10001, 10097, 10106, 10176, 10205, 10209, 10233, 10242, 10284, 10319, 10340, 10381, 10391, 10403, 10413, 10434, 10452, 10489, 10544, 10557, 10575, 10579, 10620, 10662, 10669, 10678, 10698, 10710, 10730, 10741, 10758, 10781, 10790, 10794, 10797, 10814, 10830, 10837, 10844, 10861, 10873, 10880, 10903, 10910, 10912, 10919, 10923, 10943, 10950, 10954, 10982, 11021, 11049, 11077, 11080, 11086, 11108, 11114, 11135, 11164, 11189, 11200, 11219, 11232, 11242, 11247, 11254, 11293, 11324, 11328, 11345, 11349, 11372, 11441, 11470, 11482, 11488, 11502, 11506, 11514, 11518, 11545, 11567, 11579, 11587, 11598, 11612, 11617, 11630, 11654, 11668, 11690, 11694, 11700, 11719, 11724, 11729, 11734, 11801, 11825, 11856, 11876, 11879, 11894, 11909, 11946, 11974, 11991, 12007, 12050, 12061, 12071, 12081, 12099, 12114, 12133, 12155, 12163, 12226, 12229, 12255, 12268, 12289, 12298, 12313, 12348, 12426, 12434, 12453, 12457, 12472, 12482, 12504, 12532, 12537, 12552, 12699, 12746, 12762, 12832, 12846, 12869, 12880, 12931, 12936, 12953, 12959, 12993, 13017, 13042, 13050, 13068, 13099, 13134, 13163, 13180, 13192, 13210, 13239, 13257, 13286, 13354, 13408, 13414, 13433, 13440, 13454, 13479, 13489, 13492, 13512, 13527, 13534, 13619, 13662, 13715, 13727, 13742, 13785, 13827, 13836, 13846, 13855, 13868, 13874, 13893, 13911, 13945, 13959, 13967, 13994, 14007, 14051, 14077, 14082, 14105, 14136, 14170, 14177, 14205, 14249, 14307, 14314, 14325, 14346, 14358, 14374, 14393, 14399, 14408, 14432, 14434, 14473, 14497, 14517, 14549, 14573, 14617, 14643, 14712, 14723, 14750, 14808, 14825, 14834, 14841, 14851, 14857, 14878, 14888, 14891, 14905, 14928, 14931, 14938, 14951, 14961, 14980, 14991, 15013, 15039, 15045, 15059, 15079, 15094, 15112, 15121, 15168, 15200, 15208, 15213, 15223, 15231, 15244, 15273, 15293, 15336, 15349, 15378, 15430, 15435, 15474, 15506, 15514, 15542, 15550, 15556, 15594

■ and ■

Occurrences: 497

Positions:

3, 9, 71, 95, 157, 165, 171, 175, 178, 198, 210, 220, 232, 333, 350, 372, 441, 447, 468, 473, 484, 539, 546, 576, 586, 608, 633, 694, 729, 747, 770, 777, 785, 838, 875, 912, 954, 979, 1019, 1032, 1083, 1092, 1175, 1179, 1188, 1193, 1248, 1290, 1344, 1427, 1504, 1719, 1796, 1866, 1903, 1951, 1974, 2018, 2103, 2112, 2136, 2150, 2189, 2192, 2384, 2464, 2570, 2572, 2599, 2617, 2635, 2648, 2672, 2685, 2698, 2753, 2777, 2783, 2830, 2897, 2910, 3004, 3032, 3050, 3055, 3067, 3073, 3082, 3092, 3111, 3125, 3171, 3198, 3203, 3252, 3259, 3275, 3292, 3302, 3349, 3383, 3416, 3421, 3433, 3456, 3492, 3511, 3513, 3518, 3542, 3562, 3612, 3638, 3641, 3684, 3689, 3724, 3772, 3790, 3818, 3829, 3851, 3854, 3897, 3903, 3922, 4001, 4025, 4031, 4093, 4108, 4123, 4169, 4207, 4221, 4227, 4291, 4303, 4314, 4344, 4391, 4393, 4405, 4432,

4440, 4443, 4452, 4479, 4498, 4522, 4565, 4574, 4600, 4608, 4771, 4784, 4797, 4854, 4875, 4901, 4918, 4942, 4954, 4959, 5005, 5030, 5094, 5115, 5141, 5209, 5270, 5290, 5376, 5407, 5421, 5432, 5436, 5474, 5558, 5638, 5647, 5701, 5760, 5768, 5799, 5814, 5971, 5990, 5995, 6015, 6052, 6076, 6086, 6113, 6117, 6142, 6154, 6157, 6175, 6194, 6233, 6252, 6259, 6266, 6289, 6292, 6310, 6366, 6395, 6424, 6443, 6458, 6469, 6492, 6501, 6543, 6688, 6722, 6750, 6782, 6815, 6849, 6859, 6895, 6903, 6921, 6924, 7063, 7068, 7081, 7101, 7112, 7136, 7154, 7221, 7267, 7274, 7347, 7354, 7363, 7388, 7444, 7489, 7491, 7514, 7537, 7562, 7572, 7595, 7634, 7666, 7672, 7680, 7698, 7736, 7770, 7775, 7791, 7837, 7849, 7858, 7878, 7898, 7921, 7925, 7968, 7974, 8014, 8034, 8086, 8123, 8126, 8161, 8200, 8225, 8260, 8290, 8295, 8336, 8350, 8357, 8391, 8449, 8465, 8487, 8522, 8537, 8561, 8572, 8584, 8673, 8689, 8706, 8716, 8728, 8743, 8821, 8878, 8905, 8916, 8939, 8953, 8960, 8979, 9028, 9085, 9115, 9136, 9206, 9234, 9244, 9292, 9302, 9330, 9387, 9452, 9455, 9487, 9500, 9510, 9613, 9678, 9686, 9703, 9750, 9757, 9770, 9934, 9959, 9997, 10022, 10142, 10173, 10199, 10211, 10230, 10248, 10293, 10306, 10323, 10328, 10356, 10364, 10371, 10376, 10400, 10428, 10437, 10474, 10491, 10507, 10554, 10582, 10600, 10642, 10655, 10693, 10714, 10719, 10732, 10784, 10800, 10835, 10957, 11058, 11101, 11110, 11117, 11124, 11131, 11144, 11224, 11230, 11250, 11271, 11321, 11327, 11417, 11459, 11472, 11496, 11538, 11548, 11558, 11607, 11634, 11658, 11677, 11722, 11761, 11787, 11820, 11837, 11883, 11886, 11928, 11949, 12000, 12002, 12013, 12038, 12064, 12095, 12103, 12117, 12124, 12139, 12194, 12212, 12232, 12273, 12282, 12294, 12315, 12365, 12461, 12569, 12634, 12672, 12707, 12756, 12768, 12783, 12803, 12806, 12933, 12939, 12947, 12987, 12997, 13021, 13034, 13097, 13109, 13167, 13232, 13265, 13284, 13364, 13464, 13482, 13495, 13538, 13589, 13598, 13722, 13783, 13817, 13891, 13896, 13908, 13914, 13923, 13947, 13954, 13986, 14004, 14063, 14079, 14084, 14098, 14114, 14123, 14154, 14240, 14283, 14332, 14342, 14356, 14437, 14446, 14490, 14547, 14559, 14671, 14837, 14859, 14871, 14880, 14895, 14999, 15037, 15052, 15055, 15153, 15164, 15192, 15216, 15235, 15247, 15251, 15283, 15346, 15396, 15416, 15448, 15477

■ a ■

Occurrences: 389

Positions:

127, 131, 134, 139, 285, 331, 339, 416, 425, 462, 479, 482, 526, 548, 590, 673, 680, 759, 790, 881, 933, 1101, 1114, 1126, 1149, 1233, 1242, 1283, 1302, 1310, 1399, 1411, 1438, 1491, 1568, 1608, 1653, 1671, 1854, 1968, 2086, 2177, 2208, 2273, 2411, 2509, 2523, 2525, 2540, 2643, 2723, 2866, 2878, 2882, 2921, 2948, 2961, 2969, 3039, 3062, 3068, 3178, 3196, 3299, 3385, 3424, 3446, 3498, 3569, 3672, 3696, 3704, 3756, 3964, 3998, 4016, 4081, 4173, 4201, 4237, 4287, 4357, 4381, 4417, 4465, 4482, 4509, 4513, 4536, 4624, 4683, 4729, 4805, 4879, 4906, 4929, 4945, 4982, 5007, 5072, 5204, 5232, 5238, 5253, 5293, 5313, 5338, 5363, 5416, 5487, 5500, 5623, 5641, 5693, 5720, 5724, 5850, 5862, 5903, 5924, 5939, 5974, 6000, 6034, 6056, 6061, 6135, 6185, 6281, 6336, 6419, 6479, 6483, 6509, 6533, 6546,

6594, 6610, 6613, 6623, 6631, 6660, 6684, 6692, 6705, 6791, 6794, 6984, 7027, 7045, 7124, 7184, 7239, 7293, 7398, 7403, 7439, 7445, 7519, 7565, 7715, 7731, 7745, 7902, 7949, 8004, 8015, 8054, 8072, 8100, 8167, 8308, 8312, 8329, 8375, 8382, 8430, 8458, 8469, 8507, 8604, 8773, 8777, 8835, 8842, 8847, 8851, 8866, 8893, 8914, 8974, 8992, 9008, 9014, 9019, 9104, 9127, 9142, 9198, 9299, 9303, 9338, 9370, 9382, 9390, 9400, 9438, 9504, 9570, 9617, 9635, 9727, 9733, 9745, 9829, 9944, 10032, 10039, 10046, 10076, 10080, 10089, 10117, 10145, 10484, 10500, 10564, 10618, 10660, 10935, 10948, 10976, 11039, 11075, 11309, 11343, 11354, 11358, 11424, 11486, 11572, 11596, 11600, 11644, 11652, 11727, 11772, 11799, 11877, 11938, 12011, 12040, 12129, 12143, 12147, 12201, 12206, 12227, 12241, 12253, 12265, 12280, 12290, 12378, 12407, 12451, 12468, 12480, 12497, 12502, 12510, 12731, 12757, 12839, 13014, 13028, 13037, 13081, 13095, 13132, 13237, 13314, 13343, 13371, 13392, 13403, 13420, 13452, 13543, 13611, 13630, 13658, 13699, 13738, 13764, 13766, 13813, 13815, 13818, 13820, 13834, 13863, 13884, 13902, 13905, 13909, 13921, 13926, 13940, 13943, 13968, 13989, 13992, 14011, 14018, 14057, 14072, 14075, 14108, 14133, 14137, 14151, 14155, 14158, 14182, 14220, 14225, 14230, 14233, 14269, 14317, 14326, 14403, 14406, 14428, 14430, 14450, 14456, 14461, 14482, 14494, 14510, 14526, 14597, 14599, 14612, 14615, 14630, 14632, 14635, 14646, 14654, 14702, 14710, 14716, 14720, 14731, 14733, 14740, 14758, 14763, 14793, 14829, 14948, 14959, 14963, 14966, 15002, 15005, 15020, 15069, 15119, 15138, 15206, 15210, 15224, 15229, 15238, 15253, 15258, 15356, 15370, 15379, 15401, 15422, 15427, 15433, 15533, 15554

■ is ■

Occurrences: 339

Positions:

64, 152, 207, 241, 263, 269, 344, 392, 450, 478, 494, 537, 589, 602, 642, 813, 819, 852, 886, 901, 1005, 1022, 1045, 1050, 1058, 1076, 1094, 1125, 1131, 1148, 1173, 1275, 1301, 1331, 1348, 1364, 1367, 1383, 1479, 1580, 1735, 1751, 1809, 1821, 1853, 1930, 1936, 1977, 2035, 2061, 2094, 2128, 2242, 2279, 2289, 2294, 2370, 2398, 2420, 2428, 2522, 2718, 2764, 2873, 2877, 2960, 3188, 3307, 3362, 3444, 3473, 3489, 3526, 3549, 3669, 3709, 3752, 3806, 3946, 3985, 3996, 4050, 4062, 4073, 4114, 4125, 4184, 4198, 4209, 4230, 4272, 4376, 4385, 4416, 4454, 4471, 4541, 4576, 4583, 4674, 4728, 4762, 4944, 5003, 5021, 5080, 5100, 5108, 5152, 5166, 5184, 5215, 5250, 5393, 5415, 5460, 5478, 5499, 5505, 5566, 5583, 5630, 5689, 5710, 5796, 5881, 5921, 6122, 6183, 6242, 6276, 6280, 6298, 6312, 6536, 6612, 6770, 6778, 7323, 7343, 7427, 7438, 7577, 7823, 7847, 7853, 7910, 7932, 7948, 7963, 8003, 8082, 8087, 8134, 8136, 8141, 8186, 8380, 8432, 8442, 8447, 8451, 8506, 8516, 8606, 8758, 8798, 8858, 8924, 9094, 9108, 9123, 9215, 9241, 9263, 9278, 9286, 9295, 9315, 9342, 9410, 9419, 9437, 9450, 9536, 9600, 9608, 9753, 9777, 9815, 9825, 9866, 10052, 10060, 10067, 10075, 10085, 10124, 10134, 10148, 10222, 10261, 10267, 10287, 10332, 10345, 10352, 10455, 10480, 10522, 10546, 10551, 10560, 10602, 10613, 10625, 10683, 10744, 10763, 10788, 10807, 10823, 10941, 10965, 11041,

11137, 11159, 11183, 11192, 11296, 11374, 11569, 11614, 11628, 11661, 11798, 11937, 11982, 11986, 12066, 12106, 12150, 12168, 12173, 12216, 12240, 12250, 12321, 12331, 12338, 12355, 12385, 12394, 12420, 12477, 12517, 12522, 12602, 12612, 12632, 12665, 12710, 12730, 12737, 12750, 12765, 12818, 12823, 12829, 12851, 12873, 12944, 12970, 12976, 13060, 13129, 13156, 13177, 13220, 13274, 13290, 13296, 13331, 13342, 13370, 13402, 13529, 13622, 13635, 13647, 13692, 13695, 13711, 13736, 13755, 13771, 13932, 13942, 14030, 14059, 14064, 14074, 14110, 14319, 14405, 14487, 14508, 14529, 14542, 14566, 14577, 14590, 14637, 14683, 14726, 14769, 14799, 14813, 14908, 14925, 14947, 14965, 14969, 15004, 15008, 15018, 15082, 15134, 15257, 15271, 15314, 15338, 15343, 15352, 15369, 15444, 15485, 15579, 15605

■ in ■

Occurrences: 323

Positions:

16, 29, 76, 133, 230, 236, 396, 415, 461, 525, 566, 606, 643, 847, 966, 999, 1014, 1259, 1320, 1377, 1385, 1397, 1462, 1790, 1795, 1831, 1937, 2052, 2078, 2119, 2152, 2156, 2193, 2247, 2254, 2281, 2320, 2395, 2424, 2443, 2481, 2576, 2601, 2606, 2683, 2771, 2952, 2954, 3094, 3106, 3147, 3230, 3271, 3286, 3290, 3314, 3350, 3379, 3398, 3423, 3440, 3478, 3572, 3625, 3691, 3703, 3715, 3753, 3810, 3868, 3968, 3989, 4091, 4118, 4134, 4172, 4178, 4187, 4243, 4263, 4269, 4311, 4351, 4506, 4525, 4551, 4586, 4712, 4817, 4822, 4848, 4912, 4960, 5014, 5049, 5060, 5075, 5193, 5211, 5299, 5322, 5409, 5480, 5486, 5508, 5515, 5520, 5528, 5591, 5627, 5678, 5744, 5754, 5832, 5849, 5885, 6024, 6092, 6161, 6170, 6201, 6219, 6244, 6255, 6297, 6342, 6387, 6422, 6431, 6445, 6450, 6461, 6486, 6545, 6565, 6619, 6691, 6713, 6797, 6825, 6973, 7013, 7020, 7044, 7052, 7061, 7073, 7139, 7223, 7280, 7304, 7334, 7434, 7539, 7589, 7601, 7629, 7641, 7694, 7708, 7714, 7721, 7741, 7783, 7800, 7814, 7817, 7842, 7940, 7970, 7988, 8064, 8089, 8156, 8249, 8269, 8321, 8408, 8510, 8530, 8554, 8612, 8669, 8675, 8687, 8700, 8703, 8708, 8790, 8794, 8841, 8920, 8937, 8942, 9253, 9373, 9381, 9395, 9553, 9581, 9631, 9736, 9744, 9791, 9836, 9884, 9962, 9973, 9984, 10144, 10224, 10290, 10295, 10316, 10347, 10369, 10397, 10513, 10519, 10524, 10536, 10548, 10563, 10650, 10686, 10717, 10747, 10778, 10960, 10979, 10999, 11019, 11119, 11193, 11204, 11213, 11256, 11278, 11337, 11357, 11396, 11401, 11423, 11452, 11651, 11737, 11789, 11829, 11866, 11942, 12046, 12058, 12074, 12153, 12175, 12264, 12327, 12373, 12478, 12555, 12623, 12636, 12680, 12688, 12748, 12759, 12859, 13036, 13124, 13172, 13236, 13313, 13419, 13442, 13498, 13508, 13524, 13540, 13566, 13606, 13629, 13670, 13698, 13779, 13796, 13881, 13974, 14017, 14068, 14129, 14157, 14224, 14298, 14316, 14367, 14420, 14442, 14449, 14471, 14525, 14584, 14596, 14673, 14865, 14875, 14902, 15023, 15062, 15075, 15101, 15264, 15304, 15311, 15316, 15328, 15340, 15355, 15365, 15375, 15400, 15425, 15437, 15479

■ to ■

Occurrences: 322

Positions:

58, 110, 142, 428, 453, 514, 655, 703, 717, 789, 793, 824, 830, 834, 844,

888, 918, 949, 1008, 1025, 1060, 1078, 1184, 1237, 1324, 1387, 1402, 1464, 1533, 1616, 1659, 1673, 1696, 1848, 1887, 1909, 1911, 2026, 2046, 2049, 2159, 2250, 2317, 2352, 2431, 2477, 2484, 2507, 2537, 2568, 2585, 2613, 2642, 2654, 2666, 2706, 2759, 2766, 2775, 2840, 2862, 2905, 2919, 2989, 2997, 3078, 3151, 3311, 3316, 3352, 3553, 3566, 3615, 3665, 3698, 3786, 3794, 3822, 3871, 3906, 4111, 4274, 4457, 4484, 4488, 4559, 4631, 4661, 4687, 4737, 4936, 4939, 4995, 5000, 5053, 5104, 5218, 5366, 5383, 5440, 5452, 5462, 5513, 5574, 5586, 5673, 5731, 5786, 5858, 5944, 6020, 6037, 6107, 6187, 6210, 6229, 6273, 6315, 6353, 6377, 6379, 6383, 6453, 6471, 6495, 6512, 6524, 6580, 6653, 6675, 6704, 6789, 6840, 6847, 6867, 6933, 7004, 7008, 7039, 7066, 7103, 7115, 7191, 7226, 7368, 7406, 7473, 7524, 7532, 7586, 7618, 7626, 7635, 7659, 7811, 7834, 7855, 7866, 7956, 7960, 7991, 8017, 8053, 8068, 8297, 8385, 8476, 8513, 8557, 8620, 8695, 8800, 8845, 8882, 9022, 9056, 9149, 9178, 9187, 9197, 9218, 9343, 9367, 9460, 9489, 9495, 9550, 9667, 9683, 9821, 9911, 9919, 9941, 10011, 10053, 10061, 10068, 10086, 10139, 10169, 10187, 10269, 10387, 10443, 10465, 10483, 10605, 10674, 10688, 10726, 10739, 10773, 10850, 10891, 10933, 10947, 11093, 11095, 11121, 11161, 11179, 11227, 11281, 11301, 11307, 11360, 11408, 11426, 11475, 11776, 11816, 11842, 11860, 11902, 11904, 11914, 11921, 11968, 12027, 12069, 12200, 12223, 12245, 12333, 12358, 12360, 12375, 12423, 12444, 12508, 12524, 12594, 12892, 13012, 13032, 13054, 13161, 13309, 13321, 13338, 13398, 13417, 13423, 13428, 13447, 13521, 13553, 13568, 13575, 13593, 13608, 13790, 13798, 13809, 13823, 13860, 14033, 14091, 14146, 14185, 14192, 14218, 14247, 14252, 14254, 14287, 14295, 14352, 14388, 14416, 14479, 14501, 14503, 14532, 14537, 14544, 14569, 14580, 14606, 14609, 14694, 14718, 14736, 14800, 14820, 14936, 14977, 14987, 15031, 15068, 15127, 15136, 15173, 15189, 15260, 15362, 15373, 15446, 15469, 15488, 15589, 15597

■ that ■

Occurrences: 256

Positions:

28, 98, 213, 507, 511, 528, 625, 662, 732, 809, 889, 969, 1003, 1111, 1152, 1214, 1459, 1486, 1497, 1516, 1545, 1567, 1575, 1635, 1680, 1733, 1744, 1747, 1763, 1766, 1773, 1794, 1811, 1820, 1829, 1982, 2096, 2114, 2251, 2306, 2421, 2433, 2446, 2503, 2520, 2564, 2772, 2792, 2805, 2848, 2899, 2943, 3042, 3140, 3221, 3428, 3467, 3476, 3495, 3578, 3587, 3610, 3675, 3861, 3875, 3913, 3971, 4068, 4096, 4129, 4254, 4276, 4283, 4360, 4436, 4511, 4540, 4618, 4630, 4640, 4688, 4704, 4733, 4910, 4922, 5019, 5050, 5107, 5156, 5199, 5214, 5222, 5358, 5458, 5496, 5546, 5553, 5565, 5579, 5600, 5613, 5629, 5634, 5643, 5655, 5772, 5801, 5826, 5841, 5852, 5896, 5899, 5959, 6027, 6040, 6097, 6205, 6239, 6356, 6363, 6513, 6756, 6881, 6962, 7074, 7179, 7345, 7401, 7407, 7433, 7914, 7934, 7977, 8137, 8208, 8244, 8286, 8291, 8331, 8446, 8659, 8678, 8693, 8927, 9147, 9166, 9172, 9213, 9265, 9277, 9284, 9319, 9347, 9492, 9659, 9670, 9778, 9799, 9811, 9817, 9865, 9890, 9899, 10017, 10109, 10228, 10259, 10265, 10277, 10334, 10350, 10454, 10532, 10616, 10664, 10740, 10888, 11170, 11191, 11209, 11285, 11313, 11369, 11421, 11433, 11479,

11493, 11550, 11583, 11586, 11640, 11648, 11779, 11805, 11850, 11891, 11934, 11995, 12052, 12075, 12169, 12215, 12238, 12249, 12306, 12335, 12439, 12488, 12516, 12542, 12771, 12811, 12838, 12861, 12898, 12910, 12974, 12979, 13117, 13270, 13340, 13387, 13395, 13400, 13411, 13432, 13437, 13471, 13643, 13666, 13750, 13842, 13888, 14093, 14369, 14513, 14603, 14611, 14625, 14812, 14846, 14864, 14915, 14944, 14954, 14968, 15007, 15115, 15125, 15266, 15278, 15303, 15324, 15403, 15409, 15501

■ s ■

Occurrences: 170

Positions:

61, 88, 543, 615, 618, 715, 804, 850, 893, 952, 1043, 1063, 1240, 1268, 1329, 1362, 1381, 1589, 1594, 1613, 1833, 1939, 1958, 2002, 2037, 2092, 2154, 2233, 2435, 2458, 2514, 2587, 2730, 2762, 3190, 3329, 3341, 3354, 3559, 3991, 4060, 4333, 4474, 4670, 4714, 4773, 4812, 4826, 4864, 4924, 4998, 5078, 5150, 5171, 5277, 5343, 5413, 5438, 5532, 5588, 5705, 5774, 5869, 6212, 6226, 6326, 6498, 6776, 6872, 6996, 7036, 7050, 7070, 7090, 7175, 7181, 7189, 7213, 7233, 7262, 7270, 7321, 7422, 7470, 7549, 7679, 7682, 7760, 7781, 7795, 7876, 7887, 7942, 7979, 7994, 8049, 8232, 8305, 8311, 8369, 8589, 9079, 9759, 9766, 9845, 10635, 10680, 10737, 10743, 10751, 10859, 10930, 10945, 11142, 11146, 11187, 11195, 11234, 11237, 11304, 11504, 11516, 11531, 11626, 11784, 11923, 12033, 12135, 12171, 12181, 12247, 12260, 12303, 12390, 12490, 12655, 12686, 12773, 12813, 12820, 12827, 12849, 12871, 12890, 12922, 12942, 12981, 13058, 13087, 13144, 13152, 13184, 13230, 13376, 13430, 13549, 13633, 13645, 13717, 13825, 13831, 14166, 14588, 14797, 14854, 15295, 15298, 15491, 15518, 15529

■ as ■

Occurrences: 162

Positions:

90, 265, 267, 278, 296, 569, 650, 672, 864, 880, 903, 946, 1046, 1048, 1074, 1113, 1401, 1410, 1448, 1607, 1898, 1931, 1934, 2116, 2176, 2244, 2272, 2373, 2401, 2536, 2816, 2913, 2915, 2983, 3015, 3027, 3038, 3166, 3195, 3257, 3261, 3298, 3365, 3411, 3618, 3652, 3654, 3679, 4593, 4623, 4642, 4734, 4757, 4804, 4971, 4991, 5006, 5263, 5286, 5312, 5337, 5386, 5562, 5640, 5692, 5856, 5923, 5938, 5958, 5999, 6005, 6055, 6119, 6134, 6159, 6224, 6330, 6414, 6593, 6726, 6735, 7123, 7238, 7535, 7543, 7551, 7669, 7692, 7700, 7730, 8371, 8402, 8414, 8539, 8603, 8834, 8898, 8900, 8973, 9152, 9204, 9209, 9275, 9468, 9472, 9943, 10045, 10056, 10064, 10119, 10271, 10321, 10378, 10461, 10590, 10596, 10671, 10855, 10926, 10994, 11043, 11045, 11069, 11071, 11216, 11499, 11595, 11726, 11840, 12018, 12039, 12128, 12278, 12428, 12450, 12540, 12591, 12695, 12780, 13027, 13065, 13094, 13122, 13130, 13158, 13207, 13559, 13763, 13870, 13920, 14481, 14539, 14645, 14757, 14975, 14984, 15205, 15228, 15237, 15464, 15545, 15553

■ with ■

Occurrences: 134

Positions:

404, 679, 741, 758, 774, 1136, 1156, 1181, 1196, 1222, 1375, 1917, 1967, 2132, 2381, 2389, 2554, 2977, 3036, 3084, 3243, 3269, 3485, 3531, 3538, 3628, 3848, 3880, 4136, 4176, 4225, 4532, 4603, 4638, 4657, 4844, 4862,

5042, 5177, 5560, 5871, 5888, 5948, 6047, 6287, 6385, 6392, 6403, 6615, 6746, 6753, 6851, 6853, 6975, 6988, 7197, 7290, 7568, 7583, 7606, 7687, 7696, 7701, 7712, 7755, 7762, 7798, 7972, 8058, 8158, 8482, 8524, 8550, 8576, 8582, 8587, 8911, 8991, 9059, 9230, 9232, 9235, 9486, 9627, 9643, 9664, 10031, 10093, 10121, 10130, 10191, 10499, 10569, 10899, 10916, 10967, 11001, 11331, 11342, 11637, 11765, 11811, 12010, 12078, 12165, 12187, 12286, 12345, 12557, 12626, 12650, 12653, 12716, 12789, 13056, 13251, 13306, 13460, 13501, 13505, 13657, 13803, 13862, 13925, 13980, 13988, 14232, 14268, 14792, 14831, 15281, 15418, 15454, 15456

■ siratori ■

Occurrences: 122

Positions:

15, 542, 617, 675, 803, 849, 925, 943, 1042, 1099, 1122, 1215, 1267, 1328, 1361, 1380, 1588, 1612, 1832, 1957, 1964, 2001, 2036, 2060, 2091, 2153, 2283, 2586, 3313, 3558, 4131, 4233, 4575, 4633, 4647, 4669, 4713, 5034, 5077, 5197, 5245, 5276, 5307, 5843, 5868, 5894, 5943, 6045, 6090, 6127, 6167, 6225, 6279, 6325, 6396, 6475, 6775, 6779, 7548, 7993, 8559, 9765, 10634, 10639, 10679, 10727, 10736, 10783, 10821, 10858, 10944, 11132, 11145, 11236, 11275, 11335, 11625, 11682, 11711, 11852, 12032, 12065, 12134, 12170, 12180, 12246, 12259, 12302, 12343, 12389, 12440, 12489, 12520, 12611, 12654, 12713, 12772, 12812, 12870, 12941, 12980, 13086, 13143, 13151, 13194, 13258, 13375, 13429, 13548, 13632, 13644, 13716, 14844, 15170, 15270, 15297, 15392, 15443, 15490, 15517, 15528, 15559

■ this ■

Occurrences: 113

Positions:

201, 261, 313, 493, 536, 594, 1378, 1434, 1578, 1722, 1807, 1842, 1913, 2023, 2241, 2292, 2539, 2965, 3134, 3231, 3263, 3441, 3503, 3601, 3667, 3750, 3934, 4179, 4197, 4241, 4271, 4371, 4398, 4494, 4566, 5040, 5165, 5384, 5539, 5580, 5601, 5669, 5745, 5811, 5907, 5954, 6120, 6400, 6559, 6647, 6719, 6889, 6953, 6981, 7170, 7357, 7818, 7843, 7930, 7964, 8184, 8362, 8412, 8490, 8562, 8766, 8946, 8969, 9075, 9254, 9396, 9407, 9423, 9535, 9752, 9968, 10028, 10101, 10220, 10291, 10624, 10761, 10992, 11087, 11133, 11157, 11370, 11552, 11706, 11812, 12019, 12166, 12382, 12418, 12474, 12527, 12562, 12589, 12620, 12702, 12764, 13173, 13190, 13218, 13300, 13369, 13438, 13708, 14351, 14565, 14973, 15063, 15366

■ it ■

Occurrences: 104

Positions:

268, 300, 519, 641, 697, 906, 1035, 1049, 1123, 1158, 1300, 1366, 1863, 1935, 2044, 2327, 2330, 2427, 2773, 2876, 2951, 3028, 3167, 3306, 3488, 3655, 3820, 3945, 4124, 4438, 4697, 5144, 5164, 5741, 5802, 6123, 6426, 7900, 7962, 8254, 8304, 8310, 8440, 8515, 8907, 8923, 8955, 9122, 9348, 9359, 9403, 9418, 9443, 9824, 10006, 10094, 10123, 10137, 10147, 10249, 10272, 10279, 10331, 10351, 10424, 10447, 10672, 10822, 11092, 11409, 11446, 11521, 11985, 12076, 12085, 12087, 12089, 12091, 12093, 12330, 12406, 12429, 12574, 12576, 12720, 12886, 13118, 13128, 13302, 13330, 13694, 13761, 13917, 14528, 14578, 14663, 14729, 14788, 14814, 14985, 15017, 15368, 15546, 15564

5983, 6038, 6245, 6616, 6736, 7107, 7456, 7474, 7807, 7915, 8364, 8569, 8769, 8887, 8957, 9095, 9124, 9153, 9457, 9483, 9496, 9515, 9590, 9628, 9639, 9931, 10157, 10274, 10449, 10462, 10701, 10815, 11151, 11298, 11615, 11707, 11918, 11972, 11988, 12399, 12592, 12696, 12752, 12781, 13048, 13066, 13164, 13178, 13181, 13208, 13213, 14400, 14540, 14776, 15083, 15091, 15151, 15162, 15217, 15397, 15431, 15467

■ or ■

Occurrences: 103

Positions:

56, 103, 218, 384, 565, 1663, 1827, 1838, 2206, 2213, 2222, 2227, 2235, 2261, 2323, 2362, 2552, 2800, 3164, 3337, 3407, 3436, 3523, 3843, 3899, 3954, 4008, 4075, 4400, 4554, 4645, 4987, 5134, 5962, 6302, 6333, 6382, 6557, 6833, 6936, 7031, 7146, 7939, 8214, 8419, 8610, 8663, 8683, 8737, 8793, 8869, 8876, 9046, 9073, 9120, 9416, 9638, 9691, 9732, 10161, 10396, 10460, 10630, 11155, 11168, 11174, 11206, 11377, 11526, 11542, 11602, 11605, 11610, 11970, 12029, 12262, 12484, 12834, 12836, 12877, 12906, 12908, 12914, 12968, 13003, 13137, 13205, 13212, 13325, 13335, 13504, 13650, 14045, 14140, 14361, 14397, 14414, 14458, 14523, 14634, 14748, 15085, 15421

■ an ■

Occurrences: 91

Positions:

186, 322, 521, 947, 1020, 1205, 1449, 1604, 2220, 2374, 2402, 2751, 3253, 4053, 4260, 4594, 4758, 5081, 5123, 5130, 5264, 5327, 5396, 5402, 5549, 5611, 5631, 5886, 5934,

■ by ■

Occurrences: 88

Positions:

43, 294, 297, 325, 346, 465, 604, 629, 1071, 1815, 2004, 2064, 2072, 2501, 2865, 3007, 3388, 3438, 3658, 3888, 4006, 4010, 4408, 4795, 4872, 4887, 4898, 5092, 5593, 6150, 6198, 6555, 6904, 6939, 7001, 7119, 8010, 8120, 8129, 8166, 8190, 8195, 8283, 8631, 8760, 8810, 8934, 8948, 9013, 9042, 9069, 9194, 9707, 9867, 9893, 10151, 10178, 10196, 10252, 10325, 10394, 10593, 11263, 11445, 11620, 11696, 11881, 12252, 12258, 12466, 12513, 12544, 12585, 12916, 13024, 13030, 13084, 13188, 13243, 13292, 13378, 13757, 13774, 14882, 14897, 14971, 15178, 15562

■ his ■

Occurrences: 86

Positions:

17, 65, 72, 736, 753, 866, 884, 899, 958, 1106, 1109, 1119, 1147, 1170, 1202, 1223, 1230, 1238, 1394, 1851, 2012, 2056, 2076, 2082, 2126, 2157, 2248, 2285, 2321, 2354, 2390, 2482, 3486, 4141, 4572, 4693, 4765, 4948, 4950, 4952, 4955, 4969, 4974, 5015, 5046, 5113, 5120, 5435, 5665, 5878, 6093, 6132, 6237, 6240, 7610, 7642, 7722, 7767, 7801, 8646, 8912, 9379, 9742, 10681, 11279, 11456, 11460, 11754, 11844, 12156, 12217, 12328, 12336, 12346, 12525, 12881, 12895, 13008, 13196, 13571, 13620, 13734, 14044, 14917, 15457, 15494

■ not ■

Occurrences: 86

Positions:

291, 438, 451, 638, 1153, 1349, 1581, 1784, 1836, 2262, 2342, 2350, 2823, 2837, 2946, 2987, 3475, 3917, 4051, 4199, 4273, 4455, 4979, 5022, 5865, 6299, 6328, 6554, 7528, 7597, 7719, 7752, 8187, 8306, 8359, 8407, 8479, 9216, 9411, 9577, 9754, 10009, 10126, 10441, 10456, 10481, 10510,

10540, 10552, 10561, 11173, 11176, 11375, 11381, 11386, 11400, 11523, 11575, 11960, 12043, 12140, 12174, 12816, 12852, 12874, 13332, 13458, 13577, 13641, 13740, 14180, 14190, 14210, 14320, 14530, 14567, 14641, 14652, 14727, 14761, 14790, 15029, 15332, 15344, 15353, 15521

■ for ■

Occurrences: 85

Positions:

155, 158, 311, 316, 523, 699, 1030, 1421, 2211, 2493, 3025, 3030, 3044, 3157, 3169, 3173, 3201, 3419, 3727, 3942, 4056, 4216, 4218, 4232, 4240, 4491, 4597, 4707, 4856, 4947, 5173, 5306, 5454, 5596, 5717, 5764, 6068, 6793, 6931, 6950, 6992, 7164, 7254, 7484, 7487, 7703, 7733, 7951, 8006, 8392, 8436, 9050, 9191, 9268, 9296, 9399, 9514, 9538, 9772, 9826, 9831, 9879, 9948, 10048, 10809, 10820, 10857, 11011, 11128, 11290, 11447, 11665, 11675, 11681, 12146, 12209, 12786, 13899, 14117, 14275, 14335, 14371, 14468, 14493, 14715

■ work ■

Occurrences: 69

Positions:

544, 737, 754, 805, 851, 885, 900, 959, 1107, 1330, 1363, 1852, 1940, 1959, 2013, 2083, 2127, 2155, 3096, 4813, 4970, 5016, 5079, 5121, 5151, 5195, 5392, 5414, 5668, 5810, 5839, 5957, 6213, 6227, 6241, 6327, 6777, 7051, 7182, 7204, 7550, 7888, 7980, 7995, 8081, 8344, 8413, 8523, 9391, 9767, 10682, 10729, 10738, 10806, 11147, 11756, 11957, 12060, 12248, 12512, 12882, 13088, 13133, 13634, 13646, 13718, 13735, 15519, 15530

■ be ■

Occurrences: 65

Positions:

1738, 1783, 1813, 2449, 2469, 2590, 2935, 3616, 3650, 3787, 3823, 4004, 4044, 4236, 4549, 5310, 5645, 5854, 5945, 6043, 6351, 6563, 6591, 6673, 6702, 6786, 7058, 7533, 8178, 8218, 8480, 8564, 8601, 8696, 8740, 8832, 9040, 9067, 9219, 9251, 9273, 9321, 9551, 9649, 10572, 10705, 10774, 11177, 11211, 11394, 11650, 11900, 12442, 12445, 13090, 13120, 13487, 13522, 13810, 14219, 14621, 14691, 14956, 15137, 15363

■ from ■

Occurrences: 64

Positions:

726, 928, 1313, 1433, 1600, 1667, 1724, 1803, 3568, 3604, 4481, 4928, 4934, 5138, 5187, 5198, 5237, 5257, 5269, 5571, 5671, 5695, 5780, 5821, 6013, 6466, 6489, 6602, 6888, 7186, 7242, 7420, 7614, 7923, 8181, 8745, 8826, 9007, 9091, 9796, 9955, 10014, 10159, 10217, 10280, 10299, 10304, 10588, 10753, 11013, 11955, 12412, 12588, 12604, 13076, 13473, 13781, 13812, 13934, 14132, 14629, 15131, 15160, 15219

■ are ■

Occurrences: 63

Positions:

635, 664, 756, 981, 994, 1792, 1835, 2140, 2264, 2437, 2860, 2917, 3536, 3614, 3645, 3791, 3886, 4223, 4279, 4306, 4705, 4767, 4978, 5070, 5564, 6206, 6217, 6390, 6865, 8062, 8292, 8406, 8712, 8823, 9175, 9237, 9258, 9365, 9891, 9901, 10018, 10302, 10405, 10539, 11063, 11443, 11951, 11959, 11966, 12911, 12926, 13234, 13350, 13476, 13655, 14120, 14209, 14699, 14873, 15028, 15110, 15188, 15331

■ on ■

Occurrences: 61

Positions:

504, 1108, 1208, 1445, 1620, 2006, 2068, 2406,

2738, 3216, 3453, 3505, 3671, 3801, 3895, 4040, 4724, 5024, 5035, 5084, 5246, 5346, 5538, 5977, 6130, 6406, 6440, 6552, 7094, 7148, 7201, 7235, 7396, 7455, 7664, 7830, 7966, 8071, 8221, 8266, 8352, 8633, 9201, 9544, 9623, 9961, 10494, 11026, 11125, 11534, 11555, 11562, 11712, 12142, 12220, 12310, 12561, 13281, 14378, 15389, 15591

■ we ■

Occurrences: 58

Positions:

47, 251, 512, 660, 751, 755, 842, 985, 993, 1874, 1879, 1885, 1896, 1906, 1994, 2263, 2806, 2811, 2820, 2826, 2835, 2845, 2859, 2887, 2900, 2902, 2916, 2923, 2931, 2939, 2944, 4013, 5190, 5379, 5913, 6322, 6882, 7945, 8261, 9800, 9854, 10533, 10988, 11029, 11958, 12683, 13201, 13317, 13349, 13425, 13654, 13922, 14764, 14847, 15187, 15325, 15404, 15525

■ its ■

Occurrences: 53

Positions:

302, 326, 405, 409, 488, 534, 855, 3152, 3280, 3546, 3811, 3940, 4109, 4394, 4658, 5136, 5733, 6260, 6429, 8246, 8531, 9405, 9446, 9559, 9562, 10174, 10243, 10341, 10359, 11022, 11332, 11397, 12118, 12545, 12669, 12740, 13125, 13244, 13277, 13279, 13569, 13625, 13636, 14173, 14255, 14359, 14618, 14638, 14688, 14705, 14802, 15014, 15566

■ technology ■

Occurrences: 50

Positions:

965, 992, 3194, 3244, 3246, 3270, 3439, 3452, 3592, 3611, 3648, 3690, 3694, 3728, 3828, 3882, 3921, 4011, 4112, 4177, 4258, 4284, 4555, 4601, 4900, 5880, 5941, 6715, 7261, 7361, 7479, 9078, 9134, 9448, 10570, 10589, 12706, 12802, 12841, 12864, 13211, 13273, 13295, 13367, 13410, 13466, 14236, 15161, 15195, 15561

■ which ■

Occurrences: 48

Positions:

1538, 1895, 2476, 2736, 5061, 5330, 5410, 5696, 5728, 5833, 5960, 6388, 7142, 7369, 7909, 8462, 8543, 8651, 8699, 8711, 8734, 8738, 8756, 8807, 8827, 9341, 9364, 9374, 9430, 9737, 9779, 10091, 10128, 10152, 10258, 10633, 10804, 11171, 11267, 11274, 11863, 11943, 12374, 12393, 13031, 13607, 14585, 14768

■ writing ■

Occurrences: 44

Positions:

556, 867, 1120, 1150, 1337, 1382, 1617, 1834, 1843, 2003, 4592, 4673, 4694, 4715, 4761, 6103, 6133, 6156, 6251, 6320, 7815, 8627, 10439, 10675, 11672, 11753, 12034, 12136, 12172, 12218, 12304, 12329, 12337, 12401, 12416, 12656, 12774, 12814, 12872, 12896, 12918, 13009, 13386, 13431

■ at ■

Occurrences: 41

Positions:

612, 683, 854, 1424, 1948, 2141, 2937, 3061, 4074, 4682, 4833, 5231, 5736, 5891, 6885, 8245, 8258, 8850, 9018, 9266, 9316, 9331, 9671, 10162, 11379, 11571, 11747, 12690, 12962, 13351, 13557, 13582, 13624, 13669, 13843, 14038, 14805, 14994, 15252, 15532, 15537

■ both ■

Occurrences: 41

Positions:

154, 2565, 3071, 3249, 3273, 3317, 3506, 3535, 3687, 4165, 4301, 4341, 4519, 5112, 5287, 5636, 5986, 6048, 6072, 6140, 6250, 6841, 7592, 7628,

7676, 7919, 8115, 8146, 9298, 10782, 11129, 11148, 11243, 11323, 11621, 13461, 13480, 13493, 15034, 15097, 15233

■ human ■
Occurrences: 41
Positions:
228, 366, 1702, 3594, 3636, 3677, 3699, 3768, 3824, 3914, 3927, 3994, 4071, 4156, 4167, 4264, 4277, 4605, 4621, 4678, 4895, 4908, 5067, 5928, 5988, 6001, 6029, 9138, 9611, 10216, 13052, 13070, 13793, 14138, 14244, 14251, 14279, 14476, 14724, 14929, 15364

■ language ■
Occurrences: 41
Positions:
442, 622, 924, 976, 1219, 2032, 2043, 2109, 2151, 2288, 2521, 2551, 2558, 2571, 4949, 5998, 6558, 7373, 7431, 9236, 10834, 10956, 10993, 11048, 11053, 11089, 11103, 11246, 11282, 11302, 11348, 11604, 11725, 12132, 12178, 12185, 12208, 12231, 12729, 13064, 13744

■ can ■
Occurrences: 40
Positions:
458, 2238, 4002, 4037, 4266, 4285, 4556, 5229, 5308, 5644, 5698, 5853, 6042, 6350, 6590, 6643, 6672, 6701, 6785, 8831, 9005, 9066, 9320, 9349, 9939, 10037, 10213, 10534, 10989, 11007, 11899, 12441, 12599, 12648, 13119, 13918, 14465, 14553, 14815, 15326

■ he ■
Occurrences: 38
Positions:
122, 1200, 1228, 2307, 2312, 2325, 2336, 2340, 2348, 2397, 2422, 4582, 4992, 5051, 5216, 5331, 5551, 6295, 6307, 6318, 6978, 7143, 7621, 7917, 8652, 8891, 9167, 9357, 9908, 10235, 10263, 10964, 11465, 13390, 14562, 14666, 15569, 15585

■ into ■
Occurrences: 38
Positions:
118, 471, 796, 1294, 1850, 1868, 1985, 2695, 4718, 5319, 5622, 5830, 6177, 6399, 6538, 6635, 7326, 7496, 7901, 8299, 8640, 8872, 8908, 9141, 9181, 9434, 9569, 9603, 10374, 11033, 12843, 13080, 13141, 13246, 14701, 14739, 14775, 15194

■ swarm ■
Occurrences: 38
Positions:
1, 10469, 13732, 13747, 13765, 13788, 13807, 14365, 14404, 14429, 14483, 14507, 14527, 14551, 14575, 14587, 14594, 14613, 14627, 14650, 14677, 14744, 14759, 14783, 14796, 14827, 14843, 14906, 14922, 14946, 14964, 14993, 15003, 15025, 15066, 15108, 15143, 15227

■ but ■
Occurrences: 37
Positions:
436, 1587, 1905, 2236, 2344, 2638, 2741, 2979, 3701, 4205, 5735, 5906, 6335, 6642, 8193, 8373, 8698, 8788, 9256, 9324, 9422, 9565, 9762, 9804, 9858, 11965, 12856, 12883, 13007, 13591, 13674, 13745, 14564, 14696, 15016, 15130, 15321

■ more ■
Occurrences: 37
Positions:
92, 208, 244, 516, 876, 1415, 1591, 2105, 2129, 2333, 2379, 3309, 3338, 3808, 3836, 4185, 4486, 4957, 5251, 5400, 6911, 6930, 7059, 8917, 8983, 10764, 10775, 11906, 12067, 12198, 12666, 12674, 12945, 14060, 14111, 14238, 15009

■ sense ■
Occurrences: 37

Positions:

161, 335, 411, 1379, 1927, 2445, 3232, 3707, 4180, 4495, 4517, 5063, 5723, 5746, 5851, 5966, 7276, 7717, 7844, 9583, 9618, 9675, 10146, 10292, 10349, 10836, 11371, 11399, 11405, 11878, 13127, 13174, 13684, 13910, 14373, 14598, 15367

■ writes ■

Occurrences: 37

Positions:

123, 391, 2305, 2677, 3404, 5446, 6362, 6585, 7156, 7329, 8591, 8677, 8902, 9002, 9358, 9658, 9810, 10071, 10236, 10528, 11368, 11463, 11647, 11849, 12351, 13092, 13299, 13517, 13749, 13961, 14100, 14311, 14563, 14664, 14863, 14943, 15320

■ japanese ■

Occurrences: 34

Positions:

1127, 2063, 2162, 2188, 2191, 2260, 2298, 2361, 2391, 2408, 2417, 2425, 2675, 3162, 3236, 3294, 3303, 3319, 3555, 3573, 4120, 4159, 4181, 4244, 4248, 4323, 4459, 4469, 4739, 5348, 6099, 6152, 10691, 12177

■ music ■

Occurrences: 33

Positions:

6083, 6192, 6220, 6254, 6274, 6294, 6309, 6488, 6500, 6569, 6803, 7037, 7249, 7509, 7513, 7526, 7536, 7559, 7627, 7648, 7656, 7713, 7750, 7986, 8521, 8622, 8650, 8671, 9180, 9196, 9229, 9271, 9336

■ however ■

Occurrences: 32

Positions:

264, 419, 806, 914, 1806, 1941, 2819, 2847, 2912, 3135, 3187, 4113, 4464, 5087, 5426, 5433, 6222, 7553, 7816, 8132, 9261, 9573, 9967, 10024, 10446, 11624, 12031, 12057, 13155, 13931, 14363, 15384

■ than ■

Occurrences: 32

Positions:

97, 212, 246, 379, 1409, 2388, 2439, 4700, 5395, 6927, 6955, 7026, 7087, 7959, 9222, 10026, 10766, 10776, 11561, 11913, 12205, 12496, 12571, 12597, 12668, 12677, 12726, 14243, 14258, 15010, 15157, 15386

■ abe ■

Occurrences: 31

Positions:

2310, 2369, 2434, 3360, 4219, 4723, 4744, 4756, 4791, 4811, 4825, 4863, 4923, 4965, 5020, 5149, 5170, 5178, 5201, 5202, 5342, 5428, 5453, 5531, 5547, 5587, 5663, 10699, 11751, 12028, 12921

■ avant ■

Occurrences: 31

Positions:

1177, 2299, 2462, 3237, 3266, 3295, 3304, 3400, 3500, 4193, 4433, 4750, 4769, 4808, 4975, 5047, 5350, 5481, 5533, 5935, 6246, 6464, 6516, 6835, 10645, 10695, 11670, 11910, 11979, 12109, 12923

■ one ■

Occurrences: 31

Positions:

119, 1810, 1858, 2095, 2531, 2579, 2889, 2925, 3366, 4403, 4634, 7305, 7344, 7933, 8029, 9045, 9714, 9816, 9935, 9938, 10789, 11453, 12796, 13113, 13139, 13639, 14126, 14144, 14227, 15272, 15408

■ most ■

Occurrences: 30

Positions:

711, 821, 856, 1351, 2415, 2429, 2459, 2471, 3281, 3533, 3579, 4132, 4213, 4318, 5359, 5616, 5666, 5690, 6982, 7308, 7580, 7723, 10745, 12160, 12396, 12692, 12714, 12809, 13626, 15275

■ way ■

Occurrences: 30

Positions:

591, 600, 1353, 1400, 6306, 6317, 7125, 8313, 8843, 9634, 9838, 9886, 10566, 11038, 11792, 11832, 12885, 13421, 13631, 13701, 14001, 14020, 14261, 14301, 14452, 14583, 15096, 15204, 15358, 15402

■ while ■

Occurrences: 29

Positions:

557, 915, 1942, 2059, 2928, 3115, 3883, 3919, 4046, 4144, 5476, 6709, 7034, 7481, 8039, 8138, 8504, 8534, 8579, 9681, 9787, 9812, 10819, 10925, 11140, 11870, 11977, 12920, 14338

■ new ■

Occurrences: 28

Positions:

1081, 1090, 1308, 3209, 5762, 6148, 6180, 6971, 6976, 7485, 7903, 9143, 10239, 10936, 11198, 11601, 11868, 12380, 12383, 12535, 12840, 12863, 13015, 13613, 13799, 13864, 14703, 15211

■ their ■

Occurrences: 28

Positions:

2079, 3020, 3095, 3101, 3129, 3144, 3214, 3881, 3920, 3923, 3932, 5391, 6459, 7461, 10805, 11061, 11065, 11115, 11684, 12691, 13001, 13346, 13981, 13999, 14096, 14148, 14421, 14713

■ up ■

Occurrences: 28

Positions:

846, 909, 1007, 1024, 1250, 1461, 5461, 6051, 6236, 6332, 6417, 7079, 7813, 8213, 8316, 8865, 8950, 8978, 9118, 9719, 10712, 11768, 11803, 11846, 11896, 12094, 12583, 12641

■ what ■

Occurrences: 28

Positions:

418, 684, 695, 1786, 2930, 3481, 3527, 3819, 5002, 5510, 5584, 7095, 7165, 7557, 7944, 8133, 8558, 10516, 10545, 10734, 12341, 12711, 13528, 13935, 14770, 15308, 15337, 15450

■ if ■

Occurrences: 27

Positions:

106, 223, 984, 1360, 1899, 2202, 2217, 2335, 2347, 3711, 3926, 9389, 9513, 9693, 10008, 13138, 13457, 13667, 13681, 13689, 14143, 14187, 14197, 14214, 14290, 14640, 15524

■ suggests ■

Occurrences: 27

Positions:

2393, 4196, 4252, 4380, 4512, 4548, 4629, 4839, 5018, 5180, 5203, 5357, 5578, 5676, 5686, 5795, 6880, 7178, 10928, 11284, 11432, 11890, 12054, 12438, 12973, 13269, 13841

■ art ■

Occurrences: 26

Positions:

1093, 2594, 2676, 2694, 2833, 2858, 2994, 3003, 3037, 3256, 4651, 5473, 6077, 6874, 7790, 7924, 9393, 9436, 10210, 10229, 10237, 10266, 10289, 12894, 13136, 15054

■ like ■

Occurrences: 26

Positions:

1739, 2597, 2680, 3327, 3392, 3840, 4286, 4383, 5369, 5840, 6474, 7016, 7432, 9279, 9307, 9723, 9764, 10421, 10885, 12675, 13147, 14181, 14322, 14453, 15182, 15289

■ sound ■

Occurrences: 26

Positions:

1902, 6290, 6311, 6433, 6697, 6784, 6824, 7105, 7117, 7140, 7152, 7202, 7231, 7237, 7266, 7289, 7467, 7488, 7785, 9003,

10423, 10629, 11052, 11154, 13108, 13150

■ cyberpunk ■
Occurrences: 25
Positions:
853, 865, 1057, 1128, 2466, 2487, 2497, 2510, 3287, 3289, 3300, 3320, 3372, 3394, 3560, 3805, 3846, 3960, 4470, 4846, 10692, 12718, 12723, 13381, 13623

■ digital ■
Occurrences: 25
Positions:
432, 1168, 1690, 5910, 6049, 6087, 6346, 6716, 6742, 10962, 11258, 11632, 11858, 13019, 13025, 13105, 13294, 13315, 13409, 13465, 13506, 14070, 14649, 14676, 14743

■ may ■
Occurrences: 25
Positions:
2084, 2467, 2532, 2934, 3649, 3877, 4235, 4546, 5429, 5444, 8428, 8547, 8739, 9039, 9480, 9519, 9970, 10183, 11175, 12023, 13426, 14127, 14228, 14955, 15117

■ so ■
Occurrences: 25
Positions:
292, 377, 1753, 1966, 2073, 2194, 2313, 2534, 3009, 4544, 4731, 4980, 4989, 5495, 5797, 6208, 6906, 9226, 9960, 10180, 10251, 11383, 12866, 13412, 13697

■ was ■
Occurrences: 25
Positions:
1636, 2328, 2349, 2512, 2968, 3029, 3155, 3168, 5548, 7019, 7098, 8255, 8568, 8625, 8645, 9054, 9909, 10889, 10932, 11261, 11306, 11642, 11752, 13876, 15466

■ will ■
Occurrences: 25
Positions:
1436, 3596, 3938, 4043, 6323, 6908, 8177, 8217, 8320, 8335, 8351, 8475, 8478, 10517, 10571, 10584, 10604, 11202, 11221, 13640, 14047, 14398, 14520, 14616, 15309

■ also ■
Occurrences: 24
Positions:
709, 1907, 2704, 3138, 3550, 6207, 6427, 6644, 7622, 7861, 8110, 8194, 8381, 8580, 9325, 9588, 11055, 11871, 11987, 12024, 12721, 13592, 15019, 15406

■ artaud ■
Occurrences: 24
Positions:
892, 6112, 10731, 10742, 10785, 10810, 10929, 10974, 11130, 11141, 11186, 11194, 11233, 11260, 11303, 11367, 11431, 11448, 11503, 11515, 11530, 11641, 11676, 11703

■ garde ■
Occurrences: 24
Positions:
1178, 2300, 3238, 3267, 3296, 3401, 3501, 4194, 4434, 4751, 4770, 4809, 4976, 5351, 5936, 6247, 6465, 6517, 6836, 10646, 10696, 11671, 11980, 12924

■ has ■
Occurrences: 24
Positions:
487, 1100, 1989, 3429, 3483, 5492, 5511, 5719, 6418, 6428, 6437, 6482, 6683, 9337, 9558, 11172, 11353, 12462, 12543, 13904, 14614, 14628, 15146, 15279

■ kind ■
Occurrences: 24
Positions:
3751, 5205, 5294, 5417, 5955, 6136, 6338, 8491, 8778, 9945, 10661, 11076, 11134, 11188, 11344, 12481, 12503, 13191, 13238, 13439, 13453, 14950, 15212, 15555

■ science ■
Occurrences: 24
Positions:
1096, 3376, 3574, 3581,

3747, 3838, 3952, 4121, 4138, 4182, 4245, 4644, 4819, 4837, 4849, 4943, 4964, 5687, 5708, 5790, 8690, 8830, 10574, 15058

■ all ■

Occurrences: 23

Positions:

243, 811, 1038, 1160, 2265, 2734, 3053, 4211, 4308, 6774, 6886, 7912, 8196, 8273, 8334, 8828, 9353, 11126, 11455, 11546, 12958, 12961, 14264

■ form ■

Occurrences: 23

Positions:

1563, 2541, 2669, 2920, 2947, 3179, 3494, 4000, 6581, 6595, 6827, 7062, 7920, 8536, 9975, 10871, 11680, 12698, 12747, 13652, 14305, 15234, 15449

■ media ■

Occurrences: 23

Positions:

1031, 3211, 3373, 3776, 3830, 3924, 5297, 6436, 6749, 7998, 9881, 9920, 10799, 11639, 12627, 12956, 13264, 13507, 13570, 13590, 13800, 15047, 15246

■ xenakis ■

Occurrences: 23

Positions:

6506, 6520, 6566, 6710, 8518, 8567, 8593, 8615, 8668, 8837, 8854, 8944, 9084, 9157, 9170, 9211, 9262, 9282, 9297, 9574, 9657, 10132, 10296

■ aesthetic ■

Occurrences: 22

Positions:

1395, 3024, 3288, 4573, 5044, 5278, 5576, 5679, 9192, 9932, 10153, 10651, 10768, 11616, 11998, 12056, 12486, 12700, 12782, 12943, 13382, 15558

■ no ■

Occurrences: 22

Positions:

2797, 3588, 4418, 7804, 7870, 8001, 8106, 8565, 9287, 9609, 9614, 12322, 12966, 13951, 13956, 14534, 14657, 14659, 14707, 14765, 14785, 15147

■ agency ■

Occurrences: 21

Positions:

978, 998, 1986, 1988, 2546, 6270, 6441, 6796, 7371, 8349, 8370, 9494, 9983, 10320, 14122, 14125, 14347, 14376, 14396, 15051, 15201

■ experience ■

Occurrences: 21

Positions:

181, 338, 341, 572, 940, 1357, 1405, 2027, 4251, 4518, 7194, 9155, 9193, 9497, 9591, 9606, 9803, 9861, 10041, 11180, 12507

■ itself ■

Occurrences: 21

Positions:

430, 649, 2302, 2717, 2770, 3247, 3997, 4752, 5628, 5884, 7758, 8454, 9972, 10415, 11094, 11662, 12479, 13063, 13368, 14828, 15100

■ only ■

Occurrences: 21

Positions:

1154, 1582, 4003, 4267, 5309, 5336, 5866, 7114, 7598, 7927, 8188, 8360, 8444, 9834, 10990, 13578, 13696, 13741, 13795, 14377, 15150

■ possibility ■

Occurrences: 21

Positions:

780, 818, 2100, 3765, 3874, 4087, 4904, 5027, 5221, 7936, 8496, 8500, 9530, 10623, 11693, 11699, 12006, 12113, 12930, 14516, 15377

■ there ■

Occurrences: 21

Positions:

153, 588, 663, 2721, 3548, 3708, 3962, 4234, 8271, 9214, 9285, 9607, 11295, 12239, 12320, 12975, 13341, 13401, 15081, 15256, 15465

■ these ■

Occurrences: 21

Positions:

707, 1787, 2138, 2367, 2479, 3563, 3716, 4057, 4580, 5682, 5846, 6863, 7158, 7763, 8638, 9037, 9421, 10648, 11097, 14193, 15285

■ us ■

Occurrences: 21

Positions:

624, 637, 773, 808, 1010, 1027, 2025, 2891, 4558, 4564, 4649, 5730, 7111, 8736, 9827, 12960, 13415, 13520, 15172, 15302, 15588

■ does ■

Occurrences: 20

Positions:

437, 686, 696, 1965, 5867, 8361, 9576, 9696, 10250, 10440, 10509, 11522, 12042, 12815, 14179, 14651, 14789, 14986, 15453, 15520

■ fiction ■

Occurrences: 20

Positions:

2163, 2170, 3377, 3575, 3582, 3748, 3839, 3953, 4122, 4139, 4183, 4246, 4643, 4810, 4838, 4850, 4925, 5341, 5688, 5791

■ logic ■

Occurrences: 20

Positions:

63, 75, 3609, 3674, 3912, 3977, 3980, 5467, 5807, 5877, 8503, 8710, 8806, 9630, 9656, 9731, 10000, 10427, 12547, 13394

■ novel ■

Occurrences: 20

Positions:

1269, 1980, 4865, 5828, 5879, 5883, 5901, 5920, 5937, 5940, 5981, 10839, 10959, 10973, 11249, 11795, 11827, 12779, 13062, 13176

■ other ■

Occurrences: 20

Positions:

567, 2364, 2864, 3393, 3803, 4726, 5037, 5248, 5300, 6922, 7351, 8041, 8183, 9221, 10099, 10107, 11714, 14141, 14260, 15041

■ our ■

Occurrences: 20

Positions:

160, 1017, 1727, 1891, 1918, 2842, 2871, 2958, 4296, 5139, 5161, 5516, 10869, 11027, 11975, 12787, 13074, 13077, 13499, 15543

■ century ■

Occurrences: 19

Positions:

32, 46, 87, 117, 240, 321, 389, 4655, 6449, 7315, 9844, 9875, 9966, 10479, 11742, 13445, 13849, 14869, 15483

■ granular ■

Occurrences: 19

Positions:

7, 6084, 6340, 6348, 6435, 6522, 6570, 8525, 8859, 8896, 8986, 9031, 9052, 9101, 9464, 9775, 10035, 10181, 10435

■ literary ■

Occurrences: 19

Positions:

687, 1203, 1391, 2409, 2418, 2473, 3357, 4782, 5320, 5349, 5424, 5581, 5620, 5625, 6234, 6337, 10653, 10722, 11926

■ process ■

Occurrences: 19

Positions:

6560, 6720, 6731, 7171, 7405, 7594, 7929, 7931, 7967, 8529, 8862, 8962, 8970, 8982, 9065, 9107, 11710, 11786, 15439

■ through ■

Occurrences: 19

Positions:

185, 1862, 2475, 2779, 4250, 7478, 8044, 8489, 9352, 9362, 9651, 9991, 10114, 10116, 11185, 11686, 12727, 13384, 14271

■ where ■

Occurrences: 19

Positions:

490, 540, 646, 814, 1316, 1730, 1987, 2240, 5490, 7211, 7450, 8096, 9133,

14463, 15071, 15573, 15576, 15581, 15601

■ about ■
Occurrences: 18
Positions:
281, 972, 2021, 2832, 3448, 4386, 8235, 8596, 9306, 9351, 9823, 10078, 10707, 12377, 12387, 13260, 13610, 13973

■ cut ■
Occurrences: 18
Positions:
908, 1249, 6050, 6088, 6235, 6331, 6416, 6527, 7071, 7608, 7812, 9117, 9718, 10711, 11270, 11767, 11802, 11845

■ have ■
Occurrences: 18
Positions:
48, 252, 1789, 2796, 2807, 2827, 4858, 5430, 6373, 7453, 8279, 9082, 12684, 13111, 13202, 13704, 13859, 14709

■ i ■
Occurrences: 18
Positions:
107, 124, 1451, 1618, 1774, 2345, 5897, 7864, 8151, 8278, 8327, 10864, 10896, 10914, 10970, 11384, 12577, 13114

■ individual ■
Occurrences: 18
Positions:
702, 5228, 7269, 7691, 9376, 9739, 9982, 10314, 11536, 14344, 14375, 14380, 14401, 14518, 14541, 14818, 14982, 15516

■ sounds ■
Occurrences: 18
Positions:
6600, 6680, 6894, 6902, 6917, 6959, 6972, 7132, 7279, 7561, 7668, 7705, 7710, 7735, 8599, 9690, 9769, 11099

■ system ■
Occurrences: 18
Positions:
596, 1549, 1648, 3737, 3770, 4607, 4680, 5069, 5261, 6693, 12126, 12795, 13072, 13187, 13229, 13242, 13563, 13588

■ time ■
Occurrences: 18
Positions:
233, 314, 3063, 5739, 6662, 7836, 8224, 9568, 9580, 9599, 10141, 10285, 10305, 10337, 10386, 11750, 15254, 15487

■ would ■
Occurrences: 18
Positions:
125, 529, 2589, 2795, 6561, 6979, 7057, 7546, 8211, 8527, 8966, 9081, 11314, 11649, 11780, 13858, 14162, 14620

■ body ■
Occurrences: 17
Positions:
1565, 1686, 1703, 3410, 3455, 3510, 4168, 4343, 5929, 5989, 6002, 10882, 10918, 12709, 12805, 13053, 13754

■ cage ■
Occurrences: 17
Positions:
6497, 7575, 7576, 7600, 7650, 7704, 7759, 7780, 7794, 7860, 7886, 7889, 7941, 7978, 8092, 8231, 8505

■ cruelty ■
Occurrences: 17
Positions:
896, 10759, 10983, 11220, 11294, 11350, 11351, 11373, 11392, 11410, 11434, 11449, 11483, 11507, 11519, 11568, 11618

■ future ■
Occurrences: 17
Positions:
283, 332, 782, 3425, 4885, 7646, 9099, 10383, 10515, 10521, 13857, 15166, 15313, 15360, 15383, 15391, 15399

■ information ■
Occurrences: 17
Positions:
841, 964, 991, 1072, 1955, 5639, 9185, 9293, 9924, 9995, 11735,

12435, 12616, 12673, 13272, 14498, 14592

■ rather ■
Occurrences: 17
Positions:
378, 1408, 1857, 2438, 5394, 6954, 7025, 7086, 7958, 10025, 11560, 11912, 12179, 12725, 14257, 15156, 15385

■ synthesis ■
Occurrences: 17
Positions:
8, 6085, 6341, 6349, 6523, 6571, 6598, 6698, 7358, 8526, 8860, 8897, 8987, 9053, 9102, 9465, 10036

■ because ■
Occurrences: 16
Positions:
2329, 2810, 2825, 2870, 3127, 4696, 5388, 8253, 10003, 10420, 11551, 13276, 14027, 14328, 14656, 15038

■ between ■
Occurrences: 16
Positions:
2186, 2646, 3002, 4019, 4916, 5472, 7099, 7507, 7789, 9290, 11925, 12705, 12801, 13263, 13584, 14150

■ burroughs ■
Occurrences: 16
Positions:
911, 916, 970, 1253, 2517, 6115, 7069, 9756, 10733, 11760, 11793, 11814, 11833, 11956, 12030, 12063

■ composer ■
Occurrences: 16
Positions:
6769, 6943, 6964, 7174, 7188, 7198, 7362, 7392, 7563, 7573, 7579, 7681, 7846, 8355, 8368, 9203

■ crowd ■
Occurrences: 16
Positions:
13814, 13821, 13833, 13903, 13930, 13971, 14012, 14015, 14107, 14183, 14327, 14631, 14717, 14741, 14773, 14781

■ first ■
Occurrences: 16
Positions:
239, 320, 388, 1443, 2505, 6448, 8247, 8624, 9843, 9874, 10478, 10985, 11288, 11520, 11741, 14868

■ mavo ■
Occurrences: 16
Positions:
2575, 2596, 2604, 2639, 2687, 2729, 2788, 2984, 3010, 3026, 3076, 3136, 3189, 3205, 3233, 15476

■ technologies ■
Occurrences: 16
Positions:
364, 1073, 3891, 3933, 4692, 5829, 5872, 6141, 9090, 9996, 12436, 12617, 13248, 13801, 15048, 15250

■ ultimately ■
Occurrences: 16
Positions:
2964, 3792, 4567, 4716, 5761, 7250, 8342, 8484, 9156, 10019, 10406, 12003, 12775, 13615, 15049, 15584

■ any ■
Occurrences: 15
Positions:
334, 1431, 2363, 3712, 7742, 8182, 8474, 9070, 11807, 11874, 11962, 12082, 12518, 13975, 14124

■ bifo ■
Occurrences: 15
Positions:
1877, 10527, 13748, 13936, 13962, 14002, 14101, 14195, 14310, 14424, 14535, 14862, 14942, 15144, 15319

■ history ■
Occurrences: 15
Positions:
2708, 6026, 6041, 6485, 6800, 9509, 9532, 9642, 9700, 9949, 10160, 10234, 10245, 10260, 10270

■ must ■

Occurrences: 15

Positions:

1859, 2903, 4635, 5914, 6883, 6965, 9360, 9662, 10704, 11030, 11393, 13089, 13318, 13486, 14280

■ perhaps ■

Occurrences: 15

Positions:

393, 669, 2426, 2578, 3308, 4377, 4406, 5848, 9109, 9121, 10034, 12158, 12395, 12807, 13468

■ same ■

Occurrences: 15

Positions:

2814, 3600, 3660, 4229, 4891, 5738, 7121, 7541, 8175, 9633, 11339, 11749, 11791, 11831, 14444

■ self ■

Occurrences: 15

Positions:

3415, 3746, 4107, 8493, 9304, 9549, 9615, 10362, 10365, 10410, 11656, 11659, 12505, 13544, 13547

■ semantic ■

Occurrences: 15

Positions:

563, 768, 1417, 4702, 6411, 10422, 11701, 12144, 12678, 12854, 12905, 13550, 14839, 15411, 15577

■ social ■

Occurrences: 15

Positions:

1067, 2697, 3016, 3054, 3104, 4094, 4297, 5835, 5978, 10801, 12907, 13753, 14052, 14474, 15245

■ theatre ■

Occurrences: 15

Positions:

894, 10757, 10937, 10981, 11006, 11090, 11218, 11292, 11312, 11517, 11532, 11553, 11566, 11645, 11674

■ upon ■

Occurrences: 15

Positions:

1138, 3435, 3910, 9528, 9699, 9726, 10257, 10312, 10336, 10358, 10632, 10827, 11318, 12928, 14958

■ when ■

Occurrences: 15

Positions:

501, 538, 652, 750, 1117, 1873, 2849, 5662, 5918, 9895, 12564, 13675, 13751, 14484, 15255

■ who ■

Occurrences: 15

Positions:

1130, 1775, 2377, 3018, 6284, 7521, 7545, 8574, 9476, 9904, 12149, 13356, 14086, 14754, 14911

■ without ■

Occurrences: 15

Positions:

330, 359, 365, 375, 670, 2440, 2950, 4259, 8608, 9444, 9652, 10193, 10907, 14121, 15510

■ blood ■

Occurrences: 14

Positions:

1270, 1273, 1419, 1585, 1674, 3529, 10845, 10876, 11471, 11935, 12276, 12281, 13153, 13474

■ code ■

Occurrences: 14

Positions:

740, 1082, 11255, 11606, 11887, 12204, 12233, 13312, 13344, 13404, 13418, 14282, 14286, 14289

■ electronic ■

Occurrences: 14

Positions:

6082, 6191, 6231, 6253, 6371, 6487, 6802, 7310, 7512, 7525, 8621, 11638, 11669, 12954

■ here ■

Occurrences: 14

Positions:

977, 1933, 3186, 5504, 6182, 6275, 6321, 6878, 9449, 11035, 11352, 11585, 12682, 13200

■ how ■
Occurrences: 14
Positions:
2015, 3590, 4472, 4552, 4598, 7992, 8597, 8846, 9913, 10206, 10288, 12615, 13320, 13424

■ means ■
Occurrences: 14
Positions:
1412, 1609, 3821, 6057, 7263, 7271, 8975, 8993, 9354, 11411, 11597, 11728, 12452, 15207

■ performance ■
Occurrences: 14
Positions:
3412, 7516, 7596, 7640, 7743, 7841, 7852, 7987, 8113, 8172, 8228, 8238, 8248, 8418

■ similar ■
Occurrences: 14
Positions:
1439, 2705, 5434, 6452, 6510, 7404, 7810, 7989, 8052, 8844, 10977, 12506, 13422, 14435

■ very ■
Occurrences: 14
Positions:
2099, 2198, 2867, 3741, 4076, 4612, 6576, 8338, 8499, 10255, 11692, 12459, 12546, 13104

■ were ■
Occurrences: 14
Positions:
108, 1901, 2722, 3012, 3177, 6838, 7216, 7493, 8272, 8808, 9930, 11268, 11763, 14145

■ complex ■
Occurrences: 13
Positions:
6547, 6677, 8648, 8884, 8961, 8998, 9089, 9105, 9145, 9625, 9709, 12213, 15381

■ each ■
Occurrences: 13
Positions:
2863, 2888, 2976, 6681, 6699, 7350, 8024, 8171, 8204, 8466, 9556, 13978, 15040

■ meaning ■
Occurrences: 13
Positions:
930, 1999, 3422, 3522, 4708, 9807, 9833, 9857, 10084, 11356, 12876, 13721, 15426

■ much ■
Occurrences: 13
Positions:
293, 3284, 4119, 4981, 4990, 5389, 7064, 7693, 9217, 11828, 13131, 14976, 15507

■ notes ■
Occurrences: 13
Positions:
27, 1002, 1878, 2498, 3114, 4921, 6961, 8069, 9171, 9534, 11492, 12237, 14196

■ politics ■
Occurrences: 13
Positions:
10192, 10231, 10300, 10301, 10308, 10333, 10344, 10367, 10384, 10414, 10416, 10419, 10466

■ radical ■
Occurrences: 13
Positions:
2592, 3552, 3809, 4329, 4985, 5073, 5254, 5281, 5314, 5617, 6079, 10792, 12693

■ reader ■
Occurrences: 13
Positions:
678, 1239, 1326, 1805, 5970, 11783, 11950, 12022, 12105, 12498, 12889, 12900, 13256

■ towards ■
Occurrences: 13
Positions:
931, 1845, 4325, 4373, 6478, 8772, 8776, 9242, 9369, 11150, 13451, 14024, 15440

■ tradition ■
Occurrences: 13
Positions:
1157, 2301, 2618, 4962, 6176, 6189, 6248, 6258, 7043, 8396, 10818, 10863, 12719

■ world ■
Occurrences: 13
Positions:
714, 1633, 2258, 2855, 5133, 5275, 5305, 6995, 8727, 11330, 12367, 12952, 13600

■ age ■
Occurrences: 12
Positions:
1169, 4829, 4868, 5661, 6344, 9925, 10963, 11259, 11633, 11859, 12988, 13316

■ apparatus ■
Occurrences: 12
Positions:
1359, 1376, 1662, 1699, 4505, 4614, 9921, 10004, 10050, 10122, 12791, 14836

■ cognitive ■
Occurrences: 12
Positions:
828, 2529, 4092, 4302, 4346, 4368, 5224, 5714, 5750, 14860, 15123, 15225

■ even ■
Occurrences: 12
Positions:
91, 2104, 2711, 4309, 9398, 9474, 9512, 9852, 11068, 13149, 13365, 14804

■ extension ■
Occurrences: 12
Positions:
3254, 5315, 5984, 11012, 13049, 13067, 13171, 13179, 13209, 13245, 14135, 15107

■ impersonality ■
Occurrences: 12
Positions:
6265, 6444, 6481, 7584, 8514, 9484, 9507, 9542, 9713, 9776, 9929, 10212

■ just ■
Occurrences: 12
Positions:
3165, 6004, 6223, 6413, 6725, 7913, 9044, 9616, 10595, 11215, 12141, 15463

■ makes ■
Occurrences: 12
Positions:
2790, 3583, 4084, 4437, 5740, 6101, 6718, 10005, 12111, 13254, 13301, 14010

■ nervous ■
Occurrences: 12
Positions:
3736, 3769, 4606, 4679, 5068, 5260, 12794, 13071, 13186, 13228, 13562, 13587

■ noise ■
Occurrences: 12
Positions:
474, 500, 762, 812, 1041, 6901, 7665, 11156, 11182, 12676, 13533, 15300

■ out ■
Occurrences: 12
Positions:
499, 592, 601, 1944, 2851, 6032, 8549, 10241, 11079, 11107, 12493, 12659

■ own ■
Occurrences: 12
Positions:
1919, 7462, 9560, 10244, 10342, 11976, 13078, 13637, 14000, 14619, 14714, 14919

■ political ■
Occurrences: 12
Positions:
2699, 2801, 3056, 5702, 6739, 7032, 10198, 10218, 10496, 13897, 15057, 15148

■ processes ■
Occurrences: 12
Positions:
467, 731, 2480, 4581, 7246, 7662, 7772, 9518, 10016, 13491, 13556, 13581

■ rushkoff ■
Occurrences: 12
Positions:
1001, 3576, 3720, 3858, 3907, 3943, 4059, 4195, 4253, 13268, 13298, 13483

■ such ■
Occurrences: 12
Positions:

1336, 1398, 2121, 2757, 4356, 7278, 8374, 10207, 10401, 11197, 12017, 15089

■ text ■
Occurrences: 12
Positions:
429, 440, 1435, 1606, 6358, 7088, 10631, 11885, 12458, 13020, 13023, 15284

■ twenty ■
Occurrences: 12
Positions:
238, 387, 1428, 6447, 8011, 8197, 9842, 9873, 10477, 11740, 14867, 15287

■ yet ■
Occurrences: 12
Positions:
475, 1720, 1963, 7429, 10329, 10529, 10601, 10612, 10700, 10769, 12733, 15523

■ algorithmic ■
Occurrences: 11
Positions:
352, 728, 6549, 8885, 9730, 9785, 9847, 9863, 10432, 14855, 15441

■ being ■
Occurrences: 11
Positions:
413, 2360, 3995, 4072, 4157, 4622, 6999, 8425, 10194, 14139, 14237

■ beings ■
Occurrences: 11
Positions:
3637, 3678, 3700, 3915, 3928, 4278, 13949, 14081, 14410, 14477, 14725

■ cannot ■
Occurrences: 11
Positions:
986, 1812, 1995, 2448, 9250, 9272, 9648, 10417, 11210, 14266, 14690

■ collective ■
Occurrences: 11
Positions:
791, 6030, 11540, 11603, 13767, 13885, 13912, 14600, 14647, 15060, 15139

■ consider ■
Occurrences: 11
Positions:
515, 3312, 3872, 6324, 7529, 8230, 10840, 11705, 12901, 13963, 15489

■ early ■
Occurrences: 11
Positions:
318, 3381, 4870, 6203, 6799, 7494, 7796, 8899, 9964, 11739, 15481

■ electric ■
Occurrences: 11
Positions:
1271, 1274, 1420, 1586, 1675, 3530, 10846, 11936, 12277, 13154, 13475

■ life ■
Occurrences: 11
Positions:
151, 1984, 2703, 3006, 3035, 4917, 6762, 7459, 7793, 9990, 11865

■ literature ■
Occurrences: 11
Positions:
4997, 5694, 5712, 5748, 6355, 6372, 6425, 7552, 12368, 13123, 13601

■ making ■
Occurrences: 11
Positions:
2120, 4709, 6059, 7265, 7275, 7504, 8980, 11074, 11112, 11588, 14469

■ narratives ■
Occurrences: 11
Positions:
2118, 3693, 3719, 3779, 3885, 3900, 4058, 6389, 6759, 9882, 11847

■ point ■
Occurrences: 11
Positions:
657, 685, 2088, 4061, 4561, 5090, 8435, 10059, 12162, 13373, 13714

■ present ■
Occurrences: 11
Positions:
116, 356, 735, 6036,

7806, 10526, 10538, 10550, 15318, 15330, 15342

■ production ■
Occurrences: 11
Positions:
4222, 5399, 5543, 5654, 5672, 6193, 6221, 6858, 11927, 11992, 13494

■ project ■
Occurrences: 11
Positions:
1590, 2588, 3041, 9933, 10752, 10949, 11238, 11627, 13197, 15493, 15496

■ spirit ■
Occurrences: 11
Positions:
1970, 3904, 4189, 5658, 7047, 7542, 10697, 13887, 14660, 14735, 14749

■ together ■
Occurrences: 11
Positions:
184, 2809, 8144, 11437, 11888, 14023, 14037, 14441, 14756, 14774, 15429

■ you ■
Occurrences: 11
Positions:
2203, 2218, 2237, 4036, 14188, 14198, 14208, 14265, 14291, 14302, 14552

■ after ■
Occurrences: 10
Positions:
242, 810, 1962, 4210, 4307, 6773, 6998, 7911, 8654, 14263

■ artists ■
Occurrences: 10
Positions:
2626, 2688, 2818, 2985, 3011, 3137, 3206, 6291, 6473, 15277

■ behavior ■
Occurrences: 10
Positions:
370, 13770, 13794, 13960, 14245, 14313, 14412, 14505, 15090, 15141

■ central ■
Occurrences: 10
Positions:
2765, 3735, 5259, 5798, 9159, 13185, 13227, 13372, 13561, 13586

■ content ■
Occurrences: 10
Positions:
7922, 8538, 12728, 12749, 12855, 12879, 13649, 15236, 15263, 15447

■ do ■
Occurrences: 10
Positions:
2225, 2836, 3916, 3925, 4636, 7718, 11385, 13357, 14189, 14760

■ explicitly ■
Occurrences: 10
Positions:
877, 2106, 2130, 3339, 3534, 4815, 5946, 11635, 12715, 14061

■ network ■
Occurrences: 10
Positions:
13819, 14058, 14073, 14109, 14234, 14309, 14318, 14330, 14349, 14636

■ people ■
Occurrences: 10
Positions:
3876, 4030, 4042, 4045, 8242, 13361, 14021, 14035, 14499, 14738

■ piece ■
Occurrences: 10
Positions:
7426, 7471, 7725, 7747, 7757, 8005, 8020, 8048, 8176, 8241

■ practice ■
Occurrences: 10
Positions:
2700, 3239, 3258, 3268, 5680, 8472, 8910, 8929, 12402, 12919

■ remarks ■
Occurrences: 10
Positions:
250, 2733, 3466, 3577, 3860, 4736, 4775, 5545, 11933, 14425

■ schaeffer ■
Occurrences: 10
Positions:
7049, 7089, 7133, 7166, 7180, 7195, 7212, 7232, 7518, 8583

■ some ■
Occurrences: 10
Positions:
143, 668, 4294, 4738, 4823, 4859, 8883, 9223, 11743, 14995

■ speed ■
Occurrences: 10
Positions:
54, 101, 163, 216, 381, 845, 12427, 12582, 12601, 12609

■ tetsuo ■
Occurrences: 10
Positions:
1247, 3344, 3361, 3405, 3443, 3472, 3497, 3532, 4384, 4473

■ those ■
Occurrences: 10
Positions:
5824, 6021, 7544, 8284, 9475, 11072, 11081, 13305, 13355, 14008

■ traditional ■
Occurrences: 10
Positions:
1388, 3059, 3524, 3948, 4146, 7248, 7716, 7746, 8055, 11245

■ via ■
Occurrences: 10
Positions:
861, 1338, 3047, 6144, 8971, 10088, 10607, 12388, 13198, 15104

■ ways ■
Occurrences: 10
Positions:
2561, 4353, 6451, 7225, 7255, 7990, 8555, 14368, 15077, 15265

■ whole ■
Occurrences: 10
Positions:
113, 5805, 12379, 13612, 13686, 13691, 14384, 15006, 15022, 15033

■ word ■
Occurrences: 10
Positions:
765, 4656, 6781, 11040, 11326, 11391, 11454, 11477, 12664, 13107

■ certainly ■
Occurrences: 9
Positions:
2062, 2468, 4049, 4768, 5844, 6184, 6397, 10684, 11983

■ chaos ■
Occurrences: 9
Positions:
472, 1872, 1876, 1929, 1976, 6100, 10581, 15305, 15593

■ common ■
Occurrences: 9
Positions:
1791, 8459, 9571, 13778, 13927, 13952, 13957, 14088, 14734

■ conventional ■
Occurrences: 9
Positions:
1339, 4364, 5875, 8065, 10955, 11808, 11997, 12207, 13743

■ different ■
Occurrences: 9
Positions:
1882, 2726, 3621, 7149, 8180, 11439, 11954, 12603, 14686

■ film ■
Occurrences: 9
Positions:
3343, 3403, 3447, 3487, 3502, 4339, 4382, 4413, 4415

■ glitch ■
Occurrences: 9
Positions:
11, 748, 10438, 10636, 12391, 12622, 13385, 15424, 15596

■ grains ■
Occurrences: 9
Positions:
6542, 6579, 6609, 6657, 6669, 8877, 9017, 9692, 10453

■ group ■
Occurrences: 9
Positions:
2621, 2663, 2750, 2872, 2922, 2949, 2959, 6401, 14952

■ image ■
Occurrences: 9
Positions:
194, 310, 323, 433, 456, 1164, 3992, 13110, 15282

■ machine ■
Occurrences: 9
Positions:
860, 1281, 1496, 3512, 7348, 10921, 12300, 12409, 14172

■ make ■
Occurrences: 9
Positions:
1009, 1026, 3496, 6966, 10232, 12618, 13322, 13683, 14094

■ material ■
Occurrences: 9
Positions:
4927, 5637, 6062, 6855, 7163, 7822, 9429, 11897, 12080

■ movement ■
Occurrences: 9
Positions:
2595, 2605, 2716, 2761, 2794, 4372, 11056, 12605, 12606

■ multitude ■
Occurrences: 9
Positions:
13816, 13939, 13941, 13990, 14056, 14104, 14340, 14431, 14633

■ narrative ■
Occurrences: 9
Positions:
1192, 3797, 3966, 3976, 5806, 5876, 5911, 9524, 10713

■ nature ■
Occurrences: 9
Positions:
3595, 3688, 4041, 7638, 8410, 9546, 10922, 11667, 13780

■ possibilities ■
Occurrences: 9
Positions:
5763, 6367, 6408, 6844, 7502, 10113, 10131, 11010, 15306

■ relation ■
Occurrences: 9
Positions:
3315, 3351, 4110, 8424, 10687, 10703, 11120, 13567, 13797

■ score ■
Occurrences: 9
Positions:
7190, 7633, 8050, 8057, 8109, 8140, 8170, 8453, 8456

■ shared ■
Occurrences: 9
Positions:
180, 337, 340, 571, 626, 2108, 11619, 13915, 14504

■ since ■
Occurrences: 9
Positions:
518, 1393, 2284, 4502, 6126, 6278, 6599, 8203, 12319

■ soul ■
Occurrences: 9
Positions:
1712, 1765, 13907, 14658, 14669, 14732, 14747, 15149, 15155

■ stochastic ■
Occurrences: 9
Positions:
644, 799, 6795, 8520, 8649, 8787, 9310, 9636, 10408

■ style ■
Occurrences: 9
Positions:
1151, 3491, 3517, 5013, 5114, 5176, 5183, 7336, 13148

■ they ■
Occurrences: 9
Positions:
1900, 2447, 2995, 3098, 3116, 4361, 5563, 9257, 14464

■ words ■
Occurrences: 9
Positions:
457, 568, 5301, 7603, 7943, 11016, 11196, 11214, 12687

■ act ■
Occurrences: 8
Positions:
2199, 5397, 5403, 6163, 6737, 9942, 11990, 14480

■ beyond ■
Occurrences: 8
Positions:
3133, 4515, 7895, 9301, 9420, 9586, 13449, 15565

■ brain ■
Occurrences: 8
Positions:
1454, 1734, 4170, 5992, 13204, 13267, 14589, 14920

■ constitutive ■
Occurrences: 8
Positions:
3965, 10322, 10656, 12670, 14389, 14810, 15043, 15242

■ contemporary ■
Occurrences: 8
Positions:
2161, 2169, 2274, 5448, 9173, 11835, 12021, 12270

■ culture ■
Occurrences: 8
Positions:
3060, 3321, 6054, 6172, 6556, 9786, 9848, 9864

■ effect ■
Occurrences: 8
Positions:
5952, 5976, 7342, 12566, 12637, 12770, 14904, 14923

■ extreme ■
Occurrences: 8
Positions:
857, 1176, 1846, 4672, 5857, 10690, 12697, 13628

■ had ■
Occurrences: 8
Positions:
2622, 3222, 5552, 8328, 8930, 9801, 9855, 11771

■ hand ■
Occurrences: 8
Positions:
2215, 3804, 4727, 5038, 5249, 11715, 14149, 14167

■ indeed ■
Occurrences: 8
Positions:
2125, 2291, 2465, 3297, 6763, 9697, 12340, 13467

■ instead ■
Occurrences: 8
Positions:
640, 771, 1841, 2011, 9763, 10467, 13653, 14277

■ key ■
Occurrences: 8
Positions:
1116, 2394, 2739, 4774, 5017, 5098, 5179, 5544

■ medium ■
Occurrences: 8
Positions:
6370, 9947, 11505, 12531, 12639, 12652, 12822, 13047

■ message ■
Occurrences: 8
Positions:
9231, 12631, 12825, 12828, 12850, 12868, 13223, 13278

■ modes ■
Occurrences: 8
Positions:
1340, 1389, 1817, 2780, 4365, 10208, 11199, 12536

■ over ■
Occurrences: 8
Positions:
1190, 2852, 3431, 3521, 7881, 7937, 9033, 12996

■ remains ■
Occurrences: 8
Positions:
786, 3656, 3963, 4832, 6124, 9326, 13224, 13687

■ tatsumi ■
Occurrences: 8
Positions:
2171, 2245, 4735, 5356, 5447, 5577, 11922, 12053

■ though ■
Occurrences: 8
Positions:
597, 5354, 6402, 7751, 9103, 9621, 11341, 13777

■ use ■
Occurrences: 8
Positions:
2039, 2286, 2549, 5994, 9668, 10227, 11113, 14285

■ within ■
Occurrences: 8
Positions:
2356, 6659, 8542, 10803, 11286, 13677, 14048, 14662

■ writer ■
Occurrences: 8
Positions:
1129, 3301, 4806, 5335, 5412, 11948, 12102, 12148

■ according ■
Occurrences: 7
Positions:
3905, 8881, 9918, 10725, 13822, 14387, 14605

■ along ■
Occurrences: 7
Positions:
138, 2366, 3879, 4370, 5681, 14685, 15202

■ american ■
Occurrences: 7
Positions:
3580, 3951, 4147, 6155, 7382, 7569, 10721

■ becomes ■
Occurrences: 7
Positions:
3248, 3695, 5484, 5902, 5982, 8457, 14595

■ change ■
Occurrences: 7
Positions:
3066, 3204, 3666, 3918, 10177, 12831, 14570

■ communication ■
Occurrences: 7
Positions:
1374, 4668, 4691, 9233, 9291, 12214, 13247

■ could ■
Occurrences: 7
Positions:
2945, 5332, 8600, 11450, 11484, 12499, 12578

■ dub ■
Occurrences: 7
Positions:
1658, 2544, 6106, 6166, 6181, 6215, 6301

■ emphasis ■
Occurrences: 7
Positions:
2067, 3504, 3894, 6405, 7234, 7663, 7965

■ engagement ■
Occurrences: 7
Positions:
1418, 3242, 3714, 5870, 6745, 12625, 13500

■ epistemological ■
Occurrences: 7
Positions:
4066, 5105, 5146, 5207, 5632, 6080, 10029

■ every ■
Occurrences: 7
Positions:
147, 276, 476, 485, 9426, 9986, 11122

■ example ■
Occurrences: 7
Positions:
1422, 1450, 4857, 9125, 12267, 14118, 14276

■ further ■
Occurrences: 7
Positions:
607, 1865, 1867, 7872, 9853, 15191, 15193

■ furthermore ■
Occurrences: 7
Positions:
2927, 3097, 3463, 6304, 6434, 10760, 11508

■ gesture ■
Occurrences: 7
Positions:

4983, 5932, 8379, 10771, 11149, 11981, 12487

■ going ■
Occurrences: 7
Positions:
532, 2243, 2918, 9300, 9585, 14568, 14579

■ individuals ■
Occurrences: 7
Positions:
12847, 14680, 14695, 14698, 14753, 14893, 15073

■ landscape ■
Occurrences: 7
Positions:
189, 2410, 7803, 7869, 8000, 8105, 8326

■ level ■
Occurrences: 7
Positions:
2907, 12145, 12312, 12471, 14381, 14979, 14996

■ merging ■
Occurrences: 7
Positions:
3264, 3459, 3508, 4388, 4449, 4528, 10118

■ metamusic ■
Occurrences: 7
Positions:
6503, 9169, 9294, 9314, 9502, 9575, 9587

■ non ■
Occurrences: 7
Positions:
2190, 8544, 9978, 10166, 12014, 12188, 15499

■ outside ■
Occurrences: 7
Positions:
533, 2452, 4099, 6646, 9508, 9521, 11015

■ parameters ■
Occurrences: 7
Positions:
560, 4347, 8541, 9049, 12551, 15199, 15549

■ relationship ■
Occurrences: 7
Positions:
5471, 6070, 10762, 12704, 12788, 12800, 13262

■ representation ■
Occurrences: 7
Positions:
491, 4327, 4396, 4539, 5727, 6063, 11695

■ robinson ■
Occurrences: 7
Positions:
1595, 7778, 11848, 11889, 12410, 12437, 12972

■ set ■
Occurrences: 7
Positions:
1006, 1023, 5240, 6787, 6790, 13706, 14176

■ short ■
Occurrences: 7
Positions:
848, 2396, 2953, 4526, 5076, 6577, 13541

■ signs ■
Occurrences: 7
Positions:
10055, 10070, 10079, 10100, 10108, 11073, 11082

■ something ■
Occurrences: 7
Positions:
3551, 4485, 6178, 9318, 11273, 12197, 12541

■ suvin ■
Occurrences: 7
Positions:
5685, 5704, 5718, 5773, 5794, 5819, 6006

■ terms ■
Occurrences: 7
Positions:
1015, 2955, 3107, 7590, 7630, 9555, 12154

■ them ■
Occurrences: 7
Positions:
2338, 2574, 3174, 7138, 8880, 13363, 14130

■ thought ■
Occurrences: 7
Positions:
4444, 4967, 5765, 8672, 8812, 11594, 11785

■ thus ■
Occurrences: 7
Positions:
2834, 2875, 3738, 6016, 7538, 11916, 13168

■ too ■
Occurrences: 7
Positions:
286, 8256, 9176, 13333, 13336, 14488, 14491

■ transcendence ■
Occurrences: 7
Positions:
5, 524, 647, 6268, 9597, 9602, 15215

■ two ■
Occurrences: 7
Positions:
1425, 1881, 3462, 3619, 7377, 8021, 9047

■ varèse ■
Occurrences: 7
Positions:
6494, 6945, 6960, 7018, 7035, 7482, 7702

■ whereby ■
Occurrences: 7
Positions:
764, 3245, 6532, 7340, 8473, 9517, 9595

■ whose ■
Occurrences: 7
Positions:
2414, 4760, 8519, 9239, 10083, 13769, 14411

■ works ■
Occurrences: 7
Positions:
3370, 3395, 3864, 4871, 6296, 11554, 11778

■ 4 ■
Occurrences: 6
Positions:
4830, 4869, 7726, 7805, 7871, 8002

■ aesthetics ■
Occurrences: 6
Positions:
4204, 4226, 4766, 4977, 6455, 12925

■ again ■
Occurrences: 6
Positions:
1664, 1721, 2756, 3908, 5189, 10665

■ algorithms ■
Occurrences: 6
Positions:
6347, 6360, 6394, 9467, 9471, 10002

■ alongside ■
Occurrences: 6
Positions:
3774, 3931, 6819, 10458, 10647, 12431

■ anti ■
Occurrences: 6
Positions:
897, 4763, 4802, 5095, 10640, 13729

■ artificial ■
Occurrences: 6
Positions:
7355, 13165, 13182, 13214, 13515, 14080

■ associated ■
Occurrences: 6
Positions:
4843, 7582, 7686, 7711, 7754, 13802

■ audio ■
Occurrences: 6
Positions:
6531, 6717, 7808, 8871, 8874, 9035

■ auster ■
Occurrences: 6
Positions:
5371, 5437, 5451, 5459, 12026, 12062

■ barber ■
Occurrences: 6
Positions:
1212, 10927, 11283, 11464, 11646, 12272

■ become ■
Occurrences: 6
Positions:
3430, 9139, 9481, 11084, 13112, 13679

■ certain ■
Occurrences: 6
Positions:
5784, 8059, 9246, 10098, 14296, 14809

■ characters ■
Occurrences: 6
Positions:
2319, 2355, 2436, 4349, 4951, 11109

■ conceptual ■
Occurrences: 6
Positions:
3543, 3890, 5266, 7570, 12550, 12754

■ confront ■
Occurrences: 6
Positions:
704, 718, 772, 825, 831, 835

■ consciousness ■
Occurrences: 6
Positions:
4909, 6031, 9380, 9743, 13162, 13206

■ continues ■
Occurrences: 6
Positions:
2975, 10247, 14003, 14536, 14667, 15145

■ create ■
Occurrences: 6
Positions:
6525, 6676, 11777, 11861, 11971, 13595

■ creative ■
Occurrences: 6
Positions:
5405, 5542, 5674, 11457, 11929, 12072

■ dada ■
Occurrences: 6
Positions:
2598, 2710, 3031, 3170, 10597, 15475

■ development ■
Occurrences: 6
Positions:
1195, 3624, 4024, 4262, 11018, 12433

■ effects ■
Occurrences: 6
Positions:
1802, 11163, 12903, 13041, 13280, 15044

■ engages ■
Occurrences: 6
Positions:
3847, 4816, 6046, 6169, 11636, 12077

■ era ■
Occurrences: 6
Positions:
910, 1251, 1677, 5328, 6743, 14071

■ essential ■
Occurrences: 6
Positions:
3156, 3477, 3680, 4155, 9096, 9610

■ explicit ■
Occurrences: 6
Positions:
2791, 3282, 4054, 11299, 11989, 12161

■ function ■
Occurrences: 6
Positions:
480, 549, 3642, 4202, 9340, 14548

■ gene ■
Occurrences: 6
Positions:
1505, 1657, 2543, 6105, 6165, 10893

■ grain ■
Occurrences: 6
Positions:
6611, 6632, 6650, 6664, 6682, 6700

■ hyper ■
Occurrences: 6
Positions:
2180, 8647, 9144, 9490, 9624, 9708

■ identity ■
Occurrences: 6
Positions:
2616, 3420, 6442, 9526, 9695, 13913

■ illiteracy ■
Occurrences: 6
Positions:
705, 945, 1064, 1407, 1956, 11736

■ imaginary ■
Occurrences: 6
Positions:
7802, 7868, 7999, 8104, 8325, 10065

■ interpretation ■
Occurrences: 6
Positions:
1392, 1924, 1981, 10543, 14524, 15335

■ japan ■
Occurrences: 6
Positions:
2457, 2513, 2577, 2607, 2662, 3353

■ later ■
Occurrences: 6
Positions:
3285, 6562, 6987, 7379, 11420, 11746

■ le ■
Occurrences: 6
Positions:
7002, 8577, 13829, 13850, 13878, 13900

■ machines ■
Occurrences: 6
Positions:
4032, 7658, 9907, 12994, 14085, 14119

■ many ■
Occurrences: 6
Positions:
2074, 6375, 6861, 13413, 14892, 15072

■ mass ■
Occurrences: 6
Positions:
176, 1572, 3210, 5324, 14655, 14682

■ mcluhan ■
Occurrences: 6
Positions:
12819, 12826, 12848, 12965, 13057, 13481

■ mind ■
Occurrences: 6
Positions:
1668, 6230, 9761, 9958, 13526, 13839

■ mode ■
Occurrences: 6
Positions:
2474, 3759, 4537, 4821, 5725, 13016

■ modern ■
Occurrences: 6
Positions:
150, 2661, 4667, 6761, 13044, 13271

■ modernist ■
Occurrences: 6
Positions:
2593, 3023, 4192, 6264, 6463, 6518

■ musical ■
Occurrences: 6
Positions:
6857, 7768, 7953, 8056, 8629, 8641

■ needs ■
Occurrences: 6
Positions:
829, 3664, 10385, 13446, 13808, 15361

■ once ■
Occurrences: 6
Positions:
2308, 6929, 8437, 9317, 9672, 12963

■ pattern ■
Occurrences: 6
Positions:
6550, 8886, 11582, 12837, 13233, 13958

■ performer ■
Occurrences: 6
Positions:
7360, 7678, 7857, 8030, 8042, 8467

■ place ■
Occurrences: 6
Positions:
6430, 7838, 8226, 10143, 12309, 14147

■ programming ■
Occurrences: 6
Positions:
1068, 1084, 4941, 13293, 13359, 13389

■ reading ■
Occurrences: 6
Positions:
942, 1055, 1343, 1347, 6074, 12509

■ recorded ■
Occurrences: 6
Positions:
6432, 6530, 6823, 7131, 7508, 8870

■ status ■
Occurrences: 6
Positions:
3387, 3815, 4103, 7176, 11945, 12098

■ suggest ■
Occurrences: 6
Positions:
1086, 2432, 12120, 12334, 13013, 13672

■ syntax ■
Occurrences: 6
Positions:
10090, 10102, 10619, 10831, 12314, 12671

■ t ■
Occurrences: 6
Positions:
4034, 4038, 8263, 14200, 14293, 14304

■ tape ■
Occurrences: 6
Positions:
6534, 6830, 7085, 7510, 8868, 8952

■ techno ■
Occurrences: 6
Positions:
3778, 9461, 13758, 14883, 14898, 15176

■ tendency ■
Occurrences: 6
Positions:
3570, 4242, 4324, 9240, 10559, 15351

■ transcend ■
Occurrences: 6
Positions:
689, 858, 4362, 9579, 10444, 15174

■ whether ■
Occurrences: 6
Positions:
3944, 10393, 10628, 12904, 13497, 15080

■ william ■
Occurrences: 6
Positions:
1252, 2231, 3396, 4873, 5374, 6114

■ 1 ■
Occurrences: 5
Positions:
6639, 8084, 8097, 8107, 8122

■ absence ■
Occurrences: 5
Positions:
8318, 8347, 8684, 10096, 10105

■ absolute ■
Occurrences: 5
Positions:
3045, 7023, 9458, 11418, 15414

■ acts ■
Occurrences: 5
Positions:
1112, 3176, 7729, 12070, 13762

■ affect ■
Occurrences: 5
Positions:
937, 1365, 10154, 14288, 14581

■ affective ■
Occurrences: 5
Positions:
4588, 6066, 11732, 12008, 12784

■ against ■
Occurrences: 5
Positions:
2547, 3103, 9470, 11592, 15240

■ almost ■
Occurrences: 5
Positions:
146, 5536, 11663, 11708, 12494

■ alternatives ■
Occurrences: 5
Positions:
2022, 5703, 11994, 12115, 15574

■ another ■
Occurrences: 5
Positions:
309, 2926, 3605, 14623, 15132

■ anything ■
Occurrences: 5
Positions:
5477, 8265, 8427, 8438, 11208

■ artist ■
Occurrences: 5
Positions:
2376, 2651, 3260, 6283, 7571

■ asemic ■
Occurrences: 5
Positions:
1040, 1056, 4591, 12339, 12769

■ author ■
Occurrences: 5
Positions:
1256, 4759, 6766, 7875, 12515

■ been ■
Occurrences: 5
Positions:
1992, 5431, 8281, 8931, 13705

■ behind ■
Occurrences: 5
Positions:
636, 5169, 13345, 13374, 13405

■ break ■
Occurrences: 5
Positions:
2998, 6884, 7040, 8609, 11817

■ collage ■
Occurrences: 5
Positions:
3093, 3124, 7203, 7809, 8309

■ combination ■
Occurrences: 5
Positions:
5554, 6605, 7971, 8157, 12228

■ complexity ■
Occurrences: 5
Positions:
8533, 8553, 9491, 10580, 13710

■ compositional ■
Occurrences: 5
Positions:
7593, 7661, 7670, 7771, 8511

■ computer ■
Occurrences: 5
Positions:
739, 4913, 4940, 6568, 14270

■ concrete ■
Occurrences: 5
Positions:
140, 2868, 4238, 6022, 6420

■ conductor ■
Occurrences: 5
Positions:
8016, 8202, 8356, 8401, 8464

■ consequently ■
Occurrences: 5
Positions:
2785, 4609, 5972, 8729, 12096

■ consumption ■
Occurrences: 5
Positions:
5406, 5675, 11930, 12073, 13496

■ context ■
Occurrences: 5
Positions:
2054, 10219, 10802, 13678, 15064

■ course ■
Occurrences: 5
Positions:
1346, 2893, 3278, 4447, 15167

■ cultural ■
Occurrences: 5
Positions:
2117, 5904, 9523, 9999, 14858

■ current ■
Occurrences: 5
Positions:
1816, 2256, 5834, 8829, 15508

■ demands ■
Occurrences: 5
Positions:
4535, 6744, 12897, 13519, 14845

■ destruction ■
Occurrences: 5
Positions:
3051, 10608, 11657, 11689, 11721

■ did ■
Occurrences: 5
Positions:
2341, 2822, 2986, 7527, 7599

■ direction ■
Occurrences: 5
Positions:
11340, 13217, 13977, 14445, 14572

■ doing ■
Occurrences: 5
Positions:
2195, 3008, 6905, 10179, 15445

■ dynamics ■
Occurrences: 5
Positions:
3544, 3732, 8546, 12860, 13289

■ end ■
Occurrences: 5
Positions:
3755, 4268, 4410, 10909, 13845

■ endless ■
Occurrences: 5
Positions:
196, 665, 10112, 10621, 13728

■ english ■
Occurrences: 5
Positions:
1218, 2031, 2042, 12184, 12230

■ escape ■
Occurrences: 5
Positions:
10140, 10158, 10872, 11821, 15218

■ establish ■
Occurrences: 5
Positions:
7227, 9711, 10164, 11308, 15262

■ event ■
Occurrences: 5
Positions:
7108, 7122, 7908, 7916, 9048

■ evolution ■
Occurrences: 5
Positions:
4175, 4256, 8771, 10556, 15348

■ famous ■
Occurrences: 5
Positions:
2461, 4319, 7309, 7724, 12810

■ far ■
Occurrences: 5
Positions:
2535, 3591, 5256, 7464, 11070

■ faster ■
Occurrences: 5
Positions:
4699, 12495, 12568, 12570, 12596

■ flesh ■
Occurrences: 5
Positions:
1309, 1574, 4392, 4453, 10913

■ following ■
Occurrences: 5
Positions:
1264, 1598, 1666, 4127, 14043

■ formally ■
Occurrences: 5
Positions:
4671, 8918, 12724, 13383, 13627

■ futurism ■
Occurrences: 5
Positions:
21, 2600, 3033, 3172, 15478

■ gardism ■
Occurrences: 5
Positions:
5048, 5482, 5534, 11911, 12110

■ general ■
Occurrences: 5
Positions:
2854, 3869, 8817, 11573, 13509

■ given ■
Occurrences: 5
Positions:
1183, 5239, 6661, 9020, 13976

■ gysin ■
Occurrences: 5
Positions:
913, 7067, 9758, 11762, 11770

■ her ■
Occurrences: 5
Positions:
1642, 1689, 7389, 14046, 14918

■ horizon ■
Occurrences: 5
Positions:
760, 1474, 7468, 7654, 10879

■ idea ■
Occurrences: 5
Positions:
34, 8339, 8422, 11481, 12992

■ illusions ■
Occurrences: 5
Positions:
299, 305, 554, 9705, 10402

■ indeterminate ■
Occurrences: 5
Positions:
6548, 7637, 7776, 10021, 10622

■ intense ■
Occurrences: 5
Positions:
1145, 1416, 1800, 13455, 15512

■ interfaces ■
Occurrences: 5
Positions:
6755, 13347, 13407, 13776, 14900

■ isolated ■
Occurrences: 5
Positions:
96, 211, 2403, 9010, 14679

■ lines ■
Occurrences: 5
Positions:
2368, 3622, 5683, 10843, 14687

■ listening ■
Occurrences: 5
Positions:
6928, 7102, 7113, 7193, 8420

■ living ■
Occurrences: 5
Positions:
1564, 1685, 13045, 14409, 14997

■ loop ■
Occurrences: 5
Positions:
486, 510, 620, 4289, 12736

■ machinery ■
Occurrences: 5
Positions:
863, 1473, 1644, 4553, 4599

■ made ■
Occurrences: 5
Positions:
1714, 2331, 8616, 9412, 14066

■ major ■
Occurrences: 5
Positions:
3863, 5624, 8508, 8856, 11316

■ masses ■
Occurrences: 5
Positions:
724, 10911, 13869, 13883, 14752

■ meta ■
Occurrences: 5
Positions:
9435, 10081, 10133, 10297, 12485

■ might ■
Occurrences: 5
Positions:
420, 5380, 9916, 10155, 11704

■ nationality ■
Occurrences: 5
Positions:
2065, 2365, 2441, 6158, 6173

■ necessarily ■
Occurrences: 5
Positions:
4052, 4200, 6771, 9755, 12044

■ note ■
Occurrences: 5
Positions:
2034, 5771, 8102, 10204, 10847

■ nothing ■
Occurrences: 5
Positions:
3662, 7707, 8251, 10599, 10611

■ now ■
Occurrences: 5
Positions:
9269, 9828, 14697, 15395, 15484

■ operate ■
Occurrences: 5
Positions:
3909, 9520, 9917, 11498, 15128

■ operates ■
Occurrences: 5
Positions:
1396, 1947, 14366, 14385, 14604

■ pace ■
Occurrences: 5
Positions:
1187, 4684, 12835, 13231, 13285

■ particular ■
Occurrences: 5
Positions:
3184, 6706, 7709, 11037, 14949

■ particularly ■
Occurrences: 5
Positions:
1102, 3325, 4798, 5506, 10724

■ parts ■
Occurrences: 5
Positions:
13682, 13703, 14811, 15015, 15027

■ poetics ■
Occurrences: 5
Positions:
12, 9927, 10182, 10436, 10637

■ possible ■
Occurrences: 5
Positions:
6967, 11178, 12619, 12971, 14095

■ question ■
Occurrences: 5
Positions:
682, 4507, 8680, 10668, 12978

■ radios ■
Occurrences: 5
Positions:
7799, 8008, 8028, 8210, 8268

■ recognize ■
Occurrences: 5
Positions:
661, 2846, 5732, 13399, 15470

■ result ■
Occurrences: 5
Positions:
674, 6601, 8836, 12041, 12130

■ reveals ■
Occurrences: 5
Positions:
508, 520, 648, 13391, 13436

■ revolution ■
Occurrences: 5
Positions:
1975, 3046, 4847, 10576, 13106

■ say ■
Occurrences: 5
Positions:
1875, 4275, 8243, 14533, 14610

■ schiltz ■
Occurrences: 5
Positions:
4628, 11932, 12235, 13093, 13518

■ senses ■
Occurrences: 5
Positions:
1210, 3272, 4824, 5086, 11559

■ shift ■
Occurrences: 5
Positions:
5059, 5633, 6272, 6477, 12858

■ society ■
Occurrences: 5
Positions:
3163, 3644, 5489, 5610, 13854

■ source ■
Occurrences: 5
Positions:
4946, 5568, 7162, 12079, 15087

■ spatial ■
Occurrences: 5
Positions:
6707, 9679, 9702, 10997, 11088

■ structure ■
Occurrences: 5
Positions:
3640, 8078, 8605, 11810, 12761

■ temporal ■
Occurrences: 5
Positions:
9554, 9605, 9677, 9704, 10201

■ temporality ■
Occurrences: 5
Positions:
408, 423, 10307, 10430, 10445

■ things ■
Occurrences: 5
Positions:
653, 2332, 5561, 11050, 11436

■ train ■
Occurrences: 5
Positions:
55, 102, 217, 382, 14029

■ twentieth ■
Occurrences: 5
Positions:
45, 86, 319, 7314, 15482

■ under ■
Occurrences: 5
Positions:
3224, 5243, 8813, 9162, 13000

■ 1980s ■
Occurrences: 4
Positions:
3324, 3382, 4853, 5595

■ achieve ■
Occurrences: 4
Positions:
6980, 9188, 11683, 15118

■ aimed ■
Occurrences: 4
Positions:
2612, 2774, 3043, 11570

■ airliner ■
Occurrences: 4
Positions:
57, 105, 219, 383

■ akin ■
Occurrences: 4
Positions:
887, 4487, 12068, 12199

■ alternative ■
Occurrences: 4
Positions:
2560, 10165, 10463, 15398

■ approaches ■
Occurrences: 4
Positions:
5439, 6308, 6319, 8512

■ appropriate ■
Occurrences: 4
Positions:
2280, 2472, 3310, 4501

■ around ■
Occurrences: 4
Positions:
7110, 8461, 13250, 14262

■ artistic ■
Occurrences: 4
Positions:
2843, 7907, 9428, 10567

■ arts ■
Occurrences: 4
Positions:
1091, 9661, 13463, 13503

■ asks ■
Occurrences: 4
Positions:
971, 2024, 13396, 15171

■ automated ■
Occurrences: 4
Positions:
6526, 8985, 12400, 15226

■ biases ■
Occurrences: 4
Positions:
962, 974, 989, 11241

■ biological ■
Occurrences: 4
Positions:
4070, 4304, 4531, 4613

■ bon ■
Occurrences: 4
Positions:
13830, 13851, 13879, 13901

■ borders ■
Occurrences: 4
Positions:
1950, 3001, 3974, 5785

■ boy ■
Occurrences: 4
Positions:
1484, 1655, 7320, 7346

■ bring ■
Occurrences: 4
Positions:
2020, 9350, 12376, 13609

■ chromosome ■
Occurrences: 4
Positions:
1492, 1768, 10870, 10877

■ city ■
Occurrences: 4
Positions:
1478, 1559, 3332, 13969

■ cloud ■
Occurrences: 4
Positions:
8853, 9311, 9722, 10451

■ coming ■
Occurrences: 4
Positions:
5318, 9130, 13160, 15428

■ comments ■
Occurrences: 4
Positions:
1213, 8103, 12257, 12560

■ composition ■
Occurrences: 4
Positions:
6109, 6195, 8417, 8676

■ concrète ■
Occurrences: 4
Positions:
7056, 7169, 7339, 7531

■ considered ■
Occurrences: 4
Positions:
3807, 8838, 11901, 13221

■ consumer ■
Occurrences: 4
Positions:
172, 951, 1062, 12104

■ control ■
Occurrences: 4
Positions:
1548, 2530, 8477, 13002

■ critics ■
Occurrences: 4
Positions:
2048, 3017, 4753, 4796

■ cutting ■
Occurrences: 4
Positions:
7078, 8864, 8949, 11895

■ dadaist ■
Occurrences: 4
Positions:
902, 1969, 7046, 7060

■ de ■
Occurrences: 4
Positions:
4422, 11429, 12316, 13594

■ decades ■
Occurrences: 4
Positions:
5523, 6986, 9051, 11745

■ desire ■
Occurrences: 4
Positions:
1070, 11775, 14522, 15388

■ diegetic ■
Occurrences: 4
Positions:
2110, 3853, 5951, 11809

■ difficult ■
Occurrences: 4
Positions:
2334, 10007, 12138,

13334

■ don ■
Occurrences: 4
Positions:
4033, 14199, 14292, 14303

■ during ■
Occurrences: 4
Positions:
1953, 2608, 4851, 5329

■ effectively ■
Occurrences: 4
Positions:
6168, 12613, 14357, 14509

■ employs ■
Occurrences: 4
Positions:
2172, 6007, 9466, 11716

■ entity ■
Occurrences: 4
Positions:
2963, 2967, 9146, 14778

■ everyday ■
Occurrences: 4
Positions:
129, 2702, 7792, 9154

■ everything ■
Occurrences: 4
Positions:
4639, 5483, 5498, 8789

■ evolving ■
Occurrences: 4
Positions:
3651, 4690, 6679, 13546

■ experiment ■
Occurrences: 4
Positions:
3520, 6384, 6850, 7605

■ experimental ■
Occurrences: 4
Positions:
1142, 2555, 12778, 12893

■ experiments ■
Occurrences: 4
Positions:
3561, 6864, 7147, 7797

■ expression ■
Occurrences: 4
Positions:
7684, 9356, 11201, 15093

■ familiar ■
Occurrences: 4
Positions:
128, 5759, 6958, 7667

■ follow ■
Occurrences: 4
Positions:
8691, 12984, 14201, 14417

■ force ■
Occurrences: 4
Positions:
710, 3200, 4423, 8509

■ formed ■
Occurrences: 4
Positions:
2874, 8759, 9012, 11444

■ formulation ■
Occurrences: 4
Positions:
4128, 12528, 13059, 13219

■ four ■
Occurrences: 4
Positions:
1429, 8012, 8198, 9797

■ frequently ■
Occurrences: 4
Positions:
2371, 5009, 6285, 11952

■ fundamentally ■
Occurrences: 4
Positions:
1384, 3729, 5185, 11138

■ genre ■
Occurrences: 4
Positions:
3867, 4463, 5823, 13638

■ gestures ■
Occurrences: 4
Positions:
1844, 11059, 11266, 11336

■ goes ■
Occurrences: 4
Positions:
1460, 12567, 12607, 13998

■ great ■
Occurrences: 4
Positions:
39, 50, 303, 552

■ ice ■
Occurrences: 4
Positions:
1507, 1728, 4828, 4867

■ iconoclastic ■
Occurrences: 4
Positions:
1614, 5344, 6257, 11984

■ impossible ■
Occurrences: 4
Positions:
6846, 10010, 14531, 15163

■ inhuman ■
Occurrences: 4
Positions:
466, 4490, 10015, 15269

■ inscribed ■
Occurrences: 4
Positions:
10523, 10547, 15315, 15339

■ instant ■
Occurrences: 4
Positions:
24, 5056, 5917, 9516

■ intelligence ■
Occurrences: 4
Positions:
13166, 13183, 13215, 13516

■ kenji ■
Occurrences: 4
Positions:
14, 541, 1121, 12342

■ linear ■
Occurrences: 4
Positions:
1191, 8545, 10167, 10282

■ linguistic ■
Occurrences: 4
Positions:
13572, 13759, 14884, 14899

■ links ■
Occurrences: 4
Positions:
1532, 3528, 10735, 12712

■ long ■
Occurrences: 4
Positions:
2914, 3653, 4792, 11774

■ magnetic ■
Occurrences: 4
Positions:
6829, 7084, 8867, 8951

■ man ■
Occurrences: 4
Positions:
132, 3347, 7520, 14907

■ manifest ■
Occurrences: 4
Positions:
4115, 6060, 9971, 14067

■ manipulating ■
Occurrences: 4
Positions:
7080, 9043, 13018, 13022

■ mathematics ■
Occurrences: 4
Positions:
4938, 6553, 8658, 9135

■ meaningful ■
Occurrences: 4
Positions:
2124, 4100, 4367, 4625

■ memory ■
Occurrences: 4
Positions:
275, 1292, 4914, 9612

■ methodology ■
Occurrences: 4
Positions:
10652, 11893, 12392, 12419

■ moment ■
Occurrences: 4
Positions:
489, 496, 2886, 9402

■ motion ■
Occurrences: 4
Positions:
358, 574, 1527, 4426

■ move ■
Occurrences: 4
Positions:

1860, 4514, 5670, 13448

■ multimedia ■
Occurrences: 4
Positions:
4663, 6282, 6472, 13621

■ musique ■
Occurrences: 4
Positions:
7055, 7168, 7338, 7530

■ mutating ■
Occurrences: 4
Positions:
328, 3771, 3827, 4681

■ mutations ■
Occurrences: 4
Positions:
1828, 4305, 4330, 10412

■ national ■
Occurrences: 4
Positions:
2057, 2583, 3074, 10833

■ nationhood ■
Occurrences: 4
Positions:
2102, 2148, 2569, 10670

■ negation ■
Occurrences: 4
Positions:
2782, 9969, 10115, 10615

■ noon ■
Occurrences: 4
Positions:
1938, 5382, 6211, 15294

■ notable ■
Occurrences: 4
Positions:
4860, 5975, 6438, 11512

■ offers ■
Occurrences: 4
Positions:
308, 1262, 2559, 12035

■ often ■
Occurrences: 4
Positions:
935, 2980, 3099, 4754

■ otherwise ■
Occurrences: 4
Positions:
530, 4646, 13004, 13348

■ part ■
Occurrences: 4
Positions:
2295, 3250, 5925, 14306

■ perfect ■
Occurrences: 4
Positions:
3999, 9388, 9751, 13603

■ personal ■
Occurrences: 4
Positions:
9525, 9694, 11461, 13288

■ physical ■
Occurrences: 4
Positions:
3706, 4521, 11403, 11525

■ potential ■
Occurrences: 4
Positions:
3154, 7129, 10998, 11005

■ prescribed ■
Occurrences: 4
Positions:
562, 9522, 10562, 15354

■ program ■
Occurrences: 4
Positions:
883, 2769, 8968, 10787

■ progress ■
Occurrences: 4
Positions:
36, 206, 10392, 10404

■ progressive ■
Occurrences: 4
Positions:
304, 553, 1144, 3226

■ prose ■
Occurrences: 4
Positions:
1146, 1172, 1226, 7443

■ pure ■
Occurrences: 4
Positions:
6893, 8791, 8796, 13126

■ quality ■
Occurrences: 4
Positions:
2419, 4589, 6067, 11733

■ radio ■
Occurrences: 4
Positions:
7827, 8038, 8045, 8205

■ random ■
Occurrences: 4
Positions:
6733, 8662, 9685, 9716

■ rapidly ■
Occurrences: 4
Positions:
2656, 3826, 12460, 12533

■ re ■
Occurrences: 4
Positions:
2219, 3149, 7082, 15261

■ readers ■
Occurrences: 4
Positions:
5360, 5449, 5697, 13397

■ realism ■
Occurrences: 4
Positions:
4779, 4786, 5106, 5208

■ realist ■
Occurrences: 4
Positions:
4764, 4803, 4973, 5154

■ reality ■
Occurrences: 4
Positions:
446, 4711, 5033, 5157

■ reason ■
Occurrences: 4
Positions:
4239, 5457, 5599, 14267

■ rejection ■
Occurrences: 4
Positions:
3049, 10793, 10813, 10860

■ relentless ■
Occurrences: 4
Positions:
1079, 1171, 1224, 10825

■ remain ■
Occurrences: 4
Positions:
3597, 4098, 5230, 5837

■ rhythm ■
Occurrences: 4
Positions:
1916, 1922, 9561, 10339

■ russolo ■
Occurrences: 4
Positions:
6491, 6871, 6879, 7017

■ second ■
Occurrences: 4
Positions:
6671, 8644, 9869, 11529

■ seems ■
Occurrences: 4
Positions:
2045, 6128, 13011, 14415

■ shifts ■
Occurrences: 4
Positions:
5677, 5753, 7183, 10649

■ simply ■
Occurrences: 4
Positions:
4282, 6329, 9578, 10407

■ single ■
Occurrences: 4
Positions:
9009, 9401, 12511, 12519

■ situated ■
Occurrences: 4
Positions:
4578, 6243, 10457, 10808

■ take ■
Occurrences: 4
Positions:
1441, 11031, 12308, 15526

■ takes ■
Occurrences: 4
Positions:
10203, 12219, 13140, 14730

■ technological ■
Occurrences: 4
Positions:
4023, 4534, 9665, 15106

■ think ■
Occurrences: 4
Positions:
1011, 1996, 10418, 13259

■ thinking ■
Occurrences: 4
Positions:
2563, 8595, 10190, 11165

■ three ■
Occurrences: 4
Positions:
8617, 9158, 11511, 11744

■ times ■
Occurrences: 4
Positions:
2938, 9774, 10327, 11235

■ today ■
Occurrences: 4
Positions:
248, 5361, 6214, 9063

■ tsukamoto ■
Occurrences: 4
Positions:
879, 3340, 3482, 4545

■ uncertainty ■
Occurrences: 4
Positions:
7555, 8185, 9620, 9894

■ understood ■
Occurrences: 4
Positions:
2450, 3617, 5311, 5855

■ unpredictability ■
Occurrences: 4
Positions:
6412, 8488, 9724, 10583

■ ups ■
Occurrences: 4
Positions:
6089, 6528, 7072, 7609

■ used ■
Occurrences: 4
Positions:
3208, 6564, 7862, 9820

■ uses ■
Occurrences: 4
Positions:
2556, 6357, 8093, 11853

■ verrone ■
Occurrences: 4
Positions:
3397, 3464, 4379, 4547

■ virilio ■
Occurrences: 4
Positions:
26, 60, 249, 12587

■ weisenfeld ■
Occurrences: 4
Positions:
2679, 2732, 2974, 3113

■ worlds ■
Occurrences: 4
Positions:
168, 7356, 11489, 11613

■ zero ■
Occurrences: 4
Positions:
9604, 10044, 10051, 10074

■ 1958 ■
Occurrences: 3
Positions:
6994, 7400, 8901

■ 2 ■
Occurrences: 3
Positions:
8083, 8098, 8131

■ 21st ■
Occurrences: 3
Positions:
4654, 9965, 13444

■ 5 ■
Occurrences: 3
Positions:
3726, 3845, 8073

■ accelerated ■
Occurrences: 3
Positions:
7218, 8532, 12913

■ achieves ■
Occurrences: 3
Positions:
7564, 8560, 12344

■ achieving ■
Occurrences: 3
Positions:
6952, 11599, 15209

■ acknowledge ■
Occurrences: 3
Positions:
987, 2940, 15407

■ action ■
Occurrences: 3
Positions:
4429, 11025, 15169

■ activity ■
Occurrences: 3
Positions:
7954, 8460, 8665

■ aleatoric ■
Occurrences: 3
Positions:
6499, 7774, 9720

■ although ■
Occurrences: 3
Positions:
3647, 8922, 13616

■ ambiance ■
Occurrences: 3
Positions:
3935, 4720, 7738

■ ambient ■
Occurrences: 3
Positions:
1534, 5296, 12949

■ amplitude ■
Occurrences: 3
Positions:
6617, 6690, 8033

■ analogous ■
Occurrences: 3
Positions:
1059, 10702, 11919

■ approach ■
Occurrences: 3
Positions:
1615, 4160, 11280

■ approaching ■
Occurrences: 3
Positions:
1118, 1335, 10043

■ argues ■
Occurrences: 3
Positions:
2492, 5099, 9212

■ aspect ■
Occurrences: 3
Positions:
148, 9987, 12244

■ assault ■
Occurrences: 3
Positions:
1207, 5083, 10826

■ attempts ■
Occurrences: 3
Positions:
1910, 4508, 7038

■ audience ■
Occurrences: 3
Positions:
3547, 7364, 8192

■ automatic ■
Occurrences: 3
Positions:
12415, 14876, 15152

■ automation ■
Occurrences: 3
Positions:
14169, 14887, 14937

■ away ■
Occurrences: 3
Positions:
927, 4637, 15159

■ before ■
Occurrences: 3
Positions:
9922, 12629, 12645

■ behaviour ■
Occurrences: 3
Positions:
14879, 14890, 14940

■ berio ■
Occurrences: 3
Positions:
7394, 7469, 7492

■ black ■
Occurrences: 3
Positions:
1277, 1510, 12296

■ bolton ■
Occurrences: 3
Positions:
2500, 4840, 4920

■ book ■
Occurrences: 3
Positions:
19, 12521, 15459

■ called ■
Occurrences: 3
Positions:
6541, 7144, 12398

■ calls ■
Occurrences: 3
Positions:
9168, 12405, 13937

■ case ■
Occurrences: 3
Positions:
7819, 8323, 10780

■ category ■
Occurrences: 3
Positions:
1232, 7241, 9165

■ causality ■
Occurrences: 3
Positions:
8686, 8722, 8752

■ center ■
Occurrences: 3
Positions:
616, 2143, 5225

■ chance ■
Occurrences: 3
Positions:
7859, 7880, 14721

■ changes ■
Occurrences: 3
Positions:
4090, 4354, 5961

■ characterized ■
Occurrences: 3
Positions:
3887, 4886, 5656

■ closed ■
Occurrences: 3
Positions:
595, 12125, 13240

■ come ■
Occurrences: 3
Positions:
5512, 12492, 14755

■ comes ■
Occurrences: 3
Positions:
8784, 13789, 13991

■ complicates ■
Occurrences: 3
Positions:
5039, 7172, 10666

■ conceptions ■
Occurrences: 3
Positions:
5162, 6977, 7486

■ concerned ■
Occurrences: 3
Positions:
2131, 3537, 5947

■ conditions ■
Occurrences: 3
Positions:
2659, 5979, 14472

■ confusion ■
Occurrences: 3
Positions:
2016, 3898, 4499

■ conscious ■
Occurrences: 3
Positions:
11085, 13946, 14495

■ conservative ■
Occurrences: 3
Positions:
3761, 3782, 3837

■ considering ■
Occurrences: 3
Positions:
5509, 7257, 10748

■ construction ■
Occurrences: 3
Positions:
3126, 8614, 9637

■ constructivism ■
Occurrences: 3
Positions:
3088, 4722, 4988

■ constructivist ■
Occurrences: 3
Positions:
2817, 2857, 5255

■ coordinated ■
Occurrences: 3
Positions:
14019, 14451, 15076

■ crucial ■
Occurrences: 3
Positions:
5089, 8135, 9537

■ cybernetic ■
Occurrences: 3
Positions:
956, 14062, 14134

■ dadaists ■
Occurrences: 3
Positions:
2682, 6470, 6728

■ data ■
Occurrences: 3
Positions:
1639, 9225, 10609

■ death ■
Occurrences: 3
Positions:
4742, 4747, 4919

■ define ■
Occurrences: 3
Positions:
10110, 10991, 13792

■ definition ■
Occurrences: 3
Positions:
5706, 5788, 9540

■ demonstrates ■
Occurrences: 3
Positions:
5783, 12305, 14784

■ denies ■
Occurrences: 3
Positions:
5126, 5135, 8497

■ dependent ■
Occurrences: 3
Positions:
7829, 10357, 14957

■ der ■
Occurrences: 3
Positions:
7317, 7410, 7436

■ developed ■
Occurrences: 3
Positions:
3223, 6521, 8892

■ difference ■
Occurrences: 3
Positions:
7097, 10125, 10606

■ disorder ■
Occurrences: 3
Positions:
2017, 7976, 9626

■ distinction ■
Occurrences: 3
Positions:
7788, 11924, 14624

■ documentary ■
Occurrences: 3
Positions:
5012, 5175, 5182

■ down ■
Occurrences: 3
Positions:
2999, 7325, 11873

■ drive ■
Occurrences: 3
Positions:
1227, 2207, 4215

■ dynamic ■
Occurrences: 3
Positions:
3775, 10996, 13241

■ effective ■
Occurrences: 3
Positions:
1352, 3713, 5691

■ either ■
Occurrences: 3
Positions:
5125, 8416, 12999

■ elements ■
Occurrences: 3
Positions:
3556, 7739, 7765

■ embedded ■
Occurrences: 3
Positions:
4595, 11297, 14419

■ embodied ■
Occurrences: 3
Positions:
227, 7244, 7515

■ embrace ■
Occurrences: 3
Positions:
3192, 10578, 13723

■ emerge ■
Occurrences: 3
Positions:
10518, 14719, 15310

■ emergence ■
Occurrences: 3
Positions:
3086, 13726, 14833

■ emotional ■
Occurrences: 3
Positions:
939, 1493, 4523

■ emulator ■
Occurrences: 3
Positions:
1706, 5930, 6003

■ enacts ■
Occurrences: 3
Positions:
11276, 12722, 12865

■ engaging ■
Occurrences: 3
Positions:
2553, 4171, 12642

■ entirely ■
Occurrences: 3
Positions:
5537, 8216, 10816

■ environment ■
Occurrences: 3
Positions:
3427, 14914, 14934

■ establishing ■
Occurrences: 3
Positions:
11917, 12196, 13189

■ estrangement ■
Occurrences: 3
Positions:
5715, 5716, 5751

■ exaltation ■
Occurrences: 3
Positions:
9372, 9735, 11497

■ existing ■
Occurrences: 3
Positions:
5132, 5262, 5304

■ experimentation ■
Occurrences: 3
Positions:
905, 1075, 1189

■ express ■
Occurrences: 3
Positions:
6404, 13033, 14554

■ expressed ■
Occurrences: 3
Positions:
2071, 8088, 13889

■ expressive ■
Occurrences: 3
Positions:
1368, 10995, 11002

■ extended ■
Occurrences: 3
Positions:
7890, 11064, 12915

■ fact ■
Occurrences: 3
Positions:
2942, 8270, 8701

■ feature ■
Occurrences: 3
Positions:
3402, 4467, 4878

■ features ■
Occurrences: 3
Positions:
11066, 11513, 14689

■ fecundity ■
Occurrences: 3
Positions:
816, 2137, 12123

■ find ■
Occurrences: 3
Positions:
8264, 13642, 14466

■ fragments ■
Occurrences: 3
Positions:
7215, 7328, 13665

■ free ■
Occurrences: 3
Positions:
6788, 7041, 13707

■ fundamental ■
Occurrences: 3
Positions:
3663, 8802, 9339

■ futurist ■
Occurrences: 3
Positions:
6869, 9128, 9950

■ game ■
Occurrences: 3
Positions:
14207, 14213, 14216

■ generally ■
Occurrences: 3
Positions:
1592, 2742, 4958

■ generative ■
Occurrences: 3
Positions:
6354, 11139, 12408

■ gesang ■
Occurrences: 3
Positions:
7316, 7409, 7435

■ gibson ■
Occurrences: 3
Positions:
2232, 4874, 5375

■ glitching ■
Occurrences: 3
Positions:
2029, 12203, 12792

■ goal ■
Occurrences: 3
Positions:
8330, 8780, 9406

■ governed ■
Occurrences: 3
Positions:
10355, 14116, 14242

■ hazy ■
Occurrences: 3
Positions:
9270, 9309, 9721

■ hierarchical ■
Occurrences: 3
Positions:
7983, 12048, 13872

■ humanity ■
Occurrences: 3
Positions:
3613, 4029, 12998

■ immediately ■
Occurrences: 3
Positions:
1322, 8293, 10767

■ impulse ■
Occurrences: 3
Positions:
5168, 9129, 9783

■ inclination ■
Occurrences: 3
Positions:
2815, 2869, 12051

■ incomprehensible ■
Occurrences: 3
Positions:
4085, 13680, 13688

■ independently ■
Occurrences: 3
Positions:
5159, 14386, 15129

■ indeterminacy ■
Occurrences: 3
Positions:
7973, 8148, 8486

■ innovation ■
Occurrences: 3
Positions:
376, 5570, 10568

■ instance ■
Occurrences: 3
Positions:
2275, 6932, 15600

■ intensely ■
Occurrences: 3
Positions:
983, 8958, 12946

■ intent ■
Occurrences: 3
Positions:
2673, 5023, 6129

■ inter ■
Occurrences: 3
Positions:
4827, 4866, 13287

■ internal ■
Occurrences: 3
Positions:
1522, 1921, 14786

■ internet ■
Occurrences: 3
Positions:
1135, 12465, 13805

■ intimates ■
Occurrences: 3
Positions:
5279, 5752, 10975

■ introduction ■
Occurrences: 3
Positions:
2158, 2249, 2483

■ issue ■
Occurrences: 3
Positions:
721, 2164, 2253

■ japanoid ■
Occurrences: 3
Positions:
2175, 2266, 2271

■ joyce ■
Occurrences: 3
Positions:
7399, 7421, 7620

■ jünglinge ■
Occurrences: 3
Positions:
7318, 7411, 7437

■ knowing ■
Occurrences: 3
Positions:
1819, 3468, 9445

■ least ■
Occurrences: 3
Positions:
9267, 10163, 11380

■ left ■
Occurrences: 3
Positions:
4790, 7854, 7926

■ legacy ■
Occurrences: 3
Positions:
6421, 9119, 12119

■ line ■
Occurrences: 3
Positions:
3606, 7695, 8074

■ little ■
Occurrences: 3
Positions:
3710, 12036, 12977

■ manga ■
Occurrences: 3
Positions:
2223, 4313, 4337

■ manifesto ■
Occurrences: 3
Positions:
2789, 10986, 11289

■ manner ■
Occurrences: 3
Positions:
968, 3442, 6096

■ mean ■
Occurrences: 3
Positions:
427, 698, 1880

■ mechanisms ■
Occurrences: 3
Positions:
9447, 9479, 10343

■ members ■
Occurrences: 3
Positions:
2624, 2664, 14706

■ metal ■
Occurrences: 3
Positions:
1288, 4390, 4451

■ method ■
Occurrences: 3
Positions:
7076, 11769, 15455

■ metonymical ■
Occurrences: 3
Positions:
11160, 12523, 12744

■ michael ■
Occurrences: 3
Positions:
4627, 11931, 12234

■ missed ■
Occurrences: 3
Positions:
5091, 9805, 9859

■ model ■
Occurrences: 3
Positions:
3949, 4148, 13873

■ moves ■
Occurrences: 3
Positions:
4698, 14016, 14042

■ moving ■
Occurrences: 3
Positions:
183, 14440, 14459

■ mutation ■
Occurrences: 3
Positions:
2134, 12127, 12758

■ my ■
Occurrences: 3
Positions:
1742, 1764, 6102

■ necessity ■
Occurrences: 3
Positions:
4206, 4208, 10318

■ need ■
Occurrences: 3
Positions:
513, 843, 7947

■ negative ■
Occurrences: 3
Positions:
2962, 2966, 3040

■ neurototalitarianism ■
Occurrences: 3
Positions:
826, 10594, 15116

■ notation ■
Occurrences: 3
Positions:
8066, 8095, 8642

■ novum ■
Occurrences: 3
Positions:
5778, 5793, 6012

■ number ■
Occurrences: 3
Positions:
2724, 6655, 10054

■ observation ■
Occurrences: 3
Positions:
3602, 5244, 9851

■ opening ■
Occurrences: 3
Positions:
7415, 8315, 10842

■ organism ■
Occurrences: 3
Positions:
13768, 14142, 14602

■ orientation ■
Occurrences: 3
Positions:
231, 11973, 14439

■ output ■
Occurrences: 3
Positions:
7769, 12473, 12476

■ paradoxical ■
Occurrences: 3
Positions:
9712, 12012, 12621

■ parallel ■
Occurrences: 3
Positions:
4174, 10464, 11920

■ particles ■
Occurrences: 3
Positions:
8667, 9032, 9313

■ passage ■
Occurrences: 3
Positions:
1579, 1599, 10940

■ paul ■
Occurrences: 3
Positions:
25, 5370, 12586

■ pause ■
Occurrences: 3
Positions:
11964, 15527, 15590

■ perceptual ■
Occurrences: 3
Positions:
3541, 5058, 5965

■ performed ■
Occurrences: 3
Positions:
8009, 8119, 8128

■ performers ■
Occurrences: 3
Positions:
8022, 8199, 8358

■ phenomena ■
Occurrences: 3
Positions:
5242, 8733, 15109

■ phenomenon ■
Occurrences: 3
Positions:
12563, 14953, 15070

■ philosophy ■
Occurrences: 3
Positions:
5582, 8688, 10654

■ phraseology ■
Occurrences: 3
Positions:
12381, 12384, 13614

■ pitch ■
Occurrences: 3
Positions:
6807, 9011, 15535

■ play ■
Occurrences: 3
Positions:
8548, 13558, 13583

■ plurality ■
Occurrences: 3
Positions:
13944, 14076, 14407

■ poetic ■
Occurrences: 3
Positions:
6480, 9328, 9451

■ popular ■
Occurrences: 3
Positions:
4312, 12986, 13838

■ post ■
Occurrences: 3
Positions:
2178, 4666, 13043

■ potentialities ■
Occurrences: 3
Positions:
9889, 13731, 13996

■ power ■
Occurrences: 3
Positions:
13865, 13867, 13894

■ print ■
Occurrences: 3
Positions:
6053, 7997, 11898

■ procedure ■
Occurrences: 3
Positions:
527, 7969, 14362

■ producing ■
Occurrences: 3
Positions:
1034, 12454, 12751

■ proves ■
Occurrences: 3
Positions:
4500, 10772, 12137

■ public ■
Occurrences: 3
Positions:
6075, 11574, 13485

■ purpose ■
Occurrences: 3
Positions:
2746, 14360, 14798

■ put ■
Occurrences: 3
Positions:
503, 8143, 8906

■ rapid ■
Occurrences: 3
Positions:
3065, 4686, 12667

■ ratios ■
Occurrences: 3
Positions:
5064, 5967, 8160

■ read ■
Occurrences: 3
Positions:
752, 4632, 12500

■ reconfiguration ■
Occurrences: 3
Positions:
5074, 5408, 11611

■ reconfigured ■
Occurrences: 3
Positions:
5648, 12912, 13235

■ refers ■
Occurrences: 3
Positions:
6019, 6652, 15067

■ relations ■
Occurrences: 3
Positions:
4095, 5836, 8825

■ reminds ■
Occurrences: 3
Positions:
623, 807, 15301

■ remix ■
Occurrences: 3
Positions:
6232, 6303, 6334

■ resistance ■
Occurrences: 3
Positions:
3202, 6740, 15606

■ reveal ■
Occurrences: 3
Positions:
919, 13554, 13576

■ revolt ■
Occurrences: 3
Positions:
15061, 15239, 15580

■ rigid ■
Occurrences: 3
Positions:
14113, 14174, 14239

■ roads ■
Occurrences: 3
Positions:
6587, 8963, 9001

■ rule ■
Occurrences: 3
Positions:
10354, 14115, 14241

■ rules ■
Occurrences: 3
Positions:
14204, 14391, 14418

■ run ■
Occurrences: 3
Positions:
5493, 11578, 14022

■ scale ■
Occurrences: 3
Positions:
4359, 12833, 15133

■ search ■
Occurrences: 3
Positions:
3418, 7021, 11969

■ see ■
Occurrences: 3
Positions:
2239, 5191, 12580

■ seem ■
Occurrences: 3
Positions:
3565, 5742, 15126

■ seemingly ■
Occurrences: 3
Positions:
1990, 6723, 8551

■ seen ■
Occurrences: 3
Positions:
1785, 12443, 13091

■ semantics ■
Occurrences: 3
Positions:
9335, 12307, 13673

■ sensibility ■
Occurrences: 3
Positions:
2278, 3957, 11028

■ sequential ■
Occurrences: 3
Positions:
327, 10353, 10426

■ series ■
Occurrences: 3
Positions:
3069, 7446, 11800

■ serves ■
Occurrences: 3
Positions:
10377, 13552, 13574

■ signal ■
Occurrences: 3
Positions:
6614, 8207, 9205

■ significant ■
Occurrences: 3
Positions:
5800, 6277, 8618

■ signifies ■
Occurrences: 3
Positions:
9589, 10598, 10610

■ simultaneously ■
Occurrences: 3
Positions:
5912, 10330, 15036

■ soft ■
Occurrences: 3
Positions:
1280, 12299, 15291

■ software ■
Occurrences: 3
Positions:
12449, 13324, 13329

■ sonic ■
Occurrences: 3
Positions:
6578, 6843, 8732

■ space ■
Occurrences: 3
Positions:
579, 9566, 11020

■ specific ■
Occurrences: 3
Positions:
5721, 6685, 11355

■ stage ■
Occurrences: 3
Positions:
7253, 10497, 15434

■ start ■
Occurrences: 3
Positions:
1028, 9905, 10486

■ stasis ■
Occurrences: 3
Positions:
4152, 9594, 9680

■ state ■
Occurrences: 3
Positions:
5233, 8775, 11653

■ states ■
Occurrences: 3
Positions:
2246, 5895, 6091

■ still ■
Occurrences: 3
Positions:
4831, 8277, 11008

■ stop ■
Occurrences: 3
Positions:
1033, 4425, 14036

■ structures ■
Occurrences: 3
Positions:
7141, 7984, 13895

■ substratum ■
Occurrences: 3
Positions:
9728, 10627, 15505

■ success ■
Occurrences: 3
Positions:
7961, 8341, 8483

■ systematic ■
Occurrences: 3
Positions:
14390, 14511, 14607

■ taken ■
Occurrences: 3
Positions:
4064, 7454, 11395

■ technical ■
Occurrences: 3
Positions:
744, 14203, 14933

■ technique ■
Occurrences: 3
Positions:
6589, 6711, 7625

■ teleological ■
Occurrences: 3
Positions:
4082, 4151, 13730

■ themes ■
Occurrences: 3
Positions:
4299, 7030, 11223

■ then ■
Occurrences: 3
Positions:
7332, 8636, 14284

■ theory ■
Occurrences: 3
Positions:
8705, 8894, 9186

■ therefore ■
Occurrences: 3
Positions:
4012, 13115, 14924

■ third ■
Occurrences: 3
Positions:
8855, 9760, 9957

■ timetrap ■
Occurrences: 3
Positions:
417, 463, 477

■ totalitarian ■
Occurrences: 3
Positions:
8502, 9462, 15221

■ toward ■
Occurrences: 3
Positions:
5272, 13304, 14460

■ transcendent ■
Occurrences: 3
Positions:
862, 882, 13700

■ transformed ■
Occurrences: 3
Positions:
4897, 5614, 8296

■ true ■
Occurrences: 3
Positions:
1771, 4231, 11105

■ truth ■
Occurrences: 3
Positions:
9383, 9409, 9746

■ turn ■
Occurrences: 3
Positions:
1619, 6378, 15158

■ twelve ■
Occurrences: 3
Positions:
7294, 8007, 8027

■ typically ■
Occurrences: 3
Positions:
2399, 3702, 6633

■ underlying ■
Occurrences: 3
Positions:
921, 3979, 9629

■ unique ■
Occurrences: 3
Positions:
4456, 9563, 11333

■ unlike ■
Occurrences: 3
Positions:
14054, 14102, 14779

■ unusual ■
Occurrences: 3
Positions:
4543, 11589, 12917

■ user ■
Occurrences: 3
Positions:
8990, 12644, 12647

■ virus ■
Occurrences: 3
Positions:
1669, 2524, 12732

■ visual ■
Occurrences: 3
Positions:
202, 11047, 13135

■ vital ■
Occurrences: 3
Positions:
1511, 1523, 10867

■ voice ■
Occurrences: 3
Positions:
7477, 13928, 14794

■ volume ■
Occurrences: 3
Positions:
8125, 10901, 10969

■ wave ■
Occurrences: 3
Positions:
1137, 1139, 6817

■ well ■
Occurrences: 3
Positions:
4063, 5387, 11044

■ western ■
Occurrences: 3
Positions:
3983, 8394, 10644

■ why ■
Occurrences: 3
Positions:
2311, 4378, 5818

■ writers ■
Occurrences: 3
Positions:
5368, 6376, 11622

■ wrote ■
Occurrences: 3
Positions:
2423, 5664, 9790

■ your ■
Occurrences: 3
Positions:
14555, 14557, 14560

■ 1932 ■
Occurrences: 2
Positions:
10987, 11366

■ 1941 ■
Occurrences: 2
Positions:
8921, 9795

■ 1982 ■
Occurrences: 2
Positions:
3330, 4335

■ accelerate ■
Occurrences: 2
Positions:
654, 12595

■ acceleration ■
Occurrences: 2
Positions:
51, 837

■ accelerationism ■
Occurrences: 2
Positions:
9951, 12701

■ accessible ■
Occurrences: 2
Positions:
6721, 13083

■ accidental ■
Occurrences: 2
Positions:
7734, 7764

■ account ■
Occurrences: 2
Positions:
11034, 13142

■ achieved ■
Occurrences: 2
Positions:
603, 8945

■ actions ■
Occurrences: 2
Positions:
14089, 14448

■ active ■
Occurrences: 2
Positions:
14777, 15092

■ acutely ■
Occurrences: 2
Positions:
3859, 12236

■ additive ■
Occurrences: 2
Positions:
6597, 6604

■ aesthetically ■
Occurrences: 2
Positions:
898, 5031

■ affront ■
Occurrences: 2
Positions:
8384, 9459

■ aim ■
Occurrences: 2
Positions:
9361, 10442

■ aims ■
Occurrences: 2
Positions:
9148, 10138

■ alienation ■
Occurrences: 2
Positions:
3896, 3937

■ allows ■
Occurrences: 2
Positions:
5729, 5942

■ alphabet ■
Occurrences: 2
Positions:
11078, 11190

■ already ■
Occurrences: 2
Positions:
1991, 6957

■ altogether ■
Occurrences: 2
Positions:
4542, 6179

■ amidst ■
Occurrences: 2
Positions:
1037, 3825

■ analog ■
Occurrences: 2
Positions:
948, 6714

■ anatomical ■
Occurrences: 2
Positions:
742, 4520

■ animals ■
Occurrences: 2
Positions:
1695, 14433

■ anime ■
Occurrences: 2
Positions:
2221, 4315

■ annihilation ■
Occurrences: 2
Positions:
2, 13733

■ antiquated ■
Occurrences: 2
Positions:
12363, 13596

■ antonin ■
Occurrences: 2
Positions:
891, 6111

■ apart ■
Occurrences: 2
Positions:
5268, 15197

■ apex ■
Occurrences: 2
Positions:
611, 4079

■ apocalypse ■
Occurrences: 2
Positions:
13551, 13573

■ appear ■
Occurrences: 2
Positions:
1830, 5445

■ applied ■
Occurrences: 2
Positions:
7623, 15460

■ arguably ■
Occurrences: 2
Positions:
3445, 10294

■ articulation ■
Occurrences: 2
Positions:
3283, 15500

■ asked ■
Occurrences: 2
Positions:
109, 2309

■ assemblages ■
Occurrences: 2
Positions:
766, 1793

■ assumption ■
Occurrences: 2
Positions:
3586, 4067

■ atomization ■
Occurrences: 2
Positions:
7475, 15513

■ attracted ■
Occurrences: 2
Positions:
8282, 11262

■ authentic ■
Occurrences: 2
Positions:
1231, 5427

■ automatisms ■
Occurrences: 2
Positions:
13760, 15124

■ available ■
Occurrences: 2
Positions:
7832, 12448

■ babylon ■
Occurrences: 2
Positions:
3725, 3844

■ back ■
Occurrences: 2
Positions:
2567, 14693

■ ballard ■
Occurrences: 2
Positions:
70, 78

■ ballerini ■
Occurrences: 2
Positions:
10202, 10246

■ based ■
Occurrences: 2
Positions:
6551, 9200

■ basis ■
Occurrences: 2
Positions:
5110, 8754

■ becoming ■
Occurrences: 2
Positions:
4563, 13327

■ began ■
Occurrences: 2
Positions:
6946, 8594

■ believe ■
Occurrences: 2
Positions:
5898, 15374

■ berberian ■
Occurrences: 2
Positions:
7387, 7412

■ bermel ■
Occurrences: 2
Positions:
11491, 11509

■ biased ■
Occurrences: 2
Positions:
13275, 13303

■ blank ■
Occurrences: 2
Positions:
12371, 13604

■ bloch ■
Occurrences: 2
Positions:
5782, 6014

■ bould ■
Occurrences: 2
Positions:
5767, 5813

■ broadcasts ■
Occurrences: 2
Positions:
7828, 8276

■ broken ■
Occurrences: 2
Positions:
1752, 7324

■ built ■
Occurrences: 2
Positions:
8602, 8607

■ burst ■
Occurrences: 2
Positions:
3331, 7441

■ cadaver ■
Occurrences: 2
Positions:
1477, 1558

■ call ■
Occurrences: 2
Positions:
2538, 14427

■ capacity ■
Occurrences: 2
Positions:
4999, 13308

■ captured ■
Occurrences: 2
Positions:
395, 6729

■ car ■
Occurrences: 2
Positions:
136, 192

■ caught ■
Occurrences: 2
Positions:
414, 460

■ causation ■
Occurrences: 2
Positions:
12624, 12763

■ cause ■
Occurrences: 2
Positions:
9830, 12573

■ ceaseless ■
Occurrences: 2
Positions:
199, 357

■ celebration ■
Occurrences: 2
Positions:
4893, 9832

■ changing ■
Occurrences: 2
Positions:
3730, 8090

■ chaotics ■
Occurrences: 2
Positions:
6, 15296

■ characteristically ■
Occurrences: 2
Positions:
2416, 6094

■ ching ■
Occurrences: 2
Positions:
7865, 8152

■ choice ■
Occurrences: 2
Positions:
7882, 14521

■ choose ■
Occurrences: 2
Positions:
9940, 11222

■ christian ■
Occurrences: 2
Positions:
3986, 4047

■ cinema ■
Occurrences: 2
Positions:
870, 6423

■ circle ■
Occurrences: 2
Positions:
6891, 9132

■ clips ■
Occurrences: 2
Positions:
6540, 8875

■ closely ■
Occurrences: 2
Positions:
517, 4186

■ coherence ■
Occurrences: 2
Positions:
769, 14787

■ cohesive ■
Occurrences: 2
Positions:
9880, 15382

■ collaborated ■
Occurrences: 2
Positions:
7196, 7395

■ combinations ■
Occurrences: 2
Positions:
6914, 7155

■ combined ■
Occurrences: 2
Positions:
6391, 7285

■ commitment ■
Occurrences: 2
Positions:
5103, 10931

■ commodity ■
Occurrences: 2
Positions:
5501, 5642

■ commonplace ■
Occurrences: 2
Positions:
4310, 6218

■ communicative ■
Occurrences: 2
Positions:
3197, 12538

■ complete ■
Occurrences: 2
Positions:
7566, 15423

■ composers ■
Occurrences: 2
Positions:
6507, 6837

■ comprehensible ■
Occurrences: 2
Positions:
4516, 13693

■ computers ■
Occurrences: 2
Positions:
8972, 9062

■ concatenations ■
Occurrences: 2
Positions:
749, 14345

■ conceit ■
Occurrences: 2
Positions:
1044, 4510

■ conceivable ■
Occurrences: 2
Positions:
651, 13648

■ concept ■
Occurrences: 2
Positions:
5775, 6009

■ concerns ■
Occurrences: 2
Positions:
13470, 13478

■ condition ■
Occurrences: 2
Positions:
3220, 14960

■ confrontation ■
Occurrences: 2
Positions:
13739, 14830

■ confronted ■
Occurrences: 2
Positions:
757, 13656

■ confronts ■
Occurrences: 2
Positions:
2097, 7981

■ confused ■
Occurrences: 2
Positions:
1180, 4407

■ connection ■
Occurrences: 2
Positions:
367, 9289

■ consequence ■
Occurrences: 2
Positions:
5008, 11253

■ consideration ■
Occurrences: 2
Positions:
7567, 13826

■ considers ■
Occurrences: 2
Positions:
960, 2014

■ conspiracy ■
Occurrences: 2
Positions:
922, 4889

■ constituent ■
Occurrences: 2
Positions:
444, 5291

■ constituted ■
Occurrences: 2
Positions:
10195, 10324

■ constraints ■
Occurrences: 2
Positions:
6365, 14050

■ construct ■
Occurrences: 2
Positions:
4619, 7867

■ constructive ■
Occurrences: 2
Positions:
3153, 3181

■ contrast ■
Occurrences: 2
Positions:
11000, 14674

■ contributions ■
Occurrences: 2
Positions:
8619, 9160

■ controlled ■
Occurrences: 2
Positions:
3657, 9041

■ convention ■
Occurrences: 2
Positions:
5621, 5626

■ conventions ■
Occurrences: 2
Positions:
10796, 10829

■ convictions ■
Occurrences: 2
Positions:
2844, 2896

■ corbusier ■
Occurrences: 2
Positions:
7003, 8578

■ corporate ■
Occurrences: 2
Positions:
4888, 15248

■ corpse ■
Occurrences: 2
Positions:
1649, 1707

■ created ■
Occurrences: 2
Positions:
3988, 8741

■ creating ■
Occurrences: 2
Positions:
10934, 11104

■ criteria ■
Occurrences: 2
Positions:
5847, 9190

■ critical ■
Occurrences: 2
Positions:
3145, 3241

■ criticism ■
Occurrences: 2
Positions:
3182, 9255

■ crowds ■
Occurrences: 2
Positions:
6926, 14870

■ cult ■
Occurrences: 2
Positions:
3342, 8388

■ currently ■
Occurrences: 2
Positions:
1132, 15502

■ daily ■
Occurrences: 2
Positions:
3005, 9989

■ dangerous ■
Occurrences: 2
Positions:
11311, 14221

■ dark ■
Occurrences: 2
Positions:
4439, 4881

■ dated ■
Occurrences: 2
Positions:
5485, 11363

■ david ■
Occurrences: 2
Positions:
7616, 12403

■ decade ■
Occurrences: 2
Positions:
5602, 9870

■ decentralized ■
Occurrences: 2
Positions:
8470, 15122

■ declarations ■
Occurrences: 2
Positions:
3021, 11143

■ deeper ■
Occurrences: 2
Positions:
795, 1861

■ demolishing ■
Occurrences: 2
Positions:
15179, 15232

■ demonstrating ■
Occurrences: 2
Positions:
1611, 7127

■ dense ■
Occurrences: 2
Positions:
823, 14489

■ depends ■
Occurrences: 2
Positions:
9527, 9543

■ derangement ■
Occurrences: 2
Positions:
2019, 15578

■ described ■
Occurrences: 2
Positions:
11212, 13157

■ destructive ■
Occurrences: 2
Positions:
3175, 11907

■ detect ■
Occurrences: 2
Positions:
10535, 15327

■ determines ■
Occurrences: 2
Positions:
5803, 7374

■ determinism ■
Occurrences: 2
Positions:
8792, 9463

■ deterministic ■
Occurrences: 2
Positions:
10565, 15357

■ develop ■
Occurrences: 2
Positions:
3878, 14762

■ direct ■
Occurrences: 2
Positions:
1236, 8383

■ discourse ■
Occurrences: 2
Positions:
4101, 15509

■ discussed ■
Occurrences: 2
Positions:
12152, 13121

■ disembodied ■
Occurrences: 2
Positions:
4907, 7236

■ disengages ■
Occurrences: 2
Positions:
10278, 10298

■ disillusioned ■
Occurrences: 2
Positions:
10898, 10966

■ distinct ■
Occurrences: 2
Positions:
2978, 7240

■ distinguished ■
Occurrences: 2
Positions:
13811, 13933

■ divergent ■
Occurrences: 2
Positions:
8697, 10226

■ division ■
Occurrences: 2
Positions:
4018, 15415

■ dominating ■
Occurrences: 2
Positions:
3374, 4780

■ done ■
Occurrences: 2
Positions:
3484, 10890

■ dreams ■
Occurrences: 2
Positions:
11537, 11541

■ duration ■
Occurrences: 2
Positions:
6629, 6686

■ easily ■
Occurrences: 2
Positions:
12579, 14816

■ eccentric ■
Occurrences: 2
Positions:
2038, 2290

■ ecology ■
Occurrences: 2
Positions:
3831, 5298

■ edgard ■
Occurrences: 2
Positions:
6493, 6944

■ electronically ■
Occurrences: 2
Positions:
7287, 11346

■ emancipation ■
Occurrences: 2
Positions:
9100, 10587

■ embedding ■
Occurrences: 2
Positions:
4664, 12745

■ emblematic ■
Occurrences: 2
Positions:
4675, 10856

■ emphasize ■
Occurrences: 2
Positions:
8528, 10659

■ endlessly ■
Occurrences: 2
Positions:
435, 470

■ engenders ■
Occurrences: 2
Positions:
7935, 10448

■ enlargement ■
Occurrences: 2
Positions:
8747, 8757

■ enormous ■
Occurrences: 2
Positions:
9386, 9749

■ entrails ■
Occurrences: 2
Positions:
1289, 1514

■ equally ■
Occurrences: 2
Positions:
4685, 13010

■ equation ■
Occurrences: 2
Positions:
12797, 13253

■ erasure ■
Occurrences: 2
Positions:
7674, 8365

■ escalation ■
Occurrences: 2
Positions:
5606, 5612

■ eschewing ■
Occurrences: 2
Positions:
3763, 3832

■ essentially ■
Occurrences: 2
Positions:
9327, 10135

■ established ■
Occurrences: 2
Positions:
2007, 9706

■ establishment ■
Occurrences: 2
Positions:
6146, 11609

■ europe ■
Occurrences: 2
Positions:
2602, 2684

■ evaluation ■
Occurrences: 2
Positions:
1265, 2080

■ events ■
Occurrences: 2
Positions:
6584, 9000

■ eventually ■
Occurrences: 2
Positions:
5649, 8967

■ everybody ■
Occurrences: 2
Positions:
13997, 14041

■ evokes ■
Occurrences: 2
Positions:
868, 13388

■ evolves ■
Occurrences: 2
Positions:
3593, 12430

■ exactly ■
Occurrences: 2
Positions:
3480, 8307

■ exclusion ■
Occurrences: 2
Positions:
725, 9980

■ existence ■
Occurrences: 2
Positions:
5128, 9557

■ experiencing ■
Occurrences: 2
Positions:
7100, 11169

■ expresses ■
Occurrences: 2
Positions:
8345, 15393

■ expressing ■
Occurrences: 2
Positions:
5032, 11730

■ extensions ■
Occurrences: 2
Positions:
9666, 12539

■ factory ■
Occurrences: 2
Positions:
14159, 14226

■ falls ■
Occurrences: 2
Positions:
6398, 6634

■ famously ■
Occurrences: 2
Positions:
2518, 9789

■ favoring ■
Occurrences: 2
Positions:
7879, 10175

■ feedback ■
Occurrences: 2
Positions:
4288, 10360

■ feel ■
Occurrences: 2
Positions:
2901, 5362

■ felt ■
Occurrences: 2
Positions:
4793, 4993

■ feti ■
Occurrences: 2
Positions:
1650, 1708

■ fictional ■
Occurrences: 2
Positions:
4820, 12202

■ figure ■
Occurrences: 2
Positions:
2405, 4730

■ films ■
Occurrences: 2
Positions:
3326, 3334

■ finally ■
Occurrences: 2
Positions:
8707, 11549

■ fisher ■
Occurrences: 2
Positions:
307, 390

■ fit ■
Occurrences: 2
Positions:
8298, 12045

■ fluid ■
Occurrences: 2
Positions:
1556, 10883

■ followed ■
Occurrences: 2
Positions:
6508, 7402

■ forces ■
Occurrences: 2
Positions:
3661, 15587

■ formal ■
Occurrences: 2
Positions:
3519, 12483

■ forms ■
Occurrences: 2
Positions:
6381, 6386

■ found ■
Occurrences: 2
Positions:
7784, 7821

■ foundation ■
Occurrences: 2
Positions:
12372, 13605

■ founded ■
Occurrences: 2
Positions:
3670, 10262

■ fragmentation ■
Occurrences: 2
Positions:
3089, 6457

■ frame ■
Occurrences: 2
Positions:
506, 12969

■ french ■
Occurrences: 2
Positions:
6153, 6942

■ frustrated ■
Occurrences: 2
Positions:
407, 422

■ fundamentalism ■
Occurrences: 2
Positions:
3987, 4048

■ fused ■
Occurrences: 2
Positions:
3034, 9140

■ futurists ■
Occurrences: 2
Positions:
6468, 9281

■ gardist ■
Occurrences: 2
Positions:
2463, 3305

■ gathering ■
Occurrences: 2
Positions:
2970, 14722

■ gave ■
Occurrences: 2
Positions:
2315, 2337

■ generators ■
Occurrences: 2
Positions:
6808, 6818

■ get ■
Occurrences: 2
Positions:
459, 6909

■ gif ■
Occurrences: 2
Positions:
403, 426

■ give ■
Occurrences: 2
Positions:
12366, 13599

■ goals ■
Occurrences: 2
Positions:
13916, 13983

■ govern ■
Occurrences: 2
Positions:
733, 6757

■ grammar ■
Occurrences: 2
Positions:
2527, 10276

■ grammatical ■
Occurrences: 2
Positions:
12189, 12325

■ habitual ■
Occurrences: 2
Positions:
2548, 11593

■ han ■
Occurrences: 2
Positions:
13824, 14665

■ happens ■
Occurrences: 2
Positions:
8439, 14217

■ having ■
Occurrences: 2
Positions:
5973, 11083

■ heightened ■
Occurrences: 2
Positions:
3893, 13038

■ hell ■
Occurrences: 2
Positions:
1260, 1315

■ help ■
Occurrences: 2
Positions:
9645, 9654

■ henry ■
Occurrences: 2
Positions:
7200, 7615

■ historiography ■
Occurrences: 2
Positions:
9511, 10172

■ humans ■
Occurrences: 2
Positions:
9900, 14083

■ hunter ■
Occurrences: 2
Positions:
1255, 12274

■ hybrid ■
Occurrences: 2
Positions:
2277, 6138

■ hybridity ■
Occurrences: 2
Positions:
2133, 12121

■ hyperconsumerist ■
Occurrences: 2
Positions:
5488, 5609

■ hypermodern ■
Occurrences: 2
Positions:
15419, 15495

■ iannis ■
Occurrences: 2
Positions:
6505, 8517

■ iconoclasm ■
Occurrences: 2
Positions:
11136, 11687

■ ideas ■
Occurrences: 2
Positions:
4021, 7033

■ identify ■
Occurrences: 2
Positions:
2776, 13919

■ ill ■
Occurrences: 2
Positions:
159, 1621

■ illusion ■
Occurrences: 2
Positions:
8888, 10390

■ imagery ■
Occurrences: 2
Positions:
1186, 4431

■ images ■
Occurrences: 2
Positions:
8639, 10063

■ imagine ■
Occurrences: 2
Positions:
5333, 10156

■ imagined ■
Occurrences: 2
Positions:
2122, 13852

■ immediate ■
Occurrences: 2
Positions:
9384, 9747

■ imperial ■
Occurrences: 2
Positions:
3745, 4106

■ implies ■
Occurrences: 2
Positions:
8768, 14331

■ important ■
Occurrences: 2
Positions:
2745, 6209

■ impossibility ■
Occurrences: 2
Positions:
1371, 14642

■ impress ■
Occurrences: 2
Positions:
10309, 10335

■ indebted ■
Occurrences: 2
Positions:
6866, 7585

■ independence ■
Occurrences: 2
Positions:
5137, 5236

■ indicates ■
Occurrences: 2
Positions:
10103, 11510

■ indicative ■
Occurrences: 2
Positions:
10942, 15111

■ induce ■
Occurrences: 2
Positions:
1403, 1799

■ inevitable ■
Occurrences: 2
Positions:
3458, 10286

■ infinite ■
Occurrences: 2
Positions:
6898, 8552

■ influence ■
Occurrences: 2
Positions:
2149, 5345

■ informational ■
Occurrences: 2
Positions:
12955, 15540

■ inner ■
Occurrences: 2
Positions:
82, 578

■ innovations ■
Occurrences: 2
Positions:
4842, 6023

■ insanity ■
Occurrences: 2
Positions:
1489, 1748

■ instantaneity ■
Occurrences: 2
Positions:
254, 262

■ instruction ■
Occurrences: 2
Positions:
9473, 10591

■ intact ■
Occurrences: 2
Positions:
5838, 13225

■ intensified ■
Occurrences: 2
Positions:
324, 9846

■ interconnections ■
Occurrences: 2
Positions:
11118, 13102

■ interested ■
Occurrences: 2
Positions:
4550, 4585

■ intimate ■
Occurrences: 2
Positions:
1920, 1979

■ invention ■
Occurrences: 2
Positions:
4217, 4220

■ involves ■
Occurrences: 2
Positions:
6572, 12957

■ involving ■
Occurrences: 2
Positions:
7657, 7773

■ ishii ■
Occurrences: 2
Positions:
873, 3328

■ italian ■
Occurrences: 2
Positions:
6868, 7391

■ izumiya ■
Occurrences: 2
Positions:
874, 3336

■ james ■
Occurrences: 2
Positions:
7619, 8903

■ japaneseness ■
Occurrences: 2
Positions:
2070, 12157

■ john ■
Occurrences: 2
Positions:
6496, 7574

■ journeying ■
Occurrences: 2
Positions:
605, 1864

■ junk ■
Occurrences: 2
Positions:
1512, 1687

■ kinds ■
Occurrences: 2
Positions:
3717, 8713

■ knowledge ■
Occurrences: 2
Positions:
10013, 14395

■ large ■
Occurrences: 2
Positions:
8764, 12455

■ largely ■
Occurrences: 2
Positions:
3363, 4097

■ last ■
Occurrences: 2
Positions:
5522, 5526

■ late ■
Occurrences: 2
Positions:
8257, 13337

■ latter ■
Occurrences: 2
Positions:
1926, 10750

■ law ■
Occurrences: 2
Positions:
8762, 8767

■ leads ■
Occurrences: 2
Positions:
5585, 7472

■ learn ■
Occurrences: 2
Positions:
13319, 14281

■ letter ■
Occurrences: 2
Positions:
11359, 11425

■ levels ■
Occurrences: 2
Positions:
8354, 11127

■ lights ■
Occurrences: 2
Positions:
11100, 14040

■ likely ■
Occurrences: 2
Positions:
4316, 7581

■ likes ■
Occurrences: 2
Positions:
1018, 10677

■ linearity ■
Occurrences: 2
Positions:
12553, 12598

■ literacy ■
Occurrences: 2
Positions:
693, 980

■ lived ■
Occurrences: 2
Positions:
3019, 6025

■ logical ■
Occurrences: 2
Positions:
10346, 12741

■ looks ■
Occurrences: 2
Positions:
8051, 8849

■ loops ■
Occurrences: 2
Positions:
2566, 7229

■ lose ■
Occurrences: 2
Positions:
3939, 14229

■ losing ■
Occurrences: 2
Positions:
9378, 9741

■ loss ■
Occurrences: 2
Positions:
273, 3413

■ love ■
Occurrences: 2
Positions:
1754, 3902

■ luigi ■
Occurrences: 2
Positions:
6490, 6870

■ lyrical ■
Occurrences: 2
Positions:
7428, 7690

■ magazine ■
Occurrences: 2
Positions:
2506, 5893

■ mainstream ■
Occurrences: 2
Positions:
3386, 4783

■ maintain ■
Occurrences: 2
Positions:
4015, 14353

■ maintaining ■
Occurrences: 2
Positions:
8535, 12467

■ manufacture ■
Occurrences: 2
Positions:
177, 15222

■ manufacturing ■
Occurrences: 2
Positions:
11993, 14856

■ mark ■
Occurrences: 2
Positions:
306, 5766

■ materials ■
Occurrences: 2
Positions:
7671, 11841

■ mathematical ■
Occurrences: 2
Positions:
8159, 8811

■ matter ■
Occurrences: 2
Positions:
2879, 3589

■ maze ■
Occurrences: 2
Positions:
614, 5443

■ meanings ■
Occurrences: 2
Positions:
11062, 13026

■ mental ■
Occurrences: 2
Positions:
120, 14939

■ messiaen ■
Occurrences: 2
Positions:
8586, 8588

■ metaphors ■
Occurrences: 2
Positions:
2139, 4953

■ methods ■
Occurrences: 2
Positions:
2008, 7777

■ millennium ■
Occurrences: 2
Positions:
5527, 11869

■ mingles ■
Occurrences: 2
Positions:
9377, 9740

■ modernists ■
Occurrences: 2
Positions:
7588, 9819

■ money ■
Occurrences: 2
Positions:
10066, 10069

■ motor ■
Occurrences: 2
Positions:
135, 191

■ movements ■
Occurrences: 2
Positions:
1884, 14324

■ multiple ■
Occurrences: 2
Positions:
7458, 8353

■ multiplicity ■
Occurrences: 2
Positions:
4930, 13993

■ murayama ■
Occurrences: 2
Positions:
2627, 2803

■ murder ■
Occurrences: 2
Positions:
10884, 11473

■ murderous ■
Occurrences: 2
Positions:
1225, 1761

■ mutant ■
Occurrences: 2
Positions:
1314, 1640

■ mutate ■
Occurrences: 2
Positions:
439, 4610

■ mysterious ■
Occurrences: 2
Positions:
9329, 9453

■ named ■
Occurrences: 2
Positions:
7167, 8653

■ names ■
Occurrences: 2
Positions:
2316, 2339

■ naming ■
Occurrences: 2
Positions:
2731, 2763

■ nationalism ■
Occurrences: 2
Positions:
2615, 10641

■ natural ■
Occurrences: 2
Positions:
3072, 7353

■ nerve ■
Occurrences: 2
Positions:
1541, 1630

■ neural ■
Occurrences: 2
Positions:
4616, 14422

■ neuro ■
Occurrences: 2
Positions:
15105, 15249

■ nightmare ■
Occurrences: 2
Positions:
1305, 1779

■ nimbus ■
Occurrences: 2
Positions:
800, 1870

■ nineteenth ■
Occurrences: 2
Positions:
31, 13848

■ nonnarrative ■
Occurrences: 2
Positions:
6380, 6410

■ nor ■
Occurrences: 2
Positions:
6767, 14576

■ noting ■
Occurrences: 2
Positions:
2502, 8926

■ novels ■
Occurrences: 2
Positions:
2322, 12182

■ numbers ■
Occurrences: 2
Positions:
8765, 12195

■ objective ■
Occurrences: 2
Positions:
5271, 9189

■ objectively ■
Occurrences: 2
Positions:
5131, 5303

■ objectivity ■
Occurrences: 2
Positions:
2909, 12932

■ objects ■
Occurrences: 2
Positions:
9414, 11111

■ obvious ■
Occurrences: 2
Positions:
10553, 15345

■ occurring ■
Occurrences: 2
Positions:
6658, 7109

■ oeuvre ■
Occurrences: 2
Positions:
2455, 12526

■ offer ■
Occurrences: 2
Positions:
10038, 10184

■ old ■
Occurrences: 2
Positions:
7296, 12989

■ oneself ■
Occurrences: 2
Positions:
5188, 5317

■ ontologically ■
Occurrences: 2
Positions:
4972, 10020

■ operating ■
Occurrences: 2
Positions:
3013, 9682

■ opportunity ■
Occurrences: 2
Positions:
522, 12357

■ optimism ■
Occurrences: 2
Positions:
3668, 3834

■ organization ■
Occurrences: 2
Positions:
2957, 14990

■ others ■
Occurrences: 2
Positions:
8965, 13085

■ ourselves ■
Occurrences: 2
Positions:
1013, 1036

■ overall ■
Occurrences: 2
Positions:
14823, 14989

■ pacific ■
Occurrences: 2
Positions:
5518, 11759

■ paradigms ■
Occurrences: 2
Positions:
10256, 10375

■ paradise ■
Occurrences: 2
Positions:
1661, 1698

■ passages ■
Occurrences: 2
Positions:
1788, 10852

■ past ■
Occurrences: 2
Positions:
12739, 15286

■ paths ■
Occurrences: 2
Positions:
632, 8692

■ pathways ■
Occurrences: 2
Positions:
4617, 14334

■ patterns ■
Occurrences: 2
Positions:
12679, 13283

■ paying ■
Occurrences: 2
Positions:
1029, 13362

■ perceiver ■
Occurrences: 2
Positions:
5285, 12938

■ perception ■
Occurrences: 2
Positions:
7904, 11788

■ perform ■
Occurrences: 2
Positions:
8018, 14087

■ permits ■
Occurrences: 2
Positions:
9503, 14341

■ personalized ■
Occurrences: 2
Positions:
94, 351

■ pick ■
Occurrences: 2
Positions:
126, 8212

■ pierre ■
Occurrences: 2
Positions:
7048, 7199

■ planet ■
Occurrences: 2
Positions:
289, 1531

■ played ■
Occurrences: 2
Positions:
7217, 15280

■ player ■
Occurrences: 2
Positions:
8121, 8130

■ playing ■
Occurrences: 2
Positions:
13249, 14211

■ pleasure ■
Occurrences: 2
Positions:
6912, 12037

■ plot ■
Occurrences: 2
Positions:
3470, 10832

■ posited ■
Occurrences: 2
Positions:
10685, 12927

■ position ■
Occurrences: 2
Positions:
5041, 12167

■ posits ■
Occurrences: 2
Positions:
3676, 4149

■ possess ■
Occurrences: 2
Positions:
2894, 2933

■ possessed ■
Occurrences: 2
Positions:
9441, 9482

■ postmodern ■
Occurrences: 2
Positions:
3956, 12055

■ postmodernism ■
Occurrences: 2
Positions:
11915, 12116

■ practical ■
Occurrences: 2
Positions:
1855, 3276

■ prefer ■
Occurrences: 2
Positions:
5450, 12025

■ prescriptions ■
Occurrences: 2
Positions:
10541, 15333

■ pressing ■
Occurrences: 2
Positions:
720, 4214

■ primarily ■
Occurrences: 2
Positions:
4584, 13737

■ principle ■
Occurrences: 2
Positions:
8720, 8750

■ privatized ■
Occurrences: 2
Positions:
209, 349

■ problematic ■
Occurrences: 2
Positions:
3218, 12243

■ procedures ■
Occurrences: 2
Positions:
14092, 14194

■ produced ■
Occurrences: 2
Positions:
7118, 11347

■ producer ■
Occurrences: 2
Positions:
5339, 12101

■ produces ■
Occurrences: 2
Positions:
10238, 12776

■ product ■
Occurrences: 2
Positions:
1235, 13096

■ programmed ■
Occurrences: 2
Positions:
13297, 14300

■ protagonist ■
Occurrences: 2
Positions:
4475, 15186

■ prove ■
Occurrences: 2
Positions:
2085, 3785

■ provoking ■
Occurrences: 2
Positions:
932, 4445

■ proxy ■
Occurrences: 2
Positions:
12785, 13193

■ psychopathology ■
Occurrences: 2
Positions:
89, 15420

■ push ■
Occurrences: 2
Positions:
15190, 15259

■ questions ■
Occurrences: 2
Positions:
708, 2146

■ radicalism ■
Occurrences: 2
Positions:
2093, 3132

■ radically ■
Occurrences: 2
Positions:
5873, 8179

■ railways ■
Occurrences: 2
Positions:
42, 630

■ randomizing ■
Occurrences: 2
Positions:
6359, 6393

■ range ■
Occurrences: 2
Positions:
6637, 6648

■ rare ■
Occurrences: 2
Positions:
9385, 9748

■ reach ■
Occurrences: 2
Positions:
9442, 15114

■ reaching ■
Occurrences: 2
Positions:
609, 3384

■ react ■
Occurrences: 2
Positions:
14184, 14294

■ real ■
Occurrences: 2
Positions:
3499, 5004

■ rearranging ■
Occurrences: 2
Positions:
8879, 8954

■ reasonable ■
Occurrences: 2
Positions:
5220, 12332

■ reconfigure ■
Occurrences: 2
Positions:
11996, 12817

■ reconfigures ■
Occurrences: 2
Positions:
5963, 12088

■ reconstruction ■
Occurrences: 2
Positions:
11660, 11723

■ recording ■
Occurrences: 2
Positions:
6535, 11205

■ refer ■
Occurrences: 2
Positions:
1886, 1908

■ reference ■
Occurrences: 2
Positions:
6186, 10363

■ referent ■
Occurrences: 2
Positions:
4626, 12662

■ reflect ■
Occurrences: 2
Positions:
11864, 13035

■ regarding ■
Occurrences: 2
Positions:
1065, 12798

■ regardless ■
Occurrences: 2
Positions:
14392, 15078

■ rehearsal ■
Occurrences: 2
Positions:
9505, 10047

■ rehearse ■
Occurrences: 2
Positions:
5699, 10188

■ reluctant ■
Occurrences: 2
Positions:
2351, 4892

■ repeated ■
Occurrences: 2
Positions:
469, 7228

■ repeatedly ■
Occurrences: 2
Positions:
12107, 12151

■ represent ■
Occurrences: 2
Positions:
5001, 5054

■ represents ■
Occurrences: 2
Positions:
1960, 4340

■ requires ■
Occurrences: 2
Positions:
5908, 14343

■ respiration ■
Occurrences: 2
Positions:
1678, 1732

■ respond ■
Occurrences: 2
Positions:
13416, 13427

■ response ■
Occurrences: 2
Positions:
1440, 12891

■ restructures ■
Occurrences: 2
Positions:
12887, 13565

■ resulting ■
Occurrences: 2
Positions:
7851, 10315

■ results ■
Occurrences: 2
Positions:
14131, 14901

■ reverb ■
Occurrences: 2
Positions:
1278, 12297

■ revolutionary ■
Occurrences: 2
Positions:
2768, 3159

■ rhetoric ■
Occurrences: 2
Positions:
12364, 13597

■ role ■
Occurrences: 2
Positions:
6460, 7877

■ romantic ■
Occurrences: 2
Positions:
7689, 8387

■ ross ■
Occurrences: 2
Positions:
7331, 8592

■ said ■
Occurrences: 2
Positions:
2326, 10706

■ salient ■
Occurrences: 2
Positions:
4466, 10746

■ saw ■
Occurrences: 2
Positions:
5603, 13880

■ scientific ■
Occurrences: 2
Positions:
4932, 5212

■ scope ■
Occurrences: 2
Positions:
2992, 7892

■ scores ■
Occurrences: 2
Positions:
7560, 8630

■ secret ■
Occurrences: 2
Positions:
1321, 9439

■ seppuku ■
Occurrences: 2
Positions:
1282, 12301

■ sex ■
Occurrences: 2
Positions:
1526, 4007

■ shapes ■
Occurrences: 2
Positions:
14912, 14916

■ shares ■
Occurrences: 2
Positions:
2378, 10425

■ should ■
Occurrences: 2
Positions:
8563, 15405

■ sign ■
Occurrences: 2
Positions:
10077, 10082

■ signaled ■
Occurrences: 2
Positions:
188, 582

■ signify ■
Occurrences: 2
Positions:
7706, 7720

■ similarly ■
Occurrences: 2
Positions:
4880, 11851

■ simple ■
Occurrences: 2
Positions:
5456, 5598

■ situates ■
Occurrences: 2
Positions:
3408, 4130

■ sometimes ■
Occurrences: 2
Positions:
4814, 14013

■ somewhat ■
Occurrences: 2
Positions:
2719, 4116

■ sought ■
Occurrences: 2
Positions:
2665, 2996

■ speak ■
Occurrences: 2
Positions:
13924, 14791

■ special ■
Occurrences: 2
Positions:
2252, 2511

■ specifically ■
Occurrences: 2
Positions:
3014, 3117

■ stable ■
Occurrences: 2
Positions:
8448, 8774

■ star ■
Occurrences: 2
Positions:
3722, 3841

■ station ■
Occurrences: 2
Positions:
8206, 14026

■ stochasticism ■
Occurrences: 2
Positions:
9669, 9710

■ stockhausen ■
Occurrences: 2
Positions:
7284, 7490

■ stresses ■
Occurrences: 2
Positions:
9283, 10264

■ strict ■
Occurrences: 2
Positions:
3626, 4017

■ subject ■
Occurrences: 2
Positions:
5734, 9488

■ subjectivity ■
Occurrences: 2
Positions:
2182, 3817

■ suddenly ■
Occurrences: 2
Positions:
706, 11269

■ superficial ■
Occurrences: 2
Positions:
10777, 11468

■ supermodern ■
Occurrences: 2
Positions:
4, 15214

■ swirling ■
Occurrences: 2
Positions:
1889, 9725

■ taking ■
Occurrences: 2
Positions:
2545, 12995

■ technically ■
Occurrences: 2
Positions:
6300, 6313

■ tend ■
Occurrences: 2
Positions:
14478, 14500

■ term ■
Occurrences: 2
Positions:
2174, 6018

■ texts ■
Occurrences: 2
Positions:
11862, 12982

■ textual ■
Occurrences: 2
Positions:
7607, 10715

■ theorized ■
Occurrences: 2
Positions:
8919, 8933

■ thoughts ■
Occurrences: 2
Positions:
5140, 13075

■ thousands ■
Occurrences: 2
Positions:
6574, 6607

■ threat ■
Occurrences: 2
Positions:
3697, 11300

■ timbre ■
Occurrences: 2
Positions:
8035, 8127

■ total ■
Occurrences: 2
Positions:
9371, 9734

■ traces ■
Occurrences: 2
Positions:
10531, 15323

■ transformation ■
Occurrences: 2
Positions:
3160, 14930

■ trek ■
Occurrences: 2
Positions:
3723, 3842

■ tv ■
Occurrences: 2
Positions:
1506, 10894

■ typical ■
Occurrences: 2
Positions:
4659, 12266

■ tzara ■
Occurrences: 2
Positions:
7697, 9114

■ uncertain ■
Occurrences: 2
Positions:
2720, 9456

■ unconscious ■
Occurrences: 2
Positions:
449, 15103

■ undergoing ■
Occurrences: 2
Positions:
5071, 6078

■ understanding ■
Occurrences: 2
Positions:
5029, 5755

■ unified ■
Occurrences: 2
Positions:
13886, 13906

■ unit ■
Occurrences: 2
Positions:
14704, 14983

■ unknowing ■
Occurrences: 2
Positions:
802, 2028

■ unknown ■
Occurrences: 2
Positions:
144, 7498

■ unpredictable ■
Occurrences: 2
Positions:
9454, 9687

■ unprovoked ■
Occurrences: 2
Positions:
1206, 5082

■ urban ■
Occurrences: 2
Positions:
3426, 5442

■ usually ■
Occurrences: 2
Positions:
7753, 11406

■ vary ■
Occurrences: 2
Positions:
6645, 9006

■ view ■
Occurrences: 2
Positions:
4882, 10170

■ vint ■
Occurrences: 2
Positions:
5770, 5815

■ violence ■
Occurrences: 2
Positions:
1299, 11591

■ violent ■
Occurrences: 2
Positions:
936, 11265

■ vision ■
Occurrences: 2
Positions:
3984, 11305

■ whereas ■
Occurrences: 2
Positions:
5122, 14382

■ wishes ■
Occurrences: 2
Positions:
917, 5052

■ write ■
Occurrences: 2
Positions:
1776, 13310

■ written ■
Occurrences: 2
Positions:
8063, 11679

■ year ■
Occurrences: 2
Positions:
7295, 11422

■ years ■
Occurrences: 2
Positions:
7378, 15288

■ yield ■
Occurrences: 2
Positions:
1437, 10585

■ études ■
Occurrences: 2
Positions:
7145, 7159

■ 0101010101chaos0101010101chaos0101010101chaos0101010101chaos0101010101chaos ■
Occurrences: 1
Positions:
1718

■ 112 ■
Occurrences: 1
Positions:
1447

■ 13 ■
Occurrences: 1
Positions:
11364

■ 1895 ■
Occurrences: 1
Positions:
13840

■ 1913 ■
Occurrences: 1
Positions:
6877

■ 1920s ■
Occurrences: 1
Positions:
6941

■ 1922 ■
Occurrences: 1
Positions:
7424

■ 1923 ■
Occurrences: 1
Positions:
2787

■ 1930s ■
Occurrences: 1
Positions:
10755

■ 1937 ■
Occurrences: 1
Positions:
7643

■ 1940s ■
Occurrences: 1
Positions:
7054

■ 1947 ■
Occurrences: 1
Positions:
8938

■ 1950 ■
Occurrences: 1
Positions:
7210

■ 1951 ■
Occurrences: 1
Positions:
8250

■ 1955 ■
Occurrences: 1
Positions:
7281

■ 1956 ■
Occurrences: 1
Positions:
7282

■ 1959 ■
Occurrences: 1
Positions:
11794

■ 1960s ■
Occurrences: 1
Positions:
5530

■ 1964 ■
Occurrences: 1
Positions:
8943

■ 1970s ■
Occurrences: 1
Positions:
6204

■ 1971 ■
Occurrences: 1
Positions:
77

■ 1978 ■
Occurrences: 1
Positions:
7604

■ 1988 ■
Occurrences: 1
Positions:
4338

■ 1989 ■
Occurrences: 1
Positions:
3348

■ 1990 ■
Occurrences: 1
Positions:
4336

■ 1990s ■
Occurrences: 1
Positions:
4855

■ 1999 ■
Occurrences: 1
Positions:
1261

■ 2002 ■
Occurrences: 1
Positions:
1272

■ 2006 ■
Occurrences: 1
Positions:
1603

■ 2008 ■
Occurrences: 1
Positions:
1670

■ 2009 ■
Occurrences: 1
Positions:
18

■ 2011 ■
Occurrences: 1
Positions:
1726

■ 2018 ■
Occurrences: 1
Positions:
15462

■ 3 ■
Occurrences: 1
Positions:
8085

■ 33 ■
Occurrences: 1
Positions:
7727

■ 3am ■
Occurrences: 1
Positions:
5892

■ 50 ■
Occurrences: 1
Positions:
6640

■ 80s ■
Occurrences: 1
Positions:
2179

■ 90s ■
Occurrences: 1
Positions:
3391

■ abandoned ■
Occurrences: 1
Positions:
11272

■ ability ■
Occurrences: 1
Positions:
10186

■ abolition ■
Occurrences: 1
Positions:
1632

■ abound ■
Occurrences: 1
Positions:
15307

■ above ■
Occurrences: 1
Positions:
10854

■ abrasive ■
Occurrences: 1
Positions:
13145

■ absent ■
Occurrences: 1
Positions:
8426

■ absorbed ■
Occurrences: 1
Positions:
1814

■ abstract ■
Occurrences: 1
Positions:
14601

■ abstraction ■
Occurrences: 1
Positions:
14512

■ absurdities ■
Occurrences: 1
Positions:
9243

■ absurdity ■
Occurrences: 1
Positions:
1856

■ accelerates ■
Occurrences: 1
Positions:
15410

■ accelerationist ■
Occurrences: 1
Positions:
15557

■ accepting ■
Occurrences: 1
Positions:
4089

■ access ■
Occurrences: 1
Positions:
10150

■ accessibility ■
Occurrences: 1
Positions:
9080

■ accessing ■
Occurrences: 1
Positions:
7273

■ accompany ■
Occurrences: 1
Positions:
7009

■ accompanying ■
Occurrences: 1
Positions:
4261

■ accordance ■
Occurrences: 1
Positions:
6974

■ accurate ■
Occurrences: 1
Positions:
2430

■ accurately ■
Occurrences: 1
Positions:
13791

■ acid ■
Occurrences: 1
Positions:
1717

■ acknowledges ■
Occurrences: 1
Positions:
11239

■ acknowledgment ■
Occurrences: 1
Positions:
6752

■ ackroyd ■
Occurrences: 1
Positions:
5378

■ acoustic ■
Occurrences: 1
Positions:
6583

■ acquiring ■
Occurrences: 1
Positions:
13542

■ across ■
Occurrences: 1
Positions:
11757

■ actively ■
Occurrences: 1
Positions:
3207

■ activists ■
Occurrences: 1
Positions:
2652

■ actor ■
Occurrences: 1
Positions:
14402

■ actors ■
Occurrences: 1
Positions:
14519

■ actual ■
Occurrences: 1
Positions:
247

■ actually ■
Occurrences: 1
Positions:
3474

■ adam ■
Occurrences: 1
Positions:
1716

■ adapt ■
Occurrences: 1
Positions:
14191

■ add ■
Occurrences: 1
Positions:
5381

■ addresses ■
Occurrences: 1
Positions:
7996

■ adjective ■
Occurrences: 1
Positions:
8786

■ administered ■
Occurrences: 1
Positions:
628

■ adopts ■
Occurrences: 1
Positions:
5010

■ advent ■
Occurrences: 1
Positions:
6805

■ advertising ■
Occurrences: 1
Positions:
170

■ aestheticism ■
Occurrences: 1
Positions:
4435

■ affinities ■
Occurrences: 1
Positions:
4861

■ affinity ■
Occurrences: 1
Positions:
5365

■ affirming ■
Occurrences: 1
Positions:
10411

■ aficionados ■
Occurrences: 1
Positions:
12263

■ african ■
Occurrences: 1
Positions:
9247

■ agent ■
Occurrences: 1
Positions:
7376

■ agential ■
Occurrences: 1
Positions:
6751

■ aggression ■
Occurrences: 1
Positions:
166

■ aggressively ■
Occurrences: 1
Positions:
2838

■ agitation ■
Occurrences: 1
Positions:
11229

■ ahead ■
Occurrences: 1
Positions:
639

■ akira ■
Occurrences: 1
Positions:
4334

■ alain ■
Occurrences: 1
Positions:
2385

■ albert ■
Occurrences: 1
Positions:
11490

■ aleatory ■
Occurrences: 1
Positions:
14321

■ alex ■
Occurrences: 1
Positions:
7330

■ algebra ■
Occurrences: 1
Positions:
8818

■ algorithmically ■
Occurrences: 1
Positions:
368

■ alien ■
Occurrences: 1
Positions:
15571

■ alienating ■
Occurrences: 1
Positions:
12767

■ allow ■
Occurrences: 1
Positions:
14370

■ allowance ■
Occurrences: 1
Positions:
9937

■ alter ■
Occurrences: 1
Positions:
11781

■ altering ■
Occurrences: 1
Positions:
3539

■ always ■
Occurrences: 1
Positions:
8280

■ am ■
Occurrences: 1
Positions:
10897

■ amalgam ■
Occurrences: 1
Positions:
1245

■ ambiguity ■
Occurrences: 1
Positions:
2758

■ ambivalent ■
Occurrences: 1
Positions:
12703

■ america ■
Occurrences: 1
Positions:
2686

■ americans ■
Occurrences: 1
Positions:
4014

■ amnesiac ■
Occurrences: 1
Positions:
270

■ among ■
Occurrences: 1
Positions:
8964

■ amongst ■
Occurrences: 1
Positions:
4579

■ amplify ■
Occurrences: 1
Positions:
4290

■ amputated ■
Occurrences: 1
Positions:
1993

■ analogique ■
Occurrences: 1
Positions:
8913

■ analogy ■
Occurrences: 1
Positions:
13199

■ analyzed ■
Occurrences: 1
Positions:
12584

■ anarchic ■
Occurrences: 1
Positions:
8378

■ andré ■
Occurrences: 1
Positions:
11427

■ anew ■
Occurrences: 1
Positions:
10171

■ angela ■
Occurrences: 1
Positions:
5372

■ angle ■
Occurrences: 1
Positions:
12590

■ animal ■
Occurrences: 1
Positions:
14910

■ animated ■
Occurrences: 1
Positions:
402

■ animation ■
Occurrences: 1
Positions:
4427

■ annihilate ■
Occurrences: 1
Positions:
15053

■ anthology ■
Occurrences: 1
Positions:
2488

■ anthropoids ■
Occurrences: 1
Positions:
1757

■ antirationalist ■
Occurrences: 1
Positions:
5093

■ antirealist ■
Occurrences: 1
Positions:
5124

■ anxiety ■
Occurrences: 1
Positions:
1053

■ apparatuses ■
Occurrences: 1
Positions:
4703

■ appeal ■
Occurrences: 1
Positions:
14274

■ appearance ■
Occurrences: 1
Positions:
12222

■ appeared ■
Occurrences: 1
Positions:
8694

■ appreciating ■
Occurrences: 1
Positions:
3479

■ appropriately ■
Occurrences: 1
Positions:
12397

■ appropriateness ■
Occurrences: 1
Positions:
2911

■ apt ■
Occurrences: 1
Positions:
6839

■ archaic ■
Occurrences: 1
Positions:
222

■ architect ■
Occurrences: 1
Positions:
8570

■ architectural ■
Occurrences: 1
Positions:
8540

■ area ■
Occurrences: 1
Positions:
1495

■ arise ■
Occurrences: 1
Positions:
13472

■ arises ■
Occurrences: 1
Positions:
11584

■ aristocracy ■
Occurrences: 1
Positions:
13875

■ armenian ■
Occurrences: 1
Positions:
7383

■ arrested ■
Occurrences: 1
Positions:
266

■ arrives ■
Occurrences: 1
Positions:
10092

■ articles ■
Occurrences: 1
Positions:
11839

■ articulate ■
Occurrences: 1
Positions:
2778

■ articulates ■
Occurrences: 1
Positions:
15497

■ articulating ■
Occurrences: 1
Positions:
14644

■ ascension ■
Occurrences: 1
Positions:
4083

■ authoritarian ■
Occurrences: 1
Positions:
10492

■ authorship ■
Occurrences: 1
Positions:
6263

■ automatically ■
Occurrences: 1
Positions:
13772

■ automatism ■
Occurrences: 1
Positions:
14861

■ automobile ■
Occurrences: 1
Positions:
385

■ autonomous ■
Occurrences: 1
Positions:
5265

■ autos ■
Occurrences: 1
Positions:
6920

■ awaken ■
Occurrences: 1
Positions:
6028

■ awakened ■
Occurrences: 1
Positions:
13530

■ awaking ■
Occurrences: 1
Positions:
13514

■ aware ■
Occurrences: 1
Positions:
13488

■ awareness ■
Occurrences: 1
Positions:
6039

■ b ■
Occurrences: 1
Positions:
8915

■ babel ■
Occurrences: 1
Positions:
1503

■ bad ■
Occurrences: 1
Positions:
398

■ bafflement ■
Occurrences: 1
Positions:
13435

■ ballardian ■
Occurrences: 1
Positions:
15185

■ ballardianism ■
Occurrences: 1
Positions:
15461

■ banks ■
Occurrences: 1
Positions:
1293

■ barred ■
Occurrences: 1
Positions:
4420

■ basically ■
Occurrences: 1
Positions:
3598

■ baudrillard ■
Occurrences: 1
Positions:
12554

■ became ■
Occurrences: 1
Positions:
7160

■ bees ■
Occurrences: 1
Positions:
14454

■ begins ■
Occurrences: 1
Positions:
1124

■ behave ■
Occurrences: 1
Positions:
15074

■ behaviorally ■
Occurrences: 1
Positions:
4478

■ beliefs ■
Occurrences: 1
Positions:
2831

■ believes ■
Occurrences: 1
Positions:
10368

■ believing ■
Occurrences: 1
Positions:
11478

■ bell ■
Occurrences: 1
Positions:
6626

■ belong ■
Occurrences: 1
Positions:
11903

■ belt ■
Occurrences: 1
Positions:
14223

■ bend ■
Occurrences: 1
Positions:
14253

■ berserk ■
Occurrences: 1
Positions:
12291

■ beside ■
Occurrences: 1
Positions:
8433

■ best ■
Occurrences: 1
Positions:
394

■ bifurcate ■
Occurrences: 1
Positions:
585

■ bifurcating ■
Occurrences: 1
Positions:
13995

■ big ■
Occurrences: 1
Positions:
9092

■ biocapturism ■
Occurrences: 1
Positions:
1629

■ biochemistry ■
Occurrences: 1
Positions:
4935

■ biologists ■
Occurrences: 1
Positions:
14426

■ bit ■
Occurrences: 1
Positions:
277

■ blaring ■
Occurrences: 1
Positions:
15536

■ blending ■
Occurrences: 1
Positions:
4399

■ blooded ■
Occurrences: 1
Positions:
1693

■ bloody ■
Occurrences: 1
Positions:
11378

■ blunt ■
Occurrences: 1
Positions:
10812

■ blurring ■
Occurrences: 1
Positions:
7786

■ bodies ■
Occurrences: 1
Positions:
4896

■ bodily ■
Occurrences: 1
Positions:
14438

■ bold ■
Occurrences: 1
Positions:
15492

■ bombarded ■
Occurrences: 1
Positions:
12463

■ bombarding ■
Occurrences: 1
Positions:
1133

■ books ■
Occurrences: 1
Positions:
12491

■ boredom ■
Occurrences: 1
Positions:
13985

■ borrowed ■
Occurrences: 1
Positions:
5779

■ bound ■
Occurrences: 1
Positions:
2861

■ boundaries ■
Occurrences: 1
Positions:
7506

■ boundary ■
Occurrences: 1
Positions:
2185

■ brains ■
Occurrences: 1
Positions:
13079

■ branch ■
Occurrences: 1
Positions:
8656

■ breaking ■
Occurrences: 1
Positions:
11872

■ breaks ■
Occurrences: 1
Positions:
1155

■ breathes ■
Occurrences: 1
Positions:
1983

■ breathing ■
Occurrences: 1
Positions:
11963

■ brechtian ■
Occurrences: 1
Positions:
5722

■ brian ■
Occurrences: 1
Positions:
10072

■ brief ■
Occurrences: 1
Positions:
8233

■ brings ■
Occurrences: 1
Positions:
6228

■ british ■
Occurrences: 1
Positions:
66

■ broadcasting ■
Occurrences: 1
Positions:
3213

■ broader ■
Occurrences: 1
Positions:
9164

■ broadest ■
Occurrences: 1
Positions:
11398

■ brought ■
Occurrences: 1
Positions:
12386

■ bruce ■
Occurrences: 1
Positions:
2490

■ building ■
Occurrences: 1
Positions:
14455

■ bunker ■
Occurrences: 1
Positions:
62

■ bursts ■
Occurrences: 1
Positions:
15547

■ business ■
Occurrences: 1
Positions:
5475

■ bustles ■
Occurrences: 1
Positions:
13972

■ busy ■
Occurrences: 1
Positions:
13965

■ button ■
Occurrences: 1
Positions:
14152

■ byte ■
Occurrences: 1
Positions:
1679

■ cacophony ■
Occurrences: 1
Positions:
11158

■ calculation ■
Occurrences: 1
Positions:
4369

■ calculative ■
Occurrences: 1
Positions:
730

■ camp ■
Occurrences: 1
Positions:
74

■ canceled ■
Occurrences: 1
Positions:
784

■ capable ■
Occurrences: 1
Positions:
6694

■ career ■
Occurrences: 1
Positions:
11773

■ carefully ■
Occurrences: 1
Positions:
8168

■ carried ■
Occurrences: 1
Positions:
9650

■ cars ■
Occurrences: 1
Positions:
1946

■ carter ■
Occurrences: 1
Positions:
5373

■ catalyze ■
Occurrences: 1
Positions:
9344

■ catastrophe ■
Occurrences: 1
Positions:
10505

■ cells ■
Occurrences: 1
Positions:
1631

■ centered ■
Occurrences: 1
Positions:
7093

■ centralized ■
Occurrences: 1
Positions:
15086

■ cerebellum ■
Occurrences: 1
Positions:
1241

■ chain ■
Occurrences: 1
Positions:
9015

■ chains ■
Occurrences: 1
Positions:
14877

■ challenge ■
Occurrences: 1
Positions:
12004

■ challenged ■
Occurrences: 1
Positions:
4776

■ chambers ■
Occurrences: 1
Positions:
6811

■ championed ■
Occurrences: 1
Positions:
2690

■ chang ■
Occurrences: 1
Positions:
2657

■ changed ■
Occurrences: 1
Positions:
6044

■ channels ■
Occurrences: 1
Positions:
1626

■ chaotically ■
Occurrences: 1
Positions:
581

■ character ■
Occurrences: 1
Positions:
1194

■ chorister ■
Occurrences: 1
Positions:
7297

■ chose ■
Occurrences: 1
Positions:
3118

■ christopher ■
Occurrences: 1
Positions:
2499

■ chronological ■
Occurrences: 1
Positions:
9593

■ circuit ■
Occurrences: 1
Positions:
10906

■ circumference ■
Occurrences: 1
Positions:
691

■ cited ■
Occurrences: 1
Positions:
2372

■ cites ■
Occurrences: 1
Positions:
3721

■ claim ■
Occurrences: 1
Positions:
15598

■ classical ■
Occurrences: 1
Positions:
8395

■ classified ■
Occurrences: 1
Positions:
6592

■ cleansing ■
Occurrences: 1
Positions:
11494

■ clear ■
Occurrences: 1
Positions:
2798

■ climate ■
Occurrences: 1
Positions:
10504

■ clock ■
Occurrences: 1
Positions:
10380

■ clocks ■
Occurrences: 1
Positions:
10395

■ clone ■
Occurrences: 1
Positions:
1654

■ clones ■
Occurrences: 1
Positions:
1758

■ close ■
Occurrences: 1
Positions:
1342

■ closer ■
Occurrences: 1
Positions:
7065

■ closest ■
Occurrences: 1
Positions:
8556

■ clouds ■
Occurrences: 1
Positions:
9029

■ cluttered ■
Occurrences: 1
Positions:
290

■ coalesced ■
Occurrences: 1
Positions:
8702

■ codemaniacs ■
Occurrences: 1
Positions:
1634

■ codifying ■
Occurrences: 1
Positions:
11207

■ coffee ■
Occurrences: 1
Positions:
10398

■ cognitions ■
Occurrences: 1
Positions:
15572

■ cognitively ■
Occurrences: 1
Positions:
3930

■ cohesion ■
Occurrences: 1
Positions:
564

■ coins ■
Occurrences: 1
Positions:
8155

■ cold ■
Occurrences: 1
Positions:
1692

■ collaborates ■
Occurrences: 1
Positions:
6286

■ collectivity ■
Occurrences: 1
Positions:
14967

■ combining ■
Occurrences: 1
Positions:
7135

■ commentaries ■
Occurrences: 1
Positions:
3215

■ commercial ■
Occurrences: 1
Positions:
13146

■ commingling ■
Occurrences: 1
Positions:
4401

■ commissioned ■
Occurrences: 1
Positions:
7000

■ committed ■
Occurrences: 1
Positions:
4994

■ commonalities ■
Occurrences: 1
Positions:
2380

■ commonly ■
Occurrences: 1
Positions:
7685

■ commotion ■
Occurrences: 1
Positions:
40

■ communicate ■
Occurrences: 1
Positions:
11485

■ communications ■
Occurrences: 1
Positions:
363

■ communities ■
Occurrences: 1
Positions:
2123

■ compelling ■
Occurrences: 1
Positions:
11939

■ complement ■
Occurrences: 1
Positions:
59

■ complementary ■
Occurrences: 1
Positions:
1883

■ complicate ■
Occurrences: 1
Positions:
9150

■ component ■
Occurrences: 1
Positions:
9097

■ composed ■
Occurrences: 1
Positions:
6991

■ comprise ■
Occurrences: 1
Positions:
12183

■ comprises ■
Occurrences: 1
Positions:
14678

■ compromise ■
Occurrences: 1
Positions:
3795

■ computational ■
Occurrences: 1
Positions:
833

■ concatenated ■
Occurrences: 1
Positions:
14896

■ concatenation ■
Occurrences: 1
Positions:
763

■ conceived ■
Occurrences: 1
Positions:
1539

■ conceptually ■
Occurrences: 1
Positions:
4577

■ concern ■
Occurrences: 1
Positions:
7092

■ concretely ■
Occurrences: 1
Positions:
14065

■ condense ■
Occurrences: 1
Positions:
111

■ conduit ■
Occurrences: 1
Positions:
7732

■ confidence ■
Occurrences: 1
Positions:
10512

■ confident ■
Occurrences: 1
Positions:
9264

■ confidently ■
Occurrences: 1
Positions:
9897

■ configurations ■
Occurrences: 1
Positions:
10283

■ configured ■
Occurrences: 1
Positions:
12633

■ confine ■
Occurrences: 1
Positions:
2353

■ conflagrating ■
Occurrences: 1
Positions:
13660

■ conflated ■
Occurrences: 1
Positions:
982

■ conflates ■
Occurrences: 1
Positions:
738

■ conflation ■
Occurrences: 1
Positions:
7259

■ conform ■
Occurrences: 1
Positions:
14502

■ conformity ■
Occurrences: 1
Positions:
3627

■ confronting ■
Occurrences: 1
Positions:
10049

■ confuses ■
Occurrences: 1
Positions:
4695

■ conjures ■
Occurrences: 1
Positions:
907

■ connected ■
Occurrences: 1
Positions:
11067

■ connections ■
Occurrences: 1
Positions:
11590

■ connective ■
Occurrences: 1
Positions:
13775

■ connectivity ■
Occurrences: 1
Positions:
14962

■ connects ■
Occurrences: 1
Positions:
11435

■ connotations ■
Occurrences: 1
Positions:
3130

■ connotative ■
Occurrences: 1
Positions:
1801

■ conquer ■
Occurrences: 1
Positions:
6896

■ consensual ■
Occurrences: 1
Positions:
9979

■ consequences ■
Occurrences: 1
Positions:
11317

■ constancy ■
Occurrences: 1
Positions:
3798

■ constant ■
Occurrences: 1
Positions:
11655

■ constants ■
Occurrences: 1
Positions:
3646

■ constitute ■
Occurrences: 1
Positions:
14653

■ constituter ■
Occurrences: 1
Positions:
5289

■ constitutes ■
Occurrences: 1
Positions:
7558

■ constructed ■
Occurrences: 1
Positions:
8833

■ consumed ■
Occurrences: 1
Positions:
5646

■ consumerism ■
Occurrences: 1
Positions:
5491

■ consumes ■
Occurrences: 1
Positions:
12084

■ consuming ■
Occurrences: 1
Positions:
5422

■ contaminated ■
Occurrences: 1
Positions:
1487

■ contamination ■
Occurrences: 1
Positions:
1823

■ contemplation ■
Occurrences: 1
Positions:
312

■ contemporaries ■
Occurrences: 1
Positions:
2392

■ contention ■
Occurrences: 1
Positions:
12164

■ contentious ■
Occurrences: 1
Positions:
681

■ contingent ■
Occurrences: 1
Positions:
8220

■ continue ■
Occurrences: 1
Positions:
5816

■ continuity ■
Occurrences: 1
Positions:
11880

■ contradicting ■
Occurrences: 1
Positions:
10253

■ contradiction ■
Occurrences: 1
Positions:
3091

■ contribution ■
Occurrences: 1
Positions:
8857

■ controllers ■
Occurrences: 1
Positions:
3685

■ controls ■
Occurrences: 1
Positions:
8031

■ conversation ■
Occurrences: 1
Positions:
12556

■ converting ■
Occurrences: 1
Positions:
8637

■ conveyer ■
Occurrences: 1
Positions:
14222

■ convincingly ■
Occurrences: 1
Positions:
6951

■ cool ■
Occurrences: 1
Positions:
2214

■ cords ■
Occurrences: 1
Positions:
1161

■ core ■
Occurrences: 1
Positions:
2644

■ corporatization ■
Occurrences: 1
Positions:
10508

■ corporatized ■
Occurrences: 1
Positions:
15046

■ corpus ■
Occurrences: 1
Positions:
7612

■ correlative ■
Occurrences: 1
Positions:
6314

■ corresponding ■
Occurrences: 1
Positions:
11226

■ corrupted ■
Occurrences: 1
Positions:
4009

■ cost ■
Occurrences: 1
Positions:
6887

■ couched ■
Occurrences: 1
Positions:
3100

■ couldn ■
Occurrences: 1
Positions:
8262

■ counterpart ■
Occurrences: 1
Positions:
67

■ country ■
Occurrences: 1
Positions:
4143

■ coupled ■
Occurrences: 1
Positions:
10498

■ cramped ■
Occurrences: 1
Positions:
287

■ crash ■
Occurrences: 1
Positions:
1304

■ creation ■
Occurrences: 1
Positions:
11442

■ creativity ■
Occurrences: 1
Positions:
5556

■ creators ■
Occurrences: 1
Positions:
3683

■ creature ■
Occurrences: 1
Positions:
1647

■ credo ■
Occurrences: 1
Positions:
7649

■ creole ■
Occurrences: 1
Positions:
2181

■ crisis ■
Occurrences: 1
Positions:
3081

■ critiques ■
Occurrences: 1
Positions:
15560

■ crucified ■
Occurrences: 1
Positions:
1291

■ cruel ■
Occurrences: 1
Positions:
1705

■ cryptic ■
Occurrences: 1
Positions:
7440

■ cultivate ■
Occurrences: 1
Positions:
11388

■ cultivates ■
Occurrences: 1
Positions:
15570

■ cultures ■
Occurrences: 1
Positions:
353

■ currency ■
Occurrences: 1
Positions:
9572

■ curtis ■
Occurrences: 1
Positions:
6586

■ curve ■
Occurrences: 1
Positions:
6627

■ cuts ■
Occurrences: 1
Positions:
12092

■ cybernetics ■
Occurrences: 1
Positions:
260

■ cyborg ■
Occurrences: 1
Positions:
1303

■ dadaism ■
Occurrences: 1
Positions:
7894

■ dangerously ■
Occurrences: 1
Positions:
4292

■ darko ■
Occurrences: 1
Positions:
5684

■ date ■
Occurrences: 1
Positions:
5463

■ dawn ■
Occurrences: 1
Positions:
1088

■ day ■
Occurrences: 1
Positions:
9427

■ dead ■
Occurrences: 1
Positions:
6772

■ debris ■
Occurrences: 1
Positions:
12285

■ decelerated ■
Occurrences: 1
Positions:
7220

■ decentralization ■
Occurrences: 1
Positions:
9087

■ decisiveness ■
Occurrences: 1
Positions:
11415

■ declares ■
Occurrences: 1
Positions:
2804

■ decline ■
Occurrences: 1
Positions:
5590

■ decoding ■
Occurrences: 1
Positions:
2010

■ deconstructing ■
Occurrences: 1
Positions:
3739

■ dedication ■
Occurrences: 1
Positions:
10946

■ defeat ■
Occurrences: 1
Positions:
10127

■ deference ■
Occurrences: 1
Positions:
12318

■ defined ■
Occurrences: 1
Positions:
14970

■ defining ■
Occurrences: 1
Positions:
2486

■ definitely ■
Occurrences: 1
Positions:
2821

■ defy ■
Occurrences: 1
Positions:
14848

■ degrees ■
Occurrences: 1
Positions:
7367

■ delimited ■
Occurrences: 1
Positions:
464

■ delimits ■
Occurrences: 1
Positions:
7365

■ delineating ■
Occurrences: 1
Positions:
6131

■ deliverance ■
Occurrences: 1
Positions:
12694

■ demand ■
Occurrences: 1
Positions:
14248

■ democratizing ■
Occurrences: 1
Positions:
9076

■ denaturalization ■
Occurrences: 1
Positions:
5756

■ dennis ■
Occurrences: 1
Positions:
8935

■ densities ■
Occurrences: 1
Positions:
6665

■ density ■
Occurrences: 1
Positions:
6651

■ deny ■
Occurrences: 1
Positions:
15050

■ denying ■
Occurrences: 1
Positions:
550

■ depend ■
Occurrences: 1
Positions:
9698

■ dependant ■
Occurrences: 1
Positions:
3434

■ deployment ■
Occurrences: 1
Positions:
8494

■ deploys ■
Occurrences: 1
Positions:
10273

■ derive ■
Occurrences: 1
Positions:
11009

■ describe ■
Occurrences: 1
Positions:
12275

■ description ■
Occurrences: 1
Positions:
1104

■ desert ■
Occurrences: 1
Positions:
1782

■ desiccations ■
Occurrences: 1
Positions:
9245

■ dialogue ■
Occurrences: 1
Positions:
11004

■ dials ■
Occurrences: 1
Positions:
8043

■ dictated ■
Occurrences: 1
Positions:
8165

■ dictates ■
Occurrences: 1
Positions:
8111

■ dictating ■
Occurrences: 1
Positions:
15088

■ dictator ■
Occurrences: 1
Positions:
8403

■ diegesis ■
Occurrences: 1
Positions:
3525

■ differed ■
Occurrences: 1
Positions:
2737

■ differently ■
Occurrences: 1
Positions:
4117

■ diligence ■
Occurrences: 1
Positions:
11413

■ diminishes ■
Occurrences: 1
Positions:
14350

■ directed ■
Occurrences: 1
Positions:
13773

■ disappear ■
Occurrences: 1
Positions:
10915

■ disappearance ■
Occurrences: 1
Positions:
10120

■ disaster ■
Occurrences: 1
Positions:
4270

■ disasters ■
Occurrences: 1
Positions:
3075

■ disavow ■
Occurrences: 1
Positions:
531

■ disciplines ■
Occurrences: 1
Positions:
4933

■ discombobulates ■
Occurrences: 1
Positions:
492

■ discontent ■
Occurrences: 1
Positions:
5559

■ discord ■
Occurrences: 1
Positions:
3090

■ discouraged ■
Occurrences: 1
Positions:
345

■ discover ■
Occurrences: 1
Positions:
14128

■ discuss ■
Occurrences: 1
Positions:
2050

■ discussing ■
Occurrences: 1
Positions:
2282

■ discussion ■
Occurrences: 1
Positions:
2090

■ disease ■
Occurrences: 1
Positions:
1694

■ disentangled ■
Occurrences: 1
Positions:
8809

■ disgrace ■
Occurrences: 1
Positions:
1772

■ disguised ■
Occurrences: 1
Positions:
3758

■ dismantle ■
Occurrences: 1
Positions:
2614

■ dismiss ■
Occurrences: 1
Positions:
7547

■ disordered ■
Occurrences: 1
Positions:
9717

■ disorientation ■
Occurrences: 1
Positions:
1847

■ disorienting ■
Occurrences: 1
Positions:
934

■ disparate ■
Occurrences: 1
Positions:
13663

■ dispatch ■
Occurrences: 1
Positions:
1312

■ displacements ■
Occurrences: 1
Positions:
14009

■ dispositives ■
Occurrences: 1
Positions:
14885

■ disrupt ■
Occurrences: 1
Positions:
5874

■ disseminated ■
Occurrences: 1
Positions:
12635

■ dissent ■
Occurrences: 1
Positions:
14538

■ dissociatory ■
Occurrences: 1
Positions:
11023

■ dissolves ■
Occurrences: 1
Positions:
4717

■ distinctions ■
Occurrences: 1
Positions:
8060

■ distinctly ■
Occurrences: 1
Positions:
3620

■ distinguish ■
Occurrences: 1
Positions:
10012

■ distinguishes ■
Occurrences: 1
Positions:
12411

■ distorted ■
Occurrences: 1
Positions:
8294

■ distorts ■
Occurrences: 1
Positions:
1576

■ diverse ■
Occurrences: 1
Positions:
2972

■ dna ■
Occurrences: 1
Positions:
1625

■ dog ■
Occurrences: 1
Positions:
10887

■ dominance ■
Occurrences: 1
Positions:
15243

■ dominated ■
Occurrences: 1
Positions:
3437

■ dominates ■
Occurrences: 1
Positions:
15503

■ donald ■
Occurrences: 1
Positions:
2303

■ doubt ■
Occurrences: 1
Positions:
13116

■ downplayed ■
Occurrences: 1
Positions:
7848

■ downplaying ■
Occurrences: 1
Positions:
7873

■ drama ■
Occurrences: 1
Positions:
164

■ draw ■
Occurrences: 1
Positions:
9368

■ drawing ■
Occurrences: 1
Positions:
8632

■ draws ■
Occurrences: 1
Positions:
11533

■ drifts ■
Occurrences: 1
Positions:
926

■ driven ■
Occurrences: 1
Positions:
14881

■ driving ■
Occurrences: 1
Positions:
137

■ drone ■
Occurrences: 1
Positions:
1554

■ dry ■
Occurrences: 1
Positions:
9793

■ dubmasters ■
Occurrences: 1
Positions:
6200

■ duchamp ■
Occurrences: 1
Positions:
7699

■ due ■
Occurrences: 1
Positions:
788

■ durations ■
Occurrences: 1
Positions:
8061

■ durée ■
Occurrences: 1
Positions:
9564

■ dwells ■
Occurrences: 1
Positions:
14661

■ dynamically ■
Occurrences: 1
Positions:
6678

■ e ■
Occurrences: 1
Positions:
10971

■ earliest ■
Occurrences: 1
Positions:
2582

■ eat ■
Occurrences: 1
Positions:
2204

■ eccentricities ■
Occurrences: 1
Positions:
12193

■ echo ■
Occurrences: 1
Positions:
6810

■ echoes ■
Occurrences: 1
Positions:
7449

■ ecologies ■
Occurrences: 1
Positions:
3777

■ ecstasy ■
Occurrences: 1
Positions:
778

■ ecstatic ■
Occurrences: 1
Positions:
10136

■ edward ■
Occurrences: 1
Positions:
1593

■ eerie ■
Occurrences: 1
Positions:
410

■ effecting ■
Occurrences: 1
Positions:
12210

■ efficiency ■
Occurrences: 1
Positions:
14355

■ efficient ■
Occurrences: 1
Positions:
8984

■ elaborate ■
Occurrences: 1
Positions:
2343

■ elaborately ■
Occurrences: 1
Positions:
187

■ elaborating ■
Occurrences: 1
Positions:
14591

■ elaboration ■
Occurrences: 1
Positions:
14496

■ electronics ■
Occurrences: 1
Positions:
9057

■ elegance ■
Occurrences: 1
Positions:
15292

■ element ■
Occurrences: 1
Positions:
8445

■ elementary ■
Occurrences: 1
Positions:
8824

■ elevate ■
Occurrences: 1
Positions:
2904

■ eliot ■
Occurrences: 1
Positions:
9788

■ ellmann ■
Occurrences: 1
Positions:
9533

■ else ■
Occurrences: 1
Positions:
8288

■ elsewhere ■
Occurrences: 1
Positions:
14941

■ elucidates ■
Occurrences: 1
Positions:
13195

■ emancipatory ■
Occurrences: 1
Positions:
9952

■ embeds ■
Occurrences: 1
Positions:
15099

■ embody ■
Occurrences: 1
Positions:
11451

■ embodying ■
Occurrences: 1
Positions:
15602

■ embraces ■
Occurrences: 1
Positions:
4161

■ embracing ■
Occurrences: 1
Positions:
1162

■ embryo ■
Occurrences: 1
Positions:
1318

■ emergent ■
Occurrences: 1
Positions:
13709

■ emoting ■
Occurrences: 1
Positions:
7683

■ emotion ■
Occurrences: 1
Positions:
1515

■ emotions ■
Occurrences: 1
Positions:
9415

■ emphasizes ■
Occurrences: 1
Positions:
13169

■ empty ■
Occurrences: 1
Positions:
7602

■ enact ■
Occurrences: 1
Positions:
8363

■ enacting ■
Occurrences: 1
Positions:
13379

■ enclosed ■
Occurrences: 1
Positions:
93

■ encompassing ■
Occurrences: 1
Positions:
1914

■ encouragement ■
Occurrences: 1
Positions:
8590

■ encourages ■
Occurrences: 1
Positions:
6374

■ encouraging ■
Occurrences: 1
Positions:
1414

■ encroaching ■
Occurrences: 1
Positions:
11252

■ encroachment ■
Occurrences: 1
Positions:
3450

■ encrusted ■
Occurrences: 1
Positions:
12284

■ endeavor ■
Occurrences: 1
Positions:
15372

■ endgame ■
Occurrences: 1
Positions:
15432

■ ends ■
Occurrences: 1
Positions:
12640

■ engage ■
Occurrences: 1
Positions:
12649

■ engaged ■
Occurrences: 1
Positions:
6160

■ engendered ■
Occurrences: 1
Positions:
10592

■ engineer ■
Occurrences: 1
Positions:
8571

■ engineering ■
Occurrences: 1
Positions:
174

■ enhance ■
Occurrences: 1
Positions:
7660

■ enhanced ■
Occurrences: 1
Positions:
12251

■ enigmatic ■
Occurrences: 1
Positions:
2752

■ enjoyed ■
Occurrences: 1
Positions:
2230

■ enjoyment ■
Occurrences: 1
Positions:
9840

■ enough ■
Occurrences: 1
Positions:
14728

■ enrichments ■
Occurrences: 1
Positions:
8717

■ ensues ■
Occurrences: 1
Positions:
8229

■ ensure ■
Occurrences: 1
Positions:
14801

■ entertains ■
Occurrences: 1
Positions:
301

■ enthusiastic ■
Occurrences: 1
Positions:
3191

■ entities ■
Occurrences: 1
Positions:
3681

■ entwines ■
Occurrences: 1
Positions:
10475

■ envelope ■
Occurrences: 1
Positions:
6618

■ environmental ■
Occurrences: 1
Positions:
1915

■ ephemera ■
Occurrences: 1
Positions:
7825

■ ephemeral ■
Occurrences: 1
Positions:
5355

■ episode ■
Occurrences: 1
Positions:
7419

■ epistemologically ■
Occurrences: 1
Positions:
4480

■ epistemologies ■
Occurrences: 1
Positions:
6149

■ epistemology ■
Occurrences: 1
Positions:
15582

■ equals ■
Occurrences: 1
Positions:
8099

■ equivalence ■
Occurrences: 1
Positions:
8819

■ erasing ■
Occurrences: 1
Positions:
8333

■ ernst ■
Occurrences: 1
Positions:
5781

■ eros ■
Occurrences: 1
Positions:
1258

■ establishes ■
Occurrences: 1
Positions:
9673

■ ethical ■
Occurrences: 1
Positions:
5117

■ ethnically ■
Occurrences: 1
Positions:
2259

■ ethnicity ■
Occurrences: 1
Positions:
6174

■ ethos ■
Occurrences: 1
Positions:
3961

■ eurocentric ■
Occurrences: 1
Positions:
9818

■ european ■
Occurrences: 1
Positions:
10718

■ eventual ■
Occurrences: 1
Positions:
5589

■ ever ■
Occurrences: 1
Positions:
10472

■ evil ■
Occurrences: 1
Positions:
4281

■ evoking ■
Occurrences: 1
Positions:
6151

■ evol ■
Occurrences: 1
Positions:
1551

■ evolve ■
Occurrences: 1
Positions:
3929

■ exact ■
Occurrences: 1
Positions:
8223

■ exactitude ■
Occurrences: 1
Positions:
8163

■ exaggerate ■
Occurrences: 1
Positions:
4293

■ examine ■
Occurrences: 1
Positions:
2478

■ examines ■
Occurrences: 1
Positions:
3406

■ examining ■
Occurrences: 1
Positions:
7500

■ excellent ■
Occurrences: 1
Positions:
15458

■ exception ■
Occurrences: 1
Positions:
9260

■ excerpt ■
Occurrences: 1
Positions:
1723

■ excess ■
Occurrences: 1
Positions:
13377

■ excesses ■
Occurrences: 1
Positions:
11718

■ excessive ■
Occurrences: 1
Positions:
12475

■ exclaim ■
Occurrences: 1
Positions:
1750

■ exclusive ■
Occurrences: 1
Positions:
2936

■ exclusively ■
Occurrences: 1
Positions:
11382

■ exemplary ■
Occurrences: 1
Positions:
1583

■ exercise ■
Occurrences: 1
Positions:
8468

■ exhausted ■
Occurrences: 1
Positions:
4404

■ exhaustion ■
Occurrences: 1
Positions:
4497

■ exist ■
Occurrences: 1
Positions:
15035

■ exists ■
Occurrences: 1
Positions:
5158

■ exits ■
Occurrences: 1
Positions:
666

■ expanded ■
Occurrences: 1
Positions:
2641

■ expectations ■
Occurrences: 1
Positions:
12001

■ expected ■
Occurrences: 1
Positions:
14032

■ expense ■
Occurrences: 1
Positions:
14807

■ experienced ■
Occurrences: 1
Positions:
8189

■ experimentalism ■
Occurrences: 1
Positions:
688

■ experimentalist ■
Occurrences: 1
Positions:
3358

■ experimenting ■
Occurrences: 1
Positions:
11764

■ explains ■
Occurrences: 1
Positions:
5817

■ explanation ■
Occurrences: 1
Positions:
8724

■ explanations ■
Occurrences: 1
Positions:
2727

■ exploded ■
Occurrences: 1
Positions:
1498

■ exploiting ■
Occurrences: 1
Positions:
12446

■ explore ■
Occurrences: 1
Positions:
6842

■ extending ■
Occurrences: 1
Positions:
13073

■ extent ■
Occurrences: 1
Positions:
5860

■ extra ■
Occurrences: 1
Positions:
5950

■ extremely ■
Occurrences: 1
Positions:
11277

■ extremis ■
Occurrences: 1
Positions:
3291

■ eye ■
Occurrences: 1
Positions:
12225

■ eyeball ■
Occurrences: 1
Positions:
1743

■ fabric ■
Occurrences: 1
Positions:
11855

■ facebook ■
Occurrences: 1
Positions:
1004

■ facing ■
Occurrences: 1
Positions:
10027

■ faecal ■
Occurrences: 1
Positions:
1509

■ failure ■
Occurrences: 1
Positions:
7957

■ fair ■
Occurrences: 1
Positions:
6997

■ faith ■
Occurrences: 1
Positions:
5210

■ fall ■
Occurrences: 1
Positions:
9161

■ falling ■
Occurrences: 1
Positions:
1943

■ fame ■
Occurrences: 1
Positions:
5321

■ fan ■
Occurrences: 1
Positions:
2224

■ fans ■
Occurrences: 1
Positions:
12261

■ fascinating ■
Occurrences: 1
Positions:
6484

■ fashion ■
Occurrences: 1
Positions:
13039

■ fast ■
Occurrences: 1
Positions:
14492

■ feeling ■
Occurrences: 1
Positions:
1683

■ feelings ■
Occurrences: 1
Positions:
3079

■ feels ■
Occurrences: 1
Positions:
783

■ feral ■
Occurrences: 1
Positions:
1500

■ fetishes ■
Occurrences: 1
Positions:
5652

■ fever ■
Occurrences: 1
Positions:
15534

■ few ■
Occurrences: 1
Positions:
6985

■ fi ■
Occurrences: 1
Positions:
12991

■ fibre ■
Occurrences: 1
Positions:
1467

■ fictiton ■
Occurrences: 1
Positions:
5709

■ fifteen ■
Occurrences: 1
Positions:
2649

■ filters ■
Occurrences: 1
Positions:
6809

■ final ■
Occurrences: 1
Positions:
1311

■ finds ■
Occurrences: 1
Positions:
3279

■ finesse ■
Occurrences: 1
Positions:
12288

■ finest ■
Occurrences: 1
Positions:
11755

■ fish ■
Occurrences: 1
Positions:
13786

■ fission ■
Occurrences: 1
Positions:
5192

■ five ■
Occurrences: 1
Positions:
2623

■ fixations ■
Occurrences: 1
Positions:
9363

■ flames ■
Occurrences: 1
Positions:
1463

■ flattening ■
Occurrences: 1
Positions:
13892

■ flawed ■
Occurrences: 1
Positions:
12269

■ fleshy ■
Occurrences: 1
Positions:
1470

■ flight ■
Occurrences: 1
Positions:
631

■ floats ■
Occurrences: 1
Positions:
4911

■ flows ■
Occurrences: 1
Positions:
1894

■ focus ■
Occurrences: 1
Positions:
7185

■ focused ■
Occurrences: 1
Positions:
5535

■ follows ■
Occurrences: 1
Positions:
14413

■ forced ■
Occurrences: 1
Positions:
11967

■ forceful ■
Occurrences: 1
Positions:
15472

■ foreboding ■
Occurrences: 1
Positions:
4441

■ foreground ■
Occurrences: 1
Positions:
4055

■ foresee ■
Occurrences: 1
Positions:
9912

■ forget ■
Occurrences: 1
Positions:
13719

■ forgetting ■
Occurrences: 1
Positions:
13537

■ formalistically ■
Occurrences: 1
Positions:
10689

■ formalized ■
Occurrences: 1
Positions:
8670

■ formation ■
Occurrences: 1
Positions:
12681

■ formative ■
Occurrences: 1
Positions:
6748

■ formula ■
Occurrences: 1
Positions:
9199

■ formulae ■
Occurrences: 1
Positions:
9183

■ formulations ■
Occurrences: 1
Positions:
3856

■ foundationalist ■
Occurrences: 1
Positions:
5096

■ fragmentary ■
Occurrences: 1
Positions:
11264

■ fragmented ■
Occurrences: 1
Positions:
3120

■ franz ■
Occurrences: 1
Positions:
2382

■ freedom ■
Occurrences: 1
Positions:
12689

■ frequencies ■
Occurrences: 1
Positions:
9026

■ frequency ■
Occurrences: 1
Positions:
9021

■ frustrating ■
Occurrences: 1
Positions:
6118

■ full ■
Occurrences: 1
Positions:
9131

■ fully ■
Occurrences: 1
Positions:
2451

■ func ■
Occurrences: 1
Positions:
2670

■ functionalist ■
Occurrences: 1
Positions:
904

■ giving ■
Occurrences: 1
Positions:
2748

■ glissandi ■
Occurrences: 1
Positions:
9027

■ glitched ■
Occurrences: 1
Positions:
498

■ global ■
Occurrences: 1
Positions:
10501

■ go ■
Occurrences: 1
Positions:
2533

■ goallessness ■
Occurrences: 1
Positions:
8303

■ god ■
Occurrences: 1
Positions:
3990

■ godhead ■
Occurrences: 1
Positions:
1537

■ good ■
Occurrences: 1
Positions:
156

■ goods ■
Occurrences: 1
Positions:
173

■ got ■
Occurrences: 1
Positions:
9883

■ gram ■
Occurrences: 1
Positions:
1713

■ grand ■
Occurrences: 1
Positions:
4358

■ graph ■
Occurrences: 1
Positions:
8634

■ graphic ■
Occurrences: 1
Positions:
4395

■ greatest ■
Occurrences: 1
Positions:
3355

■ grillet ■
Occurrences: 1
Positions:
2387

■ ground ■
Occurrences: 1
Positions:
12362

■ groundbreaking ■
Occurrences: 1
Positions:
3850

■ groundwork ■
Occurrences: 1
Positions:
6949

■ groupings ■
Occurrences: 1
Positions:
9023

■ growing ■
Occurrences: 1
Positions:
13535

■ guarding ■
Occurrences: 1
Positions:
3630

■ gustave ■
Occurrences: 1
Positions:
13828

■ gx ■
Occurrences: 1
Positions:
12352

■ hack_ ■
Occurrences: 1
Positions:
1725

■ hallucinogenic ■
Occurrences: 1
Positions:
1234

■ halts ■
Occurrences: 1
Positions:
575

■ handle ■
Occurrences: 1
Positions:
12600

■ handling ■
Occurrences: 1
Positions:
3812

■ happen ■
Occurrences: 1
Positions:
8429

■ happened ■
Occurrences: 1
Positions:
8252

■ harley ■
Occurrences: 1
Positions:
8904

■ harmony ■
Occurrences: 1
Positions:
14766

■ harsh ■
Occurrences: 1
Positions:
15299

■ hated ■
Occurrences: 1
Positions:
4799

■ hayles ■
Occurrences: 1
Positions:
6361

■ hazier ■
Occurrences: 1
Positions:
7517

■ heard ■
Occurrences: 1
Positions:
7740

■ heart ■
Occurrences: 1
Positions:
1741

■ helix ■
Occurrences: 1
Positions:
1566

■ helpful ■
Occurrences: 1
Positions:
1103

■ herein ■
Occurrences: 1
Positions:
5464

■ heritage ■
Occurrences: 1
Positions:
10709

■ heroic ■
Occurrences: 1
Positions:
6935

■ hesitancy ■
Occurrences: 1
Positions:
792

■ heterarchical ■
Occurrences: 1
Positions:
8471

■ heterodox ■
Occurrences: 1
Positions:
2404

■ heterogeneous ■
Occurrences: 1
Positions:
15021

■ hierarchy ■
Occurrences: 1
Positions:
13898

■ hieroglyphs ■
Occurrences: 1
Positions:
11106

■ highlights ■
Occurrences: 1
Positions:
10617

■ highly ■
Occurrences: 1
Positions:
1141

■ highway ■
Occurrences: 1
Positions:
141

■ him ■
Occurrences: 1
Positions:
2051

■ himself ■
Occurrences: 1
Positions:
4966

■ historical ■
Occurrences: 1
Positions:
5700

■ historicity ■
Occurrences: 1
Positions:
10663

■ hitherto ■
Occurrences: 1
Positions:
6845

■ hive ■
Occurrences: 1
Positions:
14457

■ hoax ■
Occurrences: 1
Positions:
5864

■ holds ■
Occurrences: 1
Positions:
4419

■ homeostatic ■
Occurrences: 1
Positions:
13580

■ homeostatically ■
Occurrences: 1
Positions:
13564

■ homme ■
Occurrences: 1
Positions:
7208

■ honey ■
Occurrences: 1
Positions:
14470

■ hopeless ■
Occurrences: 1
Positions:
15165

■ horror ■
Occurrences: 1
Positions:
11389

■ host ■
Occurrences: 1
Positions:
12254

■ hourly ■
Occurrences: 1
Positions:
373

■ house ■
Occurrences: 1
Positions:
1519

■ howling ■
Occurrences: 1
Positions:
1296

■ humanism ■
Occurrences: 1
Positions:
3762

■ humanist ■
Occurrences: 1
Positions:
3783

■ humming ■
Occurrences: 1
Positions:
13659

■ hundred ■
Occurrences: 1
Positions:
1426

■ hundreds ■
Occurrences: 1
Positions:
6667

■ hunts ■
Occurrences: 1
Positions:
1319

■ husband ■
Occurrences: 1
Positions:
7390

■ hybridism ■
Occurrences: 1
Positions:
2293

■ hydro ■
Occurrences: 1
Positions:
1457

■ hydromachine ■
Occurrences: 1
Positions:
10904

■ hyperchaos ■
Occurrences: 1
Positions:
10433

■ hypercomplex ■
Occurrences: 1
Positions:
6567

■ hypercomplexity ■
Occurrences: 1
Positions:
14475

■ hyperconsumerism ■
Occurrences: 1
Positions:
13450

■ hyperparticipation ■
Occurrences: 1
Positions:
13459

■ ichiro ■
Occurrences: 1
Positions:
2212

■ icon ■
Occurrences: 1
Positions:
10868

■ identical ■
Occurrences: 1
Positions:
2828

■ identifications ■
Occurrences: 1
Positions:
9227

■ identified ■
Occurrences: 1
Positions:
79

■ ideological ■
Occurrences: 1
Positions:
2799

■ ideologically ■
Occurrences: 1
Positions:
3789

■ ideologies ■
Occurrences: 1
Positions:
3227

■ ideology ■
Occurrences: 1
Positions:
5540

■ idioms ■
Occurrences: 1
Positions:
3121

■ idoru ■
Occurrences: 1
Positions:
2234

■ illiterate ■
Occurrences: 1
Positions:
13434

■ illogical ■
Occurrences: 1
Positions:
12753

■ illustration ■
Occurrences: 1
Positions:
4320

■ imaginative ■
Occurrences: 1
Positions:
280

■ imagining ■
Occurrences: 1
Positions:
6913

■ imitate ■
Occurrences: 1
Positions:
7349

■ immanence ■
Occurrences: 1
Positions:
5282

■ immense ■
Occurrences: 1
Positions:
5353

■ immobility ■
Occurrences: 1
Positions:
659

■ immune ■
Occurrences: 1
Positions:
452

■ impasse ■
Occurrences: 1
Positions:
10030

■ imperative ■
Occurrences: 1
Positions:
15468

■ implication ■
Occurrences: 1
Positions:
8820

■ implications ■
Occurrences: 1
Positions:
6439

■ implicitly ■
Occurrences: 1
Positions:
12983

■ importance ■
Occurrences: 1
Positions:
3185

■ improve ■
Occurrences: 1
Positions:
4039

■ inappropriateness ■
Occurrences: 1
Positions:
10953

■ inaugurated ■
Occurrences: 1
Positions:
3234

■ incalculable ■
Occurrences: 1
Positions:
4375

■ incapable ■
Occurrences: 1
Positions:
995

■ included ■
Occurrences: 1
Positions:
9252

■ including ■
Occurrences: 1
Positions:
13531

■ incorporated ■
Occurrences: 1
Positions:
11834

■ incorporates ■
Occurrences: 1
Positions:
4926

■ increasingly ■
Occurrences: 1
Positions:
348

■ indefinite ■
Occurrences: 1
Positions:
1778

■ independent ■
Occurrences: 1
Positions:
13664

■ indeterminism ■
Occurrences: 1
Positions:
8797

■ indicate ■
Occurrences: 1
Positions:
10087

■ industrialized ■
Occurrences: 1
Positions:
205

■ inextricable ■
Occurrences: 1
Positions:
10303

■ infect ■
Occurrences: 1
Positions:
1452

■ infection ■
Occurrences: 1
Positions:
2135

■ infections ■
Occurrences: 1
Positions:
1826

■ infinitely ■
Occurrences: 1
Positions:
6910

■ infinity ■
Occurrences: 1
Positions:
399

■ inflection ■
Occurrences: 1
Positions:
11032

■ inflict ■
Occurrences: 1
Positions:
11315

■ influential ■
Occurrences: 1
Positions:
5667

■ informatics ■
Occurrences: 1
Positions:
9276

■ informationally ■
Occurrences: 1
Positions:
822

■ infosphere ■
Occurrences: 1
Positions:
14486

■ infuses ■
Occurrences: 1
Positions:
1570

■ ing ■
Occurrences: 1
Positions:
2658

■ inhabits ■
Occurrences: 1
Positions:
547

■ inherent ■
Occurrences: 1
Positions:
10223

■ inherently ■
Occurrences: 1
Positions:
2932

■ inheritor ■
Occurrences: 1
Positions:
9112

■ initially ■
Occurrences: 1
Positions:
8947

■ injustice ■
Occurrences: 1
Positions:
3105

■ inoculated ■
Occurrences: 1
Positions:
1480

■ inoculation ■
Occurrences: 1
Positions:
10902

■ inscrutable ■
Occurrences: 1
Positions:
13725

■ insects ■
Occurrences: 1
Positions:
13782

■ instantaneous ■
Occurrences: 1
Positions:
12951

■ instantly ■
Occurrences: 1
Positions:
1220

■ instill ■
Occurrences: 1
Positions:
10511

■ instrument ■
Occurrences: 1
Positions:
8598

■ insurgency ■
Occurrences: 1
Positions:
1098

■ intellect ■
Occurrences: 1
Positions:
11564

■ intellectual ■
Occurrences: 1
Positions:
4524

■ intellectuals ■
Occurrences: 1
Positions:
4740

■ intensifies ■
Occurrences: 1
Positions:
15413

■ intention ■
Occurrences: 1
Positions:
1762

■ intentionality ■
Occurrences: 1
Positions:
13953

■ interaction ■
Occurrences: 1
Positions:
4265

■ interactive ■
Occurrences: 1
Positions:
257

■ interconnection ■
Occurrences: 1
Positions:
14097

■ interdependency ■
Occurrences: 1
Positions:
14053

■ interest ■
Occurrences: 1
Positions:
7782

■ interesting ■
Occurrences: 1
Positions:
6125

■ interests ■
Occurrences: 1
Positions:
2982

■ interference ■
Occurrences: 1
Positions:
14186

■ interlocking ■
Occurrences: 1
Positions:
12349

■ international ■
Occurrences: 1
Positions:
2375

■ internationalism ■
Occurrences: 1
Positions:
2495

■ internationally ■
Occurrences: 1
Positions:
2460

■ internment ■
Occurrences: 1
Positions:
73

■ interoperation ■
Occurrences: 1
Positions:
14099

■ interpenetrates ■
Occurrences: 1
Positions:
10470

■ interpersonal ■
Occurrences: 1
Positions:
12909

■ interpreted ■
Occurrences: 1
Positions:
9274

■ interrogating ■
Occurrences: 1
Positions:
2145

■ interrogation ■
Occurrences: 1
Positions:
6261

■ intersection ■
Occurrences: 1
Positions:
14006

■ interspersed ■
Occurrences: 1
Positions:
12186

■ interval ■
Occurrences: 1
Positions:
6663

■ intervening ■
Occurrences: 1
Positions:
6852

■ interview ■
Occurrences: 1
Positions:
5887

■ intimately ■
Occurrences: 1
Positions:
12421

■ intimating ■
Occurrences: 1
Positions:
12614

■ intrinsically ■
Occurrences: 1
Positions:
4280

■ introduce ■
Occurrences: 1
Positions:
5827

■ introduces ■
Occurrences: 1
Positions:
12842

■ invades ■
Occurrences: 1
Positions:
1546

■ invasive ■
Occurrences: 1
Positions:
4899

■ inventive ■
Occurrences: 1
Positions:
3889

■ inventiveness ■
Occurrences: 1
Positions:
4570

■ inventor ■
Occurrences: 1
Positions:
5550

■ investigation ■
Occurrences: 1
Positions:
9640

■ invisible ■
Occurrences: 1
Positions:
955

■ invocation ■
Occurrences: 1
Positions:
2268

■ involve ■
Occurrences: 1
Positions:
11524

■ involved ■
Occurrences: 1
Positions:
14874

■ inward ■
Occurrences: 1
Positions:
667

■ ipad ■
Occurrences: 1
Positions:
1021

■ iron ■
Occurrences: 1
Positions:
3346

■ ironic ■
Occurrences: 1
Positions:
5470

■ irony ■
Occurrences: 1
Positions:
5503

■ irrationality ■
Occurrences: 1
Positions:
3109

■ irregular ■
Occurrences: 1
Positions:
8664

■ irrelevant ■
Occurrences: 1
Positions:
14543

■ irreversible ■
Occurrences: 1
Positions:
11416

■ isolation ■
Occurrences: 1
Positions:
13671

■ issey ■
Occurrences: 1
Positions:
12292

■ iteration ■
Occurrences: 1
Positions:
4460

■ j ■
Occurrences: 1
Positions:
68

■ jack ■
Occurrences: 1
Positions:
1254

■ jacket ■
Occurrences: 1
Positions:
11824

■ jamaican ■
Occurrences: 1
Positions:
6199

■ japanoids ■
Occurrences: 1
Positions:
2442

■ japonism ■
Occurrences: 1
Positions:
12271

■ jean ■
Occurrences: 1
Positions:
11361

■ jetty ■
Occurrences: 1
Positions:
13661

■ joints ■
Occurrences: 1
Positions:
1681

■ josef ■
Occurrences: 1
Positions:
7298

■ journey ■
Occurrences: 1
Positions:
794

■ judgments ■
Occurrences: 1
Positions:
8405

■ jupitter ■
Occurrences: 1
Positions:
12353

■ kadowaki ■
Occurrences: 1
Positions:
2636

■ kafka ■
Occurrences: 1
Positions:
2383

■ kamenosuke ■
Occurrences: 1
Positions:
2634

■ karaoke ■
Occurrences: 1
Positions:
2226

■ karlheinz ■
Occurrences: 1
Positions:
7283

■ kathy ■
Occurrences: 1
Positions:
7386

■ katsuhiro ■
Occurrences: 1
Positions:
4331

■ keene ■
Occurrences: 1
Positions:
2304

■ kinetics ■
Occurrences: 1
Positions:
200

■ kk ■
Occurrences: 1
Positions:
1525

■ knot ■
Occurrences: 1
Positions:
587

■ knots ■
Occurrences: 1
Positions:
10471

■ knotted ■
Occurrences: 1
Positions:
10189

■ know ■
Occurrences: 1
Positions:
9477

■ kobo ■
Occurrences: 1
Positions:
3359

■ koboyashi ■
Occurrences: 1
Positions:
2216

■ label ■
Occurrences: 1
Positions:
4801

■ laboratory ■
Occurrences: 1
Positions:
7950

■ labs ■
Occurrences: 1
Positions:
9058

■ lack ■
Occurrences: 1
Positions:
11806

■ lacking ■
Occurrences: 1
Positions:
3901

■ lacks ■
Occurrences: 1
Positions:
14745

■ lament ■
Occurrences: 1
Positions:
9814

■ landmarks ■
Occurrences: 1
Positions:
9366

■ languages ■
Occurrences: 1
Positions:
1085

■ larger ■
Occurrences: 1
Positions:
6582

■ larsen ■
Occurrences: 1
Positions:
12354

■ lation ■
Occurrences: 1
Positions:
3150

■ laws ■
Occurrences: 1
Positions:
8804

■ layers ■
Occurrences: 1
Positions:
7291

■ leading ■
Occurrences: 1
Positions:
14935

■ learned ■
Occurrences: 1
Positions:
4249

■ learning ■
Occurrences: 1
Positions:
13536

■ leave ■
Occurrences: 1
Positions:
14034

■ leaves ■
Occurrences: 1
Positions:
4402

■ less ■
Occurrences: 1
Positions:
8795

■ leveled ■
Occurrences: 1
Positions:
8377

■ liberation ■
Occurrences: 1
Positions:
7024

■ lies ■
Occurrences: 1
Positions:
5465

■ likened ■
Occurrences: 1
Positions:
6352

■ limb ■
Occurrences: 1
Positions:
14231

■ limit ■
Occurrences: 1
Positions:
2990

■ limitations ■
Occurrences: 1
Positions:
2358

■ limited ■
Occurrences: 1
Positions:
9055

■ limitless ■
Occurrences: 1
Positions:
15539

■ limits ■
Occurrences: 1
Positions:
1080

■ linked ■
Occurrences: 1
Positions:
12422

■ list ■
Occurrences: 1
Positions:
5385

■ listener ■
Occurrences: 1
Positions:
9208

■ listeners ■
Occurrences: 1
Positions:
6907

■ literate ■
Occurrences: 1
Positions:
701

■ litigious ■
Occurrences: 1
Positions:
2087

■ live ■
Occurrences: 1
Positions:
4428

■ lives ■
Occurrences: 1
Positions:
12845

■ lobe ■
Occurrences: 1
Positions:
1501

■ locale ■
Occurrences: 1
Positions:
5267

■ location ■
Occurrences: 1
Positions:
6708

■ logistics ■
Occurrences: 1
Positions:
12425

■ longer ■
Occurrences: 1
Positions:
14708

■ look ■
Occurrences: 1
Positions:
1849

■ looked ■
Occurrences: 1
Positions:
13668

■ looking ■
Occurrences: 1
Positions:
2850

■ looping ■
Occurrences: 1
Positions:
10361

■ lord ■
Occurrences: 1
Positions:
7303

■ lotringer ■
Occurrences: 1
Positions:
12559

■ loud ■
Occurrences: 1
Positions:
6925

■ loudly ■
Occurrences: 1
Positions:
3212

■ luciano ■
Occurrences: 1
Positions:
7393

■ lucid ■
Occurrences: 1
Positions:
1047

■ lunch ■
Occurrences: 1
Positions:
11797

■ machinic ■
Occurrences: 1
Positions:
9915

■ mad ■
Occurrences: 1
Positions:
9877

■ maestro ■
Occurrences: 1
Positions:
8372

■ magajin ■
Occurrences: 1
Positions:
2516

■ magazines ■
Occurrences: 1
Positions:
11836

■ main ■
Occurrences: 1
Positions:
7091

■ mainframe ■
Occurrences: 1
Positions:
9061

■ maltreatment ■
Occurrences: 1
Positions:
11528

■ mania ■
Occurrences: 1
Positions:
1458

■ manipulate ■
Occurrences: 1
Positions:
8023

■ manipulated ■
Occurrences: 1
Positions:
7222

■ manipulation ■
Occurrences: 1
Positions:
7511

■ manually ■
Occurrences: 1
Positions:
8956

■ margaret ■
Occurrences: 1
Positions:
4772

■ marinetti ■
Occurrences: 1
Positions:
12685

■ marker ■
Occurrences: 1
Positions:
203

■ market ■
Occurrences: 1
Positions:
10657

■ marks ■
Occurrences: 1
Positions:
12501

■ marshall ■
Occurrences: 1
Positions:
5890

■ masamu ■
Occurrences: 1
Positions:
2632

■ mashing ■
Occurrences: 1
Positions:
11884

■ massive ■
Occurrences: 1
Positions:
9060

■ master ■
Occurrences: 1
Positions:
15230

■ materiality ■
Occurrences: 1
Positions:
6821

■ math ■
Occurrences: 1
Positions:
8674

■ mathematic ■
Occurrences: 1
Positions:
9106

■ mathematically ■
Occurrences: 1
Positions:
9323

■ matrix ■
Occurrences: 1
Positions:
13082

■ maximize ■
Occurrences: 1
Positions:
14821

■ mayhem ■
Occurrences: 1
Positions:
1165

■ meaningfully ■
Occurrences: 1
Positions:
4133

■ meant ■
Occurrences: 1
Positions:
37

■ measured ■
Occurrences: 1
Positions:
10429

■ measures ■
Occurrences: 1
Positions:
10370

■ mechanical ■
Occurrences: 1
Positions:
5573

■ mechanism ■
Occurrences: 1
Positions:
14161

■ medial ■
Occurrences: 1
Positions:
13101

■ mediated ■
Occurrences: 1
Positions:
11184

■ medical ■
Occurrences: 1
Positions:
743

■ meets ■
Occurrences: 1
Positions:
5845

■ melancholy ■
Occurrences: 1
Positions:
3110

■ melting ■
Occurrences: 1
Positions:
14700

■ men ■
Occurrences: 1
Positions:
11547

■ mercy ■
Occurrences: 1
Positions:
13353

■ mere ■
Occurrences: 1
Positions:
7896

■ merge ■
Occurrences: 1
Positions:
4602

■ merged ■
Occurrences: 1
Positions:
9485

■ merges ■
Occurrences: 1
Positions:
15417

■ messages ■
Occurrences: 1
Positions:
9954

■ met ■
Occurrences: 1
Positions:
8481

■ metamusical ■
Occurrences: 1
Positions:
10040

■ metaphor ■
Occurrences: 1
Positions:
4596

■ metaphorical ■
Occurrences: 1
Positions:
3274

■ mezzo ■
Occurrences: 1
Positions:
7384

■ mid ■
Occurrences: 1
Positions:
3390

■ minds ■
Occurrences: 1
Positions:
15544

■ mindscapes ■
Occurrences: 1
Positions:
583

■ minuscule ■
Occurrences: 1
Positions:
8873

■ mirrorshades ■
Occurrences: 1
Positions:
2489

■ misleading ■
Occurrences: 1
Positions:
14622

■ miss ■
Occurrences: 1
Positions:
8215

■ mistake ■
Occurrences: 1
Positions:
8431

■ misunderstood ■
Occurrences: 1
Positions:
4794

■ misuse ■
Occurrences: 1
Positions:
5996

■ mix ■
Occurrences: 1
Positions:
4035

■ miyake ■
Occurrences: 1
Positions:
12293

■ mobile ■
Occurrences: 1
Positions:
1601

■ mobility ■
Occurrences: 1
Positions:
197

■ mobilizes ■
Occurrences: 1
Positions:
10638

■ modeled ■
Occurrences: 1
Positions:
9322

■ modernization ■
Occurrences: 1
Positions:
3229

■ modulators ■
Occurrences: 1
Positions:
6813

■ molten ■
Occurrences: 1
Positions:
1284

■ moral ■
Occurrences: 1
Positions:
3631

■ motions ■
Occurrences: 1
Positions:
14178

■ motorways ■
Occurrences: 1
Positions:
634

■ mould ■
Occurrences: 1
Positions:
11819

■ mozart ■
Occurrences: 1
Positions:
7523

■ msec ■
Occurrences: 1
Positions:
6641

■ multi ■
Occurrences: 1
Positions:
8376

■ multichannel ■
Occurrences: 1
Positions:
6696

■ multiplicities ■
Occurrences: 1
Positions:
329

■ multitudes ■
Occurrences: 1
Positions:
14872

■ muscle ■
Occurrences: 1
Positions:
1469

■ musicians ■
Occurrences: 1
Positions:
6288

■ mutates ■
Occurrences: 1
Positions:
4476

■ mutilate ■
Occurrences: 1
Positions:
14163

■ mystical ■
Occurrences: 1
Positions:
11709

■ mystification ■
Occurrences: 1
Positions:
9469

■ mystifying ■
Occurrences: 1
Positions:
798

■ myth ■
Occurrences: 1
Positions:
8399

■ myths ■
Occurrences: 1
Positions:
11544

■ naked ■
Occurrences: 1
Positions:
11796

■ name ■
Occurrences: 1
Positions:
2713

■ nationalities ■
Occurrences: 1
Positions:
6143

■ native ■
Occurrences: 1
Positions:
4142

■ naturalist ■
Occurrences: 1
Positions:
4778

■ naturalizing ■
Occurrences: 1
Positions:
2196

■ ndroid ■
Occurrences: 1
Positions:
1577

■ near ■
Occurrences: 1
Positions:
4077

■ nearly ■
Occurrences: 1
Positions:
9985

■ nebula ■
Occurrences: 1
Positions:
1508

■ necessitated ■
Occurrences: 1
Positions:
8742

■ neil ■
Occurrences: 1
Positions:
4876

■ neither ■
Occurrences: 1
Positions:
6764

■ neoliberalism ■
Occurrences: 1
Positions:
15098

■ nerves ■
Occurrences: 1
Positions:
11557

■ networker ■
Occurrences: 1
Positions:
14337

■ networking ■
Occurrences: 1
Positions:
5922

■ networks ■
Occurrences: 1
Positions:
14998

■ nevertheless ■
Occurrences: 1
Positions:
3857

■ newspaper ■
Occurrences: 1
Positions:
11838

■ ngel ■
Occurrences: 1
Positions:
1602

■ night ■
Occurrences: 1
Positions:
8259

■ nineteen ■
Occurrences: 1
Positions:
2610

■ nodes ■
Occurrences: 1
Positions:
12049

■ noises ■
Occurrences: 1
Positions:
6876

■ nonalighment ■
Occurrences: 1
Positions:
14561

■ nonconformist ■
Occurrences: 1
Positions:
2413

■ nonsense ■
Occurrences: 1
Positions:
15436

■ nonsensical ■
Occurrences: 1
Positions:
1174

■ norbert ■
Occurrences: 1
Positions:
8940

■ normalized ■
Occurrences: 1
Positions:
953

■ north ■
Occurrences: 1
Positions:
10720

■ nostalgic ■
Occurrences: 1
Positions:
224

■ notably ■
Occurrences: 1
Positions:
3465

■ notated ■
Occurrences: 1
Positions:
8169

■ noticeable ■
Occurrences: 1
Positions:
1323

■ notion ■
Occurrences: 1
Positions:
3742

■ novelistic ■
Occurrences: 1
Positions:
10862

■ nowhere ■
Occurrences: 1
Positions:
12610

■ nuanced ■
Occurrences: 1
Positions:
3852

■ nude ■
Occurrences: 1
Positions:
10892

■ objectify ■
Occurrences: 1
Positions:
5213

■ objectives ■
Occurrences: 1
Positions:
11501

■ obligatory ■
Occurrences: 1
Positions:
9288

■ occult ■
Occurrences: 1
Positions:
9953

■ occurs ■
Occurrences: 1
Positions:
12628

■ off ■
Occurrences: 1
Positions:
10482

■ offered ■
Occurrences: 1
Positions:
11961

■ ogata ■
Occurrences: 1
Positions:
2633

■ okama ■
Occurrences: 1
Positions:
1466

■ olivier ■
Occurrences: 1
Positions:
8585

■ ommagio ■
Occurrences: 1
Positions:
7397

■ oneiric ■
Occurrences: 1
Positions:
10275

■ ones ■
Occurrences: 1
Positions:
9903

■ online ■
Occurrences: 1
Positions:
1605

■ onomatopoeic ■
Occurrences: 1
Positions:
11102

■ onto ■
Occurrences: 1
Positions:
7465

■ ontologic ■
Occurrences: 1
Positions:
4710

■ ontological ■
Occurrences: 1
Positions:
1373

■ opaque ■
Occurrences: 1
Positions:
6095

■ operation ■
Occurrences: 1
Positions:
14546

■ operational ■
Occurrences: 1
Positions:
8803

■ opposed ■
Occurrences: 1
Positions:
10268

■ opposition ■
Occurrences: 1
Positions:
1386

■ oppositional ■
Occurrences: 1
Positions:
12015

■ optimization ■
Occurrences: 1
Positions:
14824

■ optimized ■
Occurrences: 1
Positions:
369

■ orchestra ■
Occurrences: 1
Positions:
8840

■ order ■
Occurrences: 1
Positions:
15442

■ ordered ■
Occurrences: 1
Positions:
10490

■ orderly ■
Occurrences: 1
Positions:
7975

■ organ ■
Occurrences: 1
Positions:
11123

■ organic ■
Occurrences: 1
Positions:
14078

■ organise ■
Occurrences: 1
Positions:
11096

■ organized ■
Occurrences: 1
Positions:
15084

■ organizing ■
Occurrences: 1
Positions:
7083

■ origin ■
Occurrences: 1
Positions:
2058

■ original ■
Occurrences: 1
Positions:
2620

■ originally ■
Occurrences: 1
Positions:
6196

■ originate ■
Occurrences: 1
Positions:
3567

■ originated ■
Occurrences: 1
Positions:
6712

■ orthodox ■
Occurrences: 1
Positions:
4789

■ oscilloscopes ■
Occurrences: 1
Positions:
6814

■ otomo ■
Occurrences: 1
Positions:
4332

■ outcome ■
Occurrences: 1
Positions:
14927

■ overlap ■
Occurrences: 1
Positions:
15001

■ overlapping ■
Occurrences: 1
Positions:
2981

■ overpopulation ■
Occurrences: 1
Positions:
10506

■ overpower ■
Occurrences: 1
Positions:
4557

■ owes ■
Occurrences: 1
Positions:
11091

■ peter ■
Occurrences: 1
Positions:
5377

■ phenomenal ■
Occurrences: 1
Positions:
5274

■ phonetic ■
Occurrences: 1
Positions:
7327

■ phonetics ■
Occurrences: 1
Positions:
7452

■ physically ■
Occurrences: 1
Positions:
4477

■ piano ■
Occurrences: 1
Positions:
6831

■ picture ■
Occurrences: 1
Positions:
121

■ pieces ■
Occurrences: 1
Positions:
7311

■ piercing ■
Occurrences: 1
Positions:
11153

■ piero ■
Occurrences: 1
Positions:
7883

■ pill ■
Occurrences: 1
Positions:
1704

■ placed ■
Occurrences: 1
Positions:
8070

■ plant ■
Occurrences: 1
Positions:
14462

■ players ■
Occurrences: 1
Positions:
8013

■ plays ■
Occurrences: 1
Positions:
2324

■ pleased ■
Occurrences: 1
Positions:
9083

■ plots ■
Occurrences: 1
Positions:
4956

■ poets ■
Occurrences: 1
Positions:
6519

■ poiesis ■
Occurrences: 1
Positions:
9771

■ points ■
Occurrences: 1
Positions:
2740

■ polyvalent ■
Occurrences: 1
Positions:
8709

■ polywaves ■
Occurrences: 1
Positions:
12347

■ popularity ■
Occurrences: 1
Positions:
5592

■ population ■
Occurrences: 1
Positions:
716

■ populism ■
Occurrences: 1
Positions:
10493

■ poses ■
Occurrences: 1
Positions:
676

■ positioning ■
Occurrences: 1
Positions:
235

■ possessing ■
Occurrences: 1
Positions:
997

■ postmillennial ■
Occurrences: 1
Positions:
2257

■ posture ■
Occurrences: 1
Positions:
3146

■ postwar ■
Occurrences: 1
Positions:
3356

■ potency ■
Occurrences: 1
Positions:
11685

■ potentiality ■
Occurrences: 1
Positions:
15568

■ pound ■
Occurrences: 1
Positions:
9896

■ pour ■
Occurrences: 1
Positions:
7206

■ powered ■
Occurrences: 1
Positions:
9068

■ poème ■
Occurrences: 1
Positions:
6989

■ practicality ■
Occurrences: 1
Positions:
5557

■ practiced ■
Occurrences: 1
Positions:
6197

■ practices ■
Occurrences: 1
Positions:
12417

■ practitioner ■
Occurrences: 1
Positions:
3262

■ praise ■
Occurrences: 1
Positions:
7301

■ pre ■
Occurrences: 1
Positions:
7448

■ precarity ■
Occurrences: 1
Positions:
10503

■ precedence ■
Occurrences: 1
Positions:
1182

■ precedent ■
Occurrences: 1
Positions:
6792

■ preceding ■
Occurrences: 1
Positions:
10939

■ precise ■
Occurrences: 1
Positions:
8995

■ principles ■
Occurrences: 1
Positions:
2829

■ probability ■
Occurrences: 1
Positions:
8704

■ probe ■
Occurrences: 1
Positions:
1482

■ procedurality ■
Occurrences: 1
Positions:
535

■ proceed ■
Occurrences: 1
Positions:
9663

■ processed ■
Occurrences: 1
Positions:
1637

■ produce ■
Occurrences: 1
Positions:
10388

■ productionist ■
Occurrences: 1
Positions:
5325

■ products ■
Occurrences: 1
Positions:
9433

■ profile ■
Occurrences: 1
Positions:
14711

■ profited ■
Occurrences: 1
Positions:
8744

■ programmatic ■
Occurrences: 1
Positions:
10765

■ progression ■
Occurrences: 1
Positions:
360

■ projected ■
Occurrences: 1
Positions:
7011

■ projecting ■
Occurrences: 1
Positions:
15387

■ proliferation ■
Occurrences: 1
Positions:
839

■ prolific ■
Occurrences: 1
Positions:
12470

■ promising ■
Occurrences: 1
Positions:
10485

■ pronounced ■
Occurrences: 1
Positions:
11042

■ propagation ■
Occurrences: 1
Positions:
10366

■ propelled ■
Occurrences: 1
Positions:
3788

■ prophetic ■
Occurrences: 1
Positions:
11664

■ proportional ■
Occurrences: 1
Positions:
8094

■ proposing ■
Occurrences: 1
Positions:
11643

■ prospect ■
Occurrences: 1
Positions:
4163

■ protests ■
Occurrences: 1
Positions:
3102

■ prototypical ■
Occurrences: 1
Positions:
15184

■ protscha ■
Occurrences: 1
Positions:
7299

■ proved ■
Occurrences: 1
Positions:
5352

■ provide ■
Occurrences: 1
Positions:
7005

■ provides ■
Occurrences: 1
Positions:
8988

■ providing ■
Occurrences: 1
Positions:
11060

■ provocation ■
Occurrences: 1
Positions:
7897

■ provocative ■
Occurrences: 1
Positions:
5863

■ proximity ■
Occurrences: 1
Positions:
229

■ prying ■
Occurrences: 1
Positions:
15196

■ psychedelic ■
Occurrences: 1
Positions:
11940

■ psychic ■
Occurrences: 1
Positions:
10586

■ publish ■
Occurrences: 1
Positions:
2508

■ punctuation ■
Occurrences: 1
Positions:
12190

■ purely ■
Occurrences: 1
Positions:
7286

■ pursuer ■
Occurrences: 1
Positions:
7028

■ pushed ■
Occurrences: 1
Positions:
1077

■ pushing ■
Occurrences: 1
Positions:
15563

■ qualifies ■
Occurrences: 1
Positions:
4641

■ quantifications ■
Occurrences: 1
Positions:
8822

■ quantities ■
Occurrences: 1
Positions:
12456

■ quarter ■
Occurrences: 1
Positions:
8101

■ reassembling ■
Occurrences: 1
Positions:
6734

■ rebellion ■
Occurrences: 1
Positions:
14558

■ receding ■
Occurrences: 1
Positions:
7463

■ receive ■
Occurrences: 1
Positions:
1897

■ receiver ■
Occurrences: 1
Positions:
9210

■ recited ■
Occurrences: 1
Positions:
7413

■ reckon ■
Occurrences: 1
Positions:
13861

■ recognizable ■
Occurrences: 1
Positions:
12323

■ recognized ■
Occurrences: 1
Positions:
3139

■ recognizes ■
Occurrences: 1
Positions:
12529

■ recognizing ■
Occurrences: 1
Positions:
2929

■ reconceptualizing ■
Occurrences: 1
Positions:
929

■ reconcile ■
Occurrences: 1
Positions:
1912

■ reconfiguring ■
Occurrences: 1
Positions:
3773

■ reconsidered ■
Occurrences: 1
Positions:
13676

■ record ■
Occurrences: 1
Positions:
10865

■ recursively ■
Occurrences: 1
Positions:
361

■ redeem ■
Occurrences: 1
Positions:
10214

■ redemption ■
Occurrences: 1
Positions:
10221

■ reduce ■
Occurrences: 1
Positions:
9179

■ reduces ■
Occurrences: 1
Positions:
9567

■ reducing ■
Occurrences: 1
Positions:
9195

■ redundant ■
Occurrences: 1
Positions:
1221

■ references ■
Occurrences: 1
Positions:
4660

■ referential ■
Occurrences: 1
Positions:
9305

■ referentially ■
Occurrences: 1
Positions:
13545

■ reformulates ■
Occurrences: 1
Positions:
9849

■ refusal ■
Occurrences: 1
Positions:
14556

■ refuse ■
Occurrences: 1
Positions:
3870

■ regard ■
Occurrences: 1
Positions:
4755

■ regarded ■
Occurrences: 1
Positions:
3364

■ regards ■
Occurrences: 1
Positions:
8415

■ regimented ■
Occurrences: 1
Positions:
14112

■ regulate ■
Occurrences: 1
Positions:
2841

■ rehabilitating ■
Occurrences: 1
Positions:
4996

■ rehearses ■
Occurrences: 1
Positions:
944

■ reintegration ■
Occurrences: 1
Positions:
2692

■ reiterate ■
Occurrences: 1
Positions:
584

■ reiterating ■
Occurrences: 1
Positions:
362

■ rejecting ■
Occurrences: 1
Positions:
11697

■ rejects ■
Occurrences: 1
Positions:
5820

■ related ■
Occurrences: 1
Positions:
1840

■ relates ■
Occurrences: 1
Positions:
10673

■ relating ■
Occurrences: 1
Positions:
8067

■ relational ■
Occurrences: 1
Positions:
15154

■ relationality ■
Occurrences: 1
Positions:
14972

■ relationships ■
Occurrences: 1
Positions:
957

■ relevance ■
Occurrences: 1
Positions:
15473

■ reliant ■
Occurrences: 1
Positions:
3432

■ relying ■
Occurrences: 1
Positions:
2005

■ remaking ■
Occurrences: 1
Positions:
11487

■ remarkably ■
Occurrences: 1
Positions:
12469

■ remarked ■
Occurrences: 1
Positions:
2519

■ remembering ■
Occurrences: 1
Positions:
13539

■ remixed ■
Occurrences: 1
Positions:
7333

■ remixes ■
Occurrences: 1
Positions:
12090

■ remixing ■
Occurrences: 1
Positions:
6171

■ removed ■
Occurrences: 1
Positions:
7918

■ removes ■
Occurrences: 1
Positions:
14514

■ renders ■
Occurrences: 1
Positions:
1216

■ renunciation ■
Occurrences: 1
Positions:
5618

■ renéville ■
Occurrences: 1
Positions:
11430

■ reorganization ■
Occurrences: 1
Positions:
9688

■ reorganizations ■
Occurrences: 1
Positions:
10409

■ reorganizes ■
Occurrences: 1
Positions:
10473

■ repetition ■
Occurrences: 1
Positions:
11702

■ replaced ■
Occurrences: 1
Positions:
13523

■ replaces ■
Occurrences: 1
Positions:
5650

■ replicant ■
Occurrences: 1
Positions:
1684

■ representational ■
Occurrences: 1
Positions:
4504

■ representing ■
Occurrences: 1
Positions:
1355

■ reproduce ■
Occurrences: 1
Positions:
6956

■ reproduction ■
Occurrences: 1
Positions:
6860

■ required ■
Occurrences: 1
Positions:
6674

■ requirement ■
Occurrences: 1
Positions:
5812

■ requiring ■
Occurrences: 1
Positions:
226

■ resist ■
Occurrences: 1
Positions:
767

■ resisted ■
Occurrences: 1
Positions:
11466

■ resists ■
Occurrences: 1
Positions:
9780

■ resolve ■
Occurrences: 1
Positions:
1737

■ resonances ■
Occurrences: 1
Positions:
11469

■ resonates ■
Occurrences: 1
Positions:
15531

■ resound ■
Occurrences: 1
Positions:
15522

■ resources ■
Occurrences: 1
Positions:
14467

■ respect ■
Occurrences: 1
Positions:
2924

■ respectively ■
Occurrences: 1
Positions:
12279

■ responded ■
Occurrences: 1
Positions:
3077

■ responding ■
Occurrences: 1
Positions:
2653

■ responsible ■
Occurrences: 1
Positions:
4706

■ restricting ■
Occurrences: 1
Positions:
13890

■ restrictive ■
Occurrences: 1
Positions:
6890

■ resultantly ■
Occurrences: 1
Positions:
7480

■ retro ■
Occurrences: 1
Positions:
1715

■ revealed ■
Occurrences: 1
Positions:
15135

■ reversed ■
Occurrences: 1
Positions:
7219

■ review ■
Occurrences: 1
Positions:
2167

■ reviewers ■
Occurrences: 1
Positions:
2077

■ revolutionize ■
Occurrences: 1
Positions:
2667

■ revolves ■
Occurrences: 1
Positions:
1517

■ revulsion ■
Occurrences: 1
Positions:
1973

■ rewriting ■
Occurrences: 1
Positions:
5419

■ rhythmic ■
Occurrences: 1
Positions:
8077

■ richard ■
Occurrences: 1
Positions:
5889

■ ring ■
Occurrences: 1
Positions:
6812

■ rise ■
Occurrences: 1
Positions:
14850

■ risk ■
Occurrences: 1
Positions:
13326

■ risked ■
Occurrences: 1
Positions:
1736

■ robbe ■
Occurrences: 1
Positions:
2386

■ roid ■
Occurrences: 1
Positions:
1485

■ roles ■
Occurrences: 1
Positions:
3634

■ roll ■
Occurrences: 1
Positions:
6832

■ rolland ■
Occurrences: 1
Positions:
11428

■ rom ■
Occurrences: 1
Positions:
1646

■ room ■
Occurrences: 1
Positions:
7737

■ root ■
Occurrences: 1
Positions:
2210

■ rotman ■
Occurrences: 1
Positions:
10073

■ rotor ■
Occurrences: 1
Positions:
1535

■ rubbish ■
Occurrences: 1
Positions:
295

■ rudimentary ■
Occurrences: 1
Positions:
8909

■ running ■
Occurrences: 1
Positions:
13005

■ security ■
Occurrences: 1
Positions:
11322

■ seldom ■
Occurrences: 1
Positions:
2314

■ selection ■
Occurrences: 1
Positions:
1432

■ selfhood ■
Occurrences: 1
Positions:
3800

■ sellars ■
Occurrences: 1
Positions:
15452

■ semantically ■
Occurrences: 1
Positions:
1839

■ semblance ■
Occurrences: 1
Positions:
11875

■ semen ■
Occurrences: 1
Positions:
12283

■ semio ■
Occurrences: 1
Positions:
12324

■ semiotic ■
Occurrences: 1
Positions:
1893

■ sensationalist ■
Occurrences: 1
Positions:
3692

■ sensations ■
Occurrences: 1
Positions:
9417

■ sensible ■
Occurrences: 1
Positions:
15567

■ sensitive ■
Occurrences: 1
Positions:
13948

■ sentiment ■
Occurrences: 1
Positions:
10978

■ separate ■
Occurrences: 1
Positions:
5186

■ separateness ■
Occurrences: 1
Positions:
12935

■ september ■
Occurrences: 1
Positions:
11365

■ sepulcher ■
Occurrences: 1
Positions:
1560

■ sequel ■
Occurrences: 1
Positions:
1672

■ sequence ■
Occurrences: 1
Positions:
10459

■ seriously ■
Occurrences: 1
Positions:
12242

■ serum ■
Occurrences: 1
Positions:
1524

■ serve ■
Occurrences: 1
Positions:
15267

■ served ■
Occurrences: 1
Positions:
2743

■ sets ■
Occurrences: 1
Positions:
7251

■ setting ■
Occurrences: 1
Positions:
6947

■ seul ■
Occurrences: 1
Positions:
7209

■ several ■
Occurrences: 1
Positions:
3849

■ severs ■
Occurrences: 1
Positions:
1159

■ sf ■
Occurrences: 1
Positions:
2515

■ shape ■
Occurrences: 1
Positions:
6621

■ shaping ■
Occurrences: 1
Positions:
15120

■ share ■
Occurrences: 1
Positions:
2812

■ sharing ■
Occurrences: 1
Positions:
13950

■ shaviro ■
Occurrences: 1
Positions:
9809

■ sheet ■
Occurrences: 1
Positions:
1287

■ sherryl ■
Occurrences: 1
Positions:
5769

■ shifted ■
Occurrences: 1
Positions:
11953

■ shinrō ■
Occurrences: 1
Positions:
2637

■ shinya ■
Occurrences: 1
Positions:
878

■ shoe ■
Occurrences: 1
Positions:
14156

■ shortcomings ■
Occurrences: 1
Positions:
4298

■ shouts ■
Occurrences: 1
Positions:
11098

■ showing ■
Occurrences: 1
Positions:
13955

■ shrug ■
Occurrences: 1
Positions:
10033

■ shūzō ■
Occurrences: 1
Positions:
2630

■ sight ■
Occurrences: 1
Positions:
130

■ signals ■
Occurrences: 1
Positions:
7833

■ significantly ■
Occurrences: 1
Positions:
11623

■ signification ■
Occurrences: 1
Positions:
9151

■ signified ■
Occurrences: 1
Positions:
4745

■ signifier ■
Occurrences: 1
Positions:
12658

■ silence ■
Occurrences: 1
Positions:
7728

■ silicon ■
Occurrences: 1
Positions:
14852

■ similarity ■
Occurrences: 1
Positions:
10849

■ simon ■
Occurrences: 1
Positions:
15451

■ simultaneous ■
Occurrences: 1
Positions:
9025

■ sine ■
Occurrences: 1
Positions:
6816

■ singing ■
Occurrences: 1
Positions:
7300

■ singularity ■
Occurrences: 1
Positions:
12742

■ sirens ■
Occurrences: 1
Positions:
7418

■ size ■
Occurrences: 1
Positions:
14436

■ skeleton ■
Occurrences: 1
Positions:
1115

■ skipping ■
Occurrences: 1
Positions:
455

■ skips ■
Occurrences: 1
Positions:
434

■ skull ■
Occurrences: 1
Positions:
15552

■ sky ■
Occurrences: 1
Positions:
1729

■ smartphone ■
Occurrences: 1
Positions:
9074

■ snapshot ■
Occurrences: 1
Positions:
83

■ socialist ■
Occurrences: 1
Positions:
4785

■ socially ■
Occurrences: 1
Positions:
15380

■ speech ■
Occurrences: 1
Positions:
11014

■ speeding ■
Occurrences: 1
Positions:
8977

■ sphere ■
Occurrences: 1
Positions:
8301

■ spinal ■
Occurrences: 1
Positions:
1555

■ spinning ■
Occurrences: 1
Positions:
12738

■ spiritual ■
Occurrences: 1
Positions:
11527

■ splicing ■
Occurrences: 1
Positions:
11882

■ split ■
Occurrences: 1
Positions:
6537

■ spoken ■
Occurrences: 1
Positions:
11003

■ spoons ■
Occurrences: 1
Positions:
10399

■ spurned ■
Occurrences: 1
Positions:
9773

■ stability ■
Occurrences: 1
Positions:
11320

■ staff ■
Occurrences: 1
Positions:
8075

■ stages ■
Occurrences: 1
Positions:
11440

■ stance ■
Occurrences: 1
Positions:
12016

■ standardization ■
Occurrences: 1
Positions:
371

■ started ■
Occurrences: 1
Positions:
7134

■ stated ■
Occurrences: 1
Positions:
9898

■ statement ■
Occurrences: 1
Positions:
6121

■ static ■
Occurrences: 1
Positions:
6035

■ stations ■
Occurrences: 1
Positions:
8046

■ statistical ■
Occurrences: 1
Positions:
9224

■ staying ■
Occurrences: 1
Positions:
502

■ stems ■
Occurrences: 1
Positions:
3603

■ studying ■
Occurrences: 1
Positions:
8581

■ stuttering ■
Occurrences: 1
Positions:
406

■ stylish ■
Occurrences: 1
Positions:
2754

■ stylistic ■
Occurrences: 1
Positions:
1198

■ subjected ■
Occurrences: 1
Positions:
8799

■ subjects ■
Occurrences: 1
Positions:
11225

■ sublimation ■
Occurrences: 1
Positions:
9346

■ sublime ■
Occurrences: 1
Positions:
4352

■ subordinates ■
Occurrences: 1
Positions:
9493

■ subscribes ■
Occurrences: 1
Positions:
5217

■ subservient ■
Occurrences: 1
Positions:
15030

■ substance ■
Occurrences: 1
Positions:
5118

■ substances ■
Occurrences: 1
Positions:
1471

■ substantiates ■
Occurrences: 1
Positions:
4568

■ succeed ■
Occurrences: 1
Positions:
11203

■ succeeds ■
Occurrences: 1
Positions:
9394

■ successful ■
Occurrences: 1
Positions:
7534

■ successfully ■
Occurrences: 1
Positions:
6983

■ suck ■
Occurrences: 1
Positions:
10875

■ sudden ■
Occurrences: 1
Positions:
272

■ suffering ■
Occurrences: 1
Positions:
11462

■ sullied ■
Occurrences: 1
Positions:
4005

■ sum ■
Occurrences: 1
Positions:
15012

■ summarizes ■
Occurrences: 1
Positions:
7885

■ sumo ■
Occurrences: 1
Positions:
2229

■ sun ■
Occurrences: 1
Positions:
1746

■ supermodernity ■
Occurrences: 1
Positions:
1000

■ surpassed ■
Occurrences: 1
Positions:
12548

■ surprise ■
Occurrences: 1
Positions:
8566

■ surrealists ■
Occurrences: 1
Positions:
12414

■ surround ■
Occurrences: 1
Positions:
8735

■ surrounding ■
Occurrences: 1
Positions:
1892

■ survival ■
Occurrences: 1
Positions:
14803

■ sushi ■
Occurrences: 1
Positions:
2205

■ suspended ■
Occurrences: 1
Positions:
4915

■ swarms ■
Occurrences: 1
Positions:
15000

■ swastika ■
Occurrences: 1
Positions:
1562

■ sylvère ■
Occurrences: 1
Positions:
12558

■ symbiotic ■
Occurrences: 1
Positions:
12735

■ symbol ■
Occurrences: 1
Positions:
13098

■ symbolism ■
Occurrences: 1
Positions:
11116

■ symbols ■
Occurrences: 1
Positions:
12191

■ symphonie ■
Occurrences: 1
Positions:
7205

■ symphonies ■
Occurrences: 1
Positions:
6938

■ syndrome ■
Occurrences: 1
Positions:
3632

■ synonymous ■
Occurrences: 1
Positions:
4224

■ syntactically ■
Occurrences: 1
Positions:
1837

■ syntagms ■
Occurrences: 1
Positions:
10240

■ tomoyoshi ■
Occurrences: 1
Positions:
2628

■ toms ■
Occurrences: 1
Positions:
9249

■ toop ■
Occurrences: 1
Positions:
12404

■ topoi ■
Occurrences: 1
Positions:
2111

■ topology ■
Occurrences: 1
Positions:
2113

■ tortures ■
Occurrences: 1
Positions:
1521

■ tossing ■
Occurrences: 1
Positions:
8153

■ totalitarianism ■
Occurrences: 1
Positions:
15177

■ totality ■
Occurrences: 1
Positions:
13618

■ totalizing ■
Occurrences: 1
Positions:
9782

■ tour ■
Occurrences: 1
Positions:
4421

■ towering ■
Occurrences: 1
Positions:
4732

■ toyota ■
Occurrences: 1
Positions:
2209

■ traced ■
Occurrences: 1
Positions:
14692

■ traditionally ■
Occurrences: 1
Positions:
8164

■ traditions ■
Occurrences: 1
Positions:
10723

■ traffic ■
Occurrences: 1
Positions:
14039

■ tragedy ■
Occurrences: 1
Positions:
1645

■ trajectory ■
Occurrences: 1
Positions:
6511

■ transcending ■
Occurrences: 1
Positions:
558

■ transcends ■
Occurrences: 1
Positions:
2573

■ transculture ■
Occurrences: 1
Positions:
5519

■ transferred ■
Occurrences: 1
Positions:
12108

■ transfiguration ■
Occurrences: 1
Positions:
11495

■ transformations ■
Occurrences: 1
Positions:
6081

■ transformative ■
Occurrences: 1
Positions:
3199

■ transforming ■
Occurrences: 1
Positions:
4350

■ transforms ■
Occurrences: 1
Positions:
9431

■ transgressing ■
Occurrences: 1
Positions:
2183

■ transgression ■
Occurrences: 1
Positions:
2201

■ transgressive ■
Occurrences: 1
Positions:
15276

■ transmits ■
Occurrences: 1
Positions:
1229

■ transmutation ■
Occurrences: 1
Positions:
9424

■ traversed ■
Occurrences: 1
Positions:
14894

■ treatment ■
Occurrences: 1
Positions:
1622

■ tremendous ■
Occurrences: 1
Positions:
9408

■ trigger ■
Occurrences: 1
Positions:
5905

■ trip ■
Occurrences: 1
Positions:
11941

■ trivial ■
Occurrences: 1
Positions:
9432

■ trolleys ■
Occurrences: 1
Positions:
6919

■ truly ■
Occurrences: 1
Positions:
11310

■ try ■
Occurrences: 1
Positions:
2839

■ tuning ■
Occurrences: 1
Positions:
8117

■ turned ■
Occurrences: 1
Positions:
7899

■ turns ■
Occurrences: 1
Positions:
10372

■ twenties ■
Occurrences: 1
Positions:
2611

■ twisted ■
Occurrences: 1
Positions:
1185

■ type ■
Occurrences: 1
Positions:
12083

■ types ■
Occurrences: 1
Positions:
7150

■ typographic ■
Occurrences: 1
Positions:
745

■ typographical ■
Occurrences: 1
Positions:
12192

■ ubiquitous ■
Occurrences: 1
Positions:
8485

■ ubiquity ■
Occurrences: 1
Positions:
9993

■ ultra ■
Occurrences: 1
Positions:
1643

■ ulysses ■
Occurrences: 1
Positions:
7423

■ un ■
Occurrences: 1
Positions:
7207

■ unable ■
Occurrences: 1
Positions:
9910

■ unbearably ■
Occurrences: 1
Positions:
11152

■ unbounded ■
Occurrences: 1
Positions:
9892

■ unchanging ■
Occurrences: 1
Positions:
8450

■ uncoils ■
Occurrences: 1
Positions:
15583

■ uncompromising ■
Occurrences: 1
Positions:
1143

■ uncompromisingly ■
Occurrences: 1
Positions:
15586

■ underground ■
Occurrences: 1
Positions:
3378

■ undermining ■
Occurrences: 1
Positions:
5025

■ underpinning ■
Occurrences: 1
Positions:
5147

■ understand ■
Occurrences: 1
Positions:
13339

■ understands ■
Occurrences: 1
Positions:
5635

■ understated ■
Occurrences: 1
Positions:
3608

■ undertaking ■
Occurrences: 1
Positions:
9397

■ unfamiliar ■
Occurrences: 1
Positions:
5743

■ unforgettable ■
Occurrences: 1
Positions:
4430

■ unidirectional ■
Occurrences: 1
Positions:
3673

■ unintelligible ■
Occurrences: 1
Positions:
787

■ uniquely ■
Occurrences: 1
Positions:
11629

■ unites ■
Occurrences: 1
Positions:
14672

■ uniting ■
Occurrences: 1
Positions:
7352

■ units ■
Occurrences: 1
Positions:
14819

■ unity ■
Occurrences: 1
Positions:
2802

■ unknowable ■
Occurrences: 1
Positions:
10023

■ unleashes ■
Occurrences: 1
Positions:
1201

■ unlikely ■
Occurrences: 1
Positions:
9111

■ unlikeness ■
Occurrences: 1
Positions:
14639

■ unlimited ■
Occurrences: 1
Positions:
6724

■ unparalleled ■
Occurrences: 1
Positions:
1197

■ unquantifiable ■
Occurrences: 1
Positions:
15604

■ unrelenting ■
Occurrences: 1
Positions:
11414

■ unrest ■
Occurrences: 1
Positions:
11231

■ unruly ■
Occurrences: 1
Positions:
7457

■ unsettling ■
Occurrences: 1
Positions:
4903

■ unspooling ■
Occurrences: 1
Positions:
1285

■ unstated ■
Occurrences: 1
Positions:
3585

■ unthinkable ■
Occurrences: 1
Positions:
11167

■ unveiling ■
Occurrences: 1
Positions:
10951

■ unwilling ■
Occurrences: 1
Positions:
3793

■ updated ■
Occurrences: 1
Positions:
315

■ updates ■
Occurrences: 1
Positions:
12086

■ updating ■
Occurrences: 1
Positions:
5420

■ upgrades ■
Occurrences: 1
Positions:
374

■ useful ■
Occurrences: 1
Positions:
5507

■ useless ■
Occurrences: 1
Positions:
7952

■ using ■
Occurrences: 1
Positions:
8145

■ usual ■
Occurrences: 1
Positions:
11577

■ validity ■
Occurrences: 1
Positions:
3941

■ valley ■
Occurrences: 1
Positions:
14853

■ valuated ■
Occurrences: 1
Positions:
5235

■ value ■
Occurrences: 1
Positions:
8404

■ values ■
Occurrences: 1
Positions:
11999

■ vamp ■
Occurrences: 1
Positions:
1691

■ vanguard ■
Occurrences: 1
Positions:
4835

■ vanishing ■
Occurrences: 1
Positions:
10058

■ variations ■
Occurrences: 1
Positions:
9038

■ variety ■
Occurrences: 1
Positions:
6899

■ various ■
Occurrences: 1
Positions:
7224

■ vectors ■
Occurrences: 1
Positions:
3057

■ vehicles ■
Occurrences: 1
Positions:
6923

■ vibratory ■
Occurrences: 1
Positions:
11024

■ viewer ■
Occurrences: 1
Positions:
4493

■ vignettes ■
Occurrences: 1
Positions:
11804

■ vinyl ■
Occurrences: 1
Positions:
6834

■ viral ■
Occurrences: 1
Positions:
1825

■ virtual ■
Occurrences: 1
Positions:
245

■ virtually ■
Occurrences: 1
Positions:
5497

■ virtuosic ■
Occurrences: 1
Positions:
7381

■ virulently ■
Occurrences: 1
Positions:
1243

■ visuals ■
Occurrences: 1
Positions:
7012

■ void ■
Occurrences: 1
Positions:
1297

■ wagnerian ■
Occurrences: 1
Positions:
8398

■ walks ■
Occurrences: 1
Positions:
1749

■ waning ■
Occurrences: 1
Positions:
13877

■ want ■
Occurrences: 1
Positions:
2988

■ wants ■
Occurrences: 1
Positions:
8289

■ warped ■
Occurrences: 1
Positions:
1244

■ watch ■
Occurrences: 1
Positions:
2228

■ watershed ■
Occurrences: 1
Positions:
3369

■ waveform ■
Occurrences: 1
Positions:
6687

■ webpage ■
Occurrences: 1
Positions:
1110

■ welds ■
Occurrences: 1
Positions:
14771

■ west ■
Occurrences: 1
Positions:
3970

■ whatever ■
Occurrences: 1
Positions:
13216

■ whence ■
Occurrences: 1
Positions:
8783

■ whine ■
Occurrences: 1
Positions:
9822

■ wholly ■
Occurrences: 1
Positions:
8219

■ wiener ■
Occurrences: 1
Positions:
8941

■ wired ■
Occurrences: 1
Positions:
13756

■ womb ■
Occurrences: 1
Positions:
1494

■ wonder ■
Occurrences: 1
Positions:
2346

■ worked ■
Occurrences: 1
Positions:
8575

■ worker ■
Occurrences: 1
Positions:
14165

■ worth ■
Occurrences: 1
Positions:
8925

■ worthwhile ■
Occurrences: 1
Positions:
15371

■ yanase ■
Occurrences: 1
Positions:
2631

■ young ■
Occurrences: 1
Positions:
2650

■ younger ■
Occurrences: 1
Positions:
5367

■ zeitgeist ■
Occurrences: 1
Positions:
10311

■ électronique ■
Occurrences: 1
Positions:
6990

■ ōura ■
Occurrences: 1
Positions:
2629

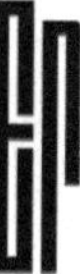

www.ingramcontent.com/pod-product-compliance
Lightning Source LLC
LaVergne TN
LVHW091120080826
845145LV00008B/1991

* 9 7 8 1 9 1 6 5 4 1 1 0 8 *